D1590886

BECOMING AMERICAN
IN CREOLE NEW ORLEANS
1896–1949

BECOMING AMERICAN
IN CREOLE NEW ORLEANS
1896–1949

Darryl Barthé Jr.

LOUISIANA STATE UNIVERSITY PRESS

BATON ROUGE

Published by Louisiana State University Press
www.lsupress.org

Manufactured in the United States of America
First printing

Designer: Barbara Neely Bourgoyne
Typefaces: Vulpa, display; Whitman, text
Printer and binder: Sheridan Books

Front jacket illustration: Group photograph at the St. Louis School (Couvent School).
Courtesy of Xavier University of Louisiana Archives and Special Collections.

Library of Congress Cataloging-in-Publication Data
Names: Barthé, Darryl, Jr., author.
Title: Becoming American in Creole New Orleans, 1896–1949 / Darryl Barthé Jr.
Description: Baton Rouge : Louisiana State University Press, 2021. | Includes
    bibliographical references and index.
Identifiers: LCCN 2020043800 (print) | LCCN 2020043801 (ebook) | ISBN 978-0-
    8071-7547-7 (cloth) | ISBN 978-0-8071-7552-1 (pdf) | ISBN 978-0-8071-7553-8 (epub)
Subjects: LCSH: Creoles—Louisiana—New Orleans—Social life and customs—
    20th century. | Creoles—Louisiana—New Orleans—History—20th century. |
    Americanization. | Creoles—Ethnic identity. | New Orleans (La.)—History.
Classification: LCC F380.C87 B37 2021 (print) | LCC F380.C87 (ebook) |
    DDC 976.3/35—dc23
LC record available at https://lccn.loc.gov/2020043800
LC ebook record available at https://lccn.loc.gov/2020043801

This book is dedicated to the memories of those who saw the beginning of this journey, but not the end, including my great-uncle Earl, and to Terry, Trudy, Lauren, and Joyce, and to my grandmother Mildred, my great-uncles Henry Oubre and Archie Rhone, to my great-aunt Sandra Rhone, my uncle Clarence Collins, to my father-in-law, William Servais, and finally, to Drs. Madelyn Powers, Michael Mizell-Nelson, and Arnold Hirsch. There is no way I could ever repay their kindness, patience, and generosity.

CONTENTS

ACKNOWLEDGMENTS

Acknowledging the assistance of everyone who contributed to this book is impossible. Works like this are, from the beginning, collaborative efforts and draw inspiration from everyone and everything the author interacts with over the course of the project. I would not have been able to complete this book had it not been for the people in my graduate school seminars, and the folks I shared Guinness and shots of Jameson's with at Pals, Finn McCool's, the Lost Love Lounge, and the Sugar Park Tavern. This book is the product of many cups of coffee at Fair Grinds in Faubourg St. Jean, but also at the Student Union at the University of Sussex. I wrote it after many conversations, and many pints of Harvey's, at the Hound and Hare, the World's End Pub, and the Waggon and Horses in Brighton.

All of my children sacrificed chunks of their childhood to their father's ambition in the production of this work, but especially Daughter #1, Marie. I can never give any of them back that time, so I will offer them my thanks, and beg their forgiveness, here.

I could not have pursued this work at all if it had not been for my wife, Joelle, and the support and encouragement of her parents. This book is dedicated, in part, to her father, but I am compelled to offer a special mention of her mother, Mary Ann McCarty Servais, who over the lifetime of my research, writing, and editing, and crises and emotional twists and turns, gave my family and me a roof over our heads and fed us. Joelle Servais is a saintly woman, and much of that she learned from her mother.

This book was written in dialogue, scholarly and otherwise, with Christophe Landry, Andrew Jolivette, Rain Prudhomme-Cranford, Carolyn

Dunn, Mary Niall Mitchell, Nikki Dugar, Rafael Delgadillo, Jari C. Honora, and with the assistance of scores of community leaders, culture producers, and knowledge bearers from New Orleans's Creole community, including my parents, Darryl Sr. and Carolyn Oubre, and James Oubre.

I would like to call attention to the archivists at Earl K. Long Library's Special Collections at the University of New Orleans, the Amistad Research Center at Tulane University, Xavier University of New Orleans, and the Main Library of the New Orleans Public Library system. They are among the most capable ambassadors of the city of New Orleans. Additionally, I would like to thank to Mrs. Lagarde at Corpus Christi Parish, who was so patient and generous with her time.

Finally, I am deeply grateful to Richard Follett, who took me as an apprentice, who never let me quit, who gave me an example of how to face horror and evil while maintaining composure and good spirits (I'm still trying to master that skill, Richard), and who taught me how to write my people's history.

BECOMING AMERICAN
IN CREOLE NEW ORLEANS
1896–1949

INTRODUCTION

In November of 2002, the Delgado Memorial Museum of Art in New Orleans hosted an exhibit titled "Raised to the Trade" featuring a number of Creole craftsmen from New Orleans. Among them was my great-uncle Earl A. Barthé. I attended the exhibit on the opening day and watched as my uncle Earl, a born "articulator" (his term), spun a tale of his grandfather's brother, Pierre Barthé, founding New Orleans Plasterers' Union Local 93 along with an Irish American named Sam Ball. As Earl told it, it was a stirring, uplifting tale of interracial cooperation just as the curtain of Jim Crow was being drawn on the Crescent City. It sounded too good to be true, but it was certainly the sort of story that drew people in and made them smile. A few days later, back at his office on Frenchmen Street, away from the crowds and strangers, I asked him for clarification.

Earl suggested that Local 93 was the first racially integrated, AFL-affiliated union local in the United States featuring "Blacks" in positions of authority. (Pierre Barthé was the first president of Local 93.) However, I knew that racial qualifiers like "black" and "white" were not always used in the same way by Louisiana Creoles in New Orleans, particularly older Creoles like my uncle. Did he mean to say that Local 93 was integrated and open to Whites and Blacks, or did he mean to say that Local 93 was integrated between Whites and Creoles?[1] Earl looked at me out of the corner of his eye and massaged his chin pensively before clarifying that the union was integrated between Whites and Creoles. When I asked him when the first African Americans were allowed in the union, he replied that he was unsure but that it was certainly after World War II.

Earl understood a difference between Blacks and Creoles. He understood that difference experientially: he grew up during a time when the animosity between downtown New Orleans Creoles and uptown New Orleans African Americans was so real that interactions between the two groups often devolved into violence. That story of ethnic antipathy among people of color in New Orleans is not a feel-good story. It is, however, a crucial part of the story that I intend to tell.

The story of Louisiana Creoles in New Orleans is a convoluted one because it is the story of an in-between people who do not fit neatly into the black and white American racial narrative. Though it may be hard for some to accept, Creoles are not Americans in the sense that white Anglo-Saxon Protestants in New York or Maryland or Georgia are Americans. The Americans, Whites and Blacks alike, were cultural "others" to the Creole people of Louisiana until the twentieth century. The story I will tell is of how these two groups, American and Creole, overcame that state of "otherness" in the twentieth century (to the extent that that state of otherness was actually overcome, a proposition both debatable and better left to a separate study).

The history of Creoles in the twentieth century is often obscured by American racial protocols utilized by historians who attempt to qualify Creoles racially by describing them as "Afro-Creoles." This practice was engaged in response to attempts in the late nineteenth century by revisionists like Charles Gayarré and Grace King to disqualify people of color from a Creole identity. However, in an effort to make the case that people of color could be Creole too, these historians have either glossed over or entirely erased the indigenous history of Louisiana Creole people. More often than not, Creoles share blood ties with Amerindian people throughout the Mississippi River Valley, from the Great Lakes to the Gulf of Mexico, making them an indigenous triracial isolate group "created" in colonial interactions between Europeans, Amerindians, and Africans in Louisiana.

While the subject of triracial isolates has been vigorously interrogated by anthropologists and sociologists like C. J. Witkop, William Pollitzer, C. L. Beane, and Eduardo Bonilla-Silva, historians have been less enthusiastic about plunging into the murky waters of this history in Louisiana. The first major contemporary attempt at a historical treatment of Lou-

isiana Creoles in New Orleans was Arnold R. Hirsch and Joseph Logsdon's *Creole New Orleans: Race and Americanization*. Hirsch and Logsdon's
work was groundbreaking and went hand in hand with Gwendolyn Midlo
Hall's *Africans in Colonial Louisiana: The Development of Afro-Creole Culture
in the Eighteenth Century*, both published in 1992. Since 1992, a host of
studies have built upon the foundations laid by these scholars, but the
best of them are those written by Creoles themselves, including Caryn
Cossé Bell's *Revolution, Romanticism, and the Afro-Creole Protest Tradition
in Louisiana, 1718–1868*.[2] These are the scholars who laid the foundations
for my work.

Two recent studies of Creoles in New Orleans in the twentieth century
have been very influential to my work. They are Wendy Ann Gaudin's
doctoral dissertation, "Autocrats and All Saints: Migration, Memory and
Modern Creole Identities," and Nikki Dugar's master's thesis, "I Am What
I Say I Am: Racial and Cultural Identity among Creoles of Color in New
Orleans."[3] My work has much in common with the scholarship of both
of these women. Among those commonalities are our interrogations of
the role of family ties, institutional associations, and race, specifically the
role of racial in-betweenness, in shaping Creole identity in the twentieth
century. Where my work differs most from Gaudin's is in my focus on
Creole identity as expressed in linguistic heritage and the transition from
a Creole to an American identity as a consequence, at least in part, of a
linguistic shift from French and Louisiana Creole to English. Gaudin does
not engage this issue at all, which is reflected in a fundamental flaw in her
analysis of the psychological distance that existed between Creoles and
African Americans. Dugar's work is more narrow in scope than my own,
but the bold assertion of Creole identity in "I Am What I Say I Am" has
definitely informed my lines of inquiry.

A relative paucity of records providing direct archival commentary,
and the inherent difficulty in engaging the history of ethno-racial identity migration, demanded that I consult a variety of sources. There are
precious few literary accounts of the Creole experience in the twentieth
century and, without oral histories, often taken from family, it would be
impossible to tell New Orleans Creoles' stories, particularly the stories of
working-class Creoles. In some cases, I employ published interviews from

journalistic sources and at other times I employ oral history interviews gleaned from other scholars (Gaudin, for example). Whenever possible, as a member of that community, I put oral accounts and family histories in dialogue with archival sources to reconstruct historical contexts that may have been heretofore inaccessible, especially to a scholar without direct access to the Creole community.

I worked extensively with organizational records for representative Creole social sodalities in New Orleans. Often, when engaging these records, I consulted oral history interviewees to clarify the murky pictures that emerged. In some cases, interviewees were able to identify people in photographs whose identities would have been impossible to glean otherwise.

Chapter 1 examines Louisiana Creoles from their ethnogenesis in the early eighteenth century to the *Plessy* verdict. Chapter 2 examines the construction of Creole identity in the wake of the *Plessy* verdict, the difficulty entailed in forcing these in-between people into black and white racial identities, and the effect of a more aggressive program of Americanization and US nationalism on the Creole community in New Orleans. Chapter 3 examines the role that Creole voluntary associations, fraternal societies, and civil rights organizations played in the rearticulation of Creole identity in the early twentieth century, as well as the assimilation of the Creole community in New Orleans to the larger American society around it. In chapter 4, I focus on work and organized labor in Creole New Orleans, specifically the history of Plasterers' Union Local 92 and the categorical exclusion of African American members until 1947. In chapter 5, I interrogate the role of English-only education in Creole New Orleans and connect the shift in Creole linguistic identity to the shift in ethno-racial identity.

For Louisiana Creoles in eighteenth-century New Orleans, "the Americans" were those who spoke English and hailed from the wild lands of Kentucky. In nineteenth-century New Orleans, the Americans were those who brought with them a racialized caste system unlike anything Creoles had experienced under the French or the Spanish, and who had dedicated themselves to the disenfranchisement of Creoles of color, despite the provisions of the Louisiana Purchase treaty that demanded that all "inhabitants" of Louisiana be afforded all rights enjoyed by US citizens. At the turn of the twentieth century in New Orleans, the Americans were those who lived above Canal Street in uptown New Orleans and who spoke 'Mericain. However, by the end of World War II, most Creoles in New Orleans were primarily Anglophone (some exclusively) and deeply invested in the African American movement for political and social equality and civil rights, with no few having served proudly under the American flag in both the European and Pacific theaters; they had become American, themselves. The aim of this work is to explore that transformation of ethnocultural (and racial) identity from Creole to American and to interrogate the historical circumstances that effected this change.

1

IDENTIFYING A HISTORIC
LOUISIANA CREOLE COMMUNITY

In 1832, iconic American author Washington Irving toured the prairies of the western frontier of the United States in what are today the states of Missouri and Oklahoma. The resulting account, Irving's *Tour of the Prairies,* is a romanticized retelling of his exploits on the US frontier. Initially, Irving's companions in this adventure were two Europeans: an Englishman, Mr. Latrobe, and a young aristocrat from Switzerland, the Count de Pourtales. Yet, in St. Louis, the three intrepid tourists found their wilderness guide in the person of Tonish:

> a personage of inferior rank, but of all-pervading and prevalent importance: the squire, the groom, the cook, the tent man.—in a word, the factotum, and, I may add, the universal meddler and marplot of our party. This was a little, swarthy, meagre, French Creole, named Antoine, but familiarly dubbed Tonish: a kind of Gil Bias of the frontiers, who had passed a scrambling life, sometimes among white men, sometimes among Indians; sometimes in the employ of traders, missionaries, and Indian agents; sometimes mingling with the Osage hunters. We picked him up at St. Louis, near which he has a small farm, an Indian wife, and a brood of half-blood children. According to his own account, however, he had a wife in every tribe; in fact, if all this little vagabond said of himself were to be believed, he was without morals, without caste, without creed, without country, and even without language; for he spoke a jargon of mingled French, English, and Osage. He was, withal, a notorious braggart, and a liar of the first water.[1]

Irving's characterization of the "French Creole" reveals much about the Anglo-American perception of the people who fell under US authority after the Louisiana Purchase. Tonish was effective, indeed indispensable, to the purposes of Irving and his companions. Yet, Irving's portrayal of Tonish also casts him as fundamentally untrustworthy, morally depraved, a compulsive liar, a sexual deviant, and a philandering polygamist. Despite this depiction as a base and unserious person, however, there is a clear menace in Irving's depiction that speaks to a larger sense of "otherness."

Upon arriving at the trading town of Chouteau, Oklahoma, Irving hired two more Creoles, both of French-Osage heritage. One was a young man, also named Antoine, who Irving described as having "a vehement propensity to do nothing, being one of the worthless brood engendered and brought up among the missions . . . a little spoiled by being really a handsome young fellow, an Adonis of the frontier, and still worse by fancying himself highly connected, his sister being concubine to an opulent white trader!" The other Creole was a hunter named Pierre Beatte, and it is with his description of Beatte that Irving was most explicit in communicating that sense of malicious "otherness" that existed between the Creoles and Irving, the American:

> I confess I did not like his looks when he was first presented to me. He was lounging about, in an old hunting-frock and metasses or leggings, of deer-skin, soiled and greased, and almost japanned by constant use. . . . His features were not bad, being shaped not unlike those of Napoleon, but sharpened up, with high Indian cheek-bones. Perhaps the dusky greenish hue of his complexion aided his resemblance to an old bronze bust I had seen of the Emperor. . . . He had altogether more of the red than the white man in his composition; and as I had been taught to look upon all half-breeds with distrust, as an uncertain and faithless race, I would gladly have dispensed with the services of Pierre Beatte.[2]

Irving takes care to speak to an image of a frontiersman that his audience would have been familiar with when describing the hunter: he racialized and exoticized Beatte, the Creole with the high "Indian" cheek-bones and the chiseled features that reminded the New Yorker of a bronze bust of Napoleon Bonaparte. Not quite civilized, being more red man than white, Beatte was devoid of pretense and wholly unconcerned with social niceties. Unkempt and filthy, he was not a "Noble Savage," as such; just savage. Indeed, it is almost as if Irving used Beatte as a literary representation of the Louisiana Territory itself: a twilight land inhabited by "a sprinkling of trappers, hunters, half-breeds, creoles, negroes of every hue; and all that other rabble rout of nondescript beings that keep about the frontiers, between civilized and savage life, as those equivocal birds, the bats, hover about the confines of light and darkness."[3] It was a wild, dangerous land, yet by the 1830s many Americans viewed the subjugation of that wild frontier—and its people—as a natural consequence of the arrival of Anglophone American settlers there, and it is in this context that the story of the Americanization of Louisiana's Creole people takes place.

It is important to, first, disambiguate, define, and analyze the interplay of creolization and Americanization, social processes that often worked in opposition to one another throughout the nineteenth century and that would continue to frame the limits of Creole identity and cultural expression in New Orleans throughout the period of this study. Much of the scholarly discourse on "creolization" has taken place among linguists, anthropologists, and sociologists. Of those historians who have grappled with the inexactitude of créolité (that is, the quality of "creoleness"), there is a wide variety of opinions and perspectives on what créolité is, how it has manifested historically, and who and/or what can be authentically identified as "Creole/creole." More than a decade ago, German linguist Eva Martha Eckkrammer observed that,

> to investigate creolization and its underlying anthropological, social and linguistic processes on general grounds, the point of departure has to be at least pan-Caribbean if not—and I personally plead for a cognate perception—a geographically much wider belt including all territories where cultural and/or racial mixing have led or are leading to the evolution of mixed cultures and new identities some of them including an independent linguistic output. If we base our considerations on such a broad definition we cannot avoid asking what the term creole means precisely. . . . the etymological exigency lies in the changing semantic

8

values transported by the word which differ across languages, chrono-logically as well as geographically.[4]

Eckkrammer's observation is useful although perhaps its greatest utility is in its presentation of the sort of problematic complexity inherent to the dialogue on creolization and creole people and languages. If creolization consists of processes of cultural and/or racial mixing that have led to the evolution of new hybrid identities, then where on Earth did creolization not occur and who on Earth is not a Creole? No one perceives Egyptians as "Nile River basin Creoles," nor have Egyptians ever identified them-selves as Creoles, yet it is undeniable that Egypt was the setting for processes of "cultural and/or racial mixing." Eckkrammer, even as she attempts to extend the interpretive device of "creolization" to wider con-texts, acknowledges that extending the limits of the "Creole World" can easily result in the term losing its meaning. Thus, the first task of this study is to define terms and to positively identify the historic Creole com-munity in Louisiana.

The ambiguity inherent to créolité, and the varied ways that créolité is manifested, make identifying historic Creole communities in Louisiana a difficult proposition at times. This is especially true, it seems, for those who have been conditioned to see "Whites," "Blacks," "African Americans," "Indians," "Germans," "Frenchmen," "Spaniards," and "Cajuns" when view-ing Creoles. Only adding to the confusion is the fact that Louisiana Creole identity is not mutually exclusive to any of those identifiers: there are white Creoles, black Creoles, and African Americans who assimilated into Creole communities in Louisiana. There are German Coast Creoles, Creole Isleños (Hispanophone), métis Creoles, Creole Houmas, Creole Ishaks, and Creole Coushattas. The very word "Cajun" is a Creole pronunciation of the word "Acadian," and many of the cultural markers of contemporary cajunéité, particularly Cajun cuisine (for example, "Cajun gumbo," "Cajun spices"), are simply not Acadian in origin, suggesting that the Cajun ethnic identity itself is inseparable from Louisiana créolité.

Créolité in Louisiana is manifested in the new modes of social in-teraction that emerged among the Africans, Amerindians, Europeans, Afro-Amerindians, Euro-Amerindians, Afro-Europeans, and Afro-Euro-

Amerindians who settled there. Creoles in Louisiana, compelled to grow new foods and to prepare old foods in new ways, were forced to expand their palettes to accommodate one another's tastes since they were all eating the same meals, even if not around the same dinner table. Enslaved Afro-Creoles who refused to relinquish their ancestral spiritual traditions continued to observe traditional African spirituality but couched their devotion in the imagery of Catholicism and found American alternatives, like tobacco and rum, to replace traditional devotional offerings that may not have been so readily available in the Americas.

Créolité in Louisiana is also manifested in language. Indeed, French-lexified Creole languages emerged everywhere in the Americas from as far north as French Canada, throughout Louisiana, and as far south as the Caribbean. Métis Creole, also referred to as Michif and French Cree, of the Métis people of Canada and the United States is influenced by French, Cree, and Ojibwé. Haitian Kréyol, one of the two official languages of Haiti, is significantly different from both Louisiana Creole French and Michif, and borrows idioms and pronunciations from both African languages and the language of Amerindian people as well. Louisiana Creole, also referred to as "Louisiana Creole French" and "Kouri-Vini," is influenced by French but also incorporates vocabulary from West African languages and Amerindian languages as well as Spanish.

Neither Virginia nor Maryland produced a community of people, of mixed heritage or otherwise, that identified itself and was recognized by others as Creoles the way that Louisiana did. However, historian Ira Berlin offers a compelling argument that the English colonies in North America, from Chesapeake Bay to the Carolina low country, were settled by "Atlantic Creoles" from West Africa. Atlantic Creoles were the products of a colonial culture of trade and exchange that began in the middle of the fifteenth century between various West African peoples and the Portuguese along the west coast of Africa. Often having ancestral connections to both Africa and Europe, Atlantic Creoles were adept at trade languages and at exploiting their in-betweenness to profit from the triangle trade. Berlin argues, however, that Atlantic Creoles were forced into new, exclusively black, identities in North America as the plantation system in the English colonies matured. That system, which would become more severe over the course of the eighteenth century, required not only that non-Whites be socially subordinate to Whites, but also that people of African descent be considered a "special species of beings," a species specifically designed for slavery. A Creole community did not endure in Virginia and Maryland because the operational ideology that promoted hybridization and promoted amalgamation (that is, creolization) was abandoned and replaced with an ideology of "radical separation of master and slave and the creation of the worlds of the Big House and the Quarters."[5]

In 1992, anthropologist Ulf Hannerz observed that "Creole cultures—like creole languages—are intrinsically of mixed origin, the confluence of two or more widely separated historical currents . . . [that] come out of multi-dimensional cultural encounters." These "multi-dimensional cultural encounters" in places like Michigan, Ontario, Mauritius, Saint-Domingue, and Louisiana all have underlying similarities that are directly related to a larger context of European colonialism, but the fact that Michif, Mauritian Creole, Haitian Creole, and Louisiana Creole are not all mutually intelligible languages speaks directly to the diverse ways that créolité is manifested, even if in every case there is cultural exchange and hybridization.[6]

Creolization is a generative process, a fact contained in the origin of the word itself: "creole" is derived from the Latin verb "creare," that is, "to create." Referencing only the original Latin, the word, when used as an adjective, is "creatus" which can be translated, roughly, as "created" in the sense of "begotten." The same word can be used as a noun in fact (or rather, as a gerund), as a synonym for "offspring." Indeed, the etymology for the word given in the *Grande Dicionário da Lingua Portuguesa* includes "infant" as an archaic use of the term.[7] With this in mind, it is not difficult to contrast the ideology and process of creolization with that of Americanization.

Anthropologist Charles Stewart describes Americanization—a process he sees as a restructuring, rearranging, and reordering of new geographical and cultural contexts on the frontier—as a form of creolization. Yet, the story of the American frontier is a story of conquest, not of amalgamation; separation, not integration; domination, not exchange. As historian Rob Kroes so concisely articulates the point: Americanization is the "story of an American cultural language traveling and of other people acquiring that language." Americanization is not the story of a new language, and new identity, emerging organically and erotically.[8]

Absent from the English colonies in North America was the sexual permissiveness that allows for the hybridity that characterizes creole contexts. Indeed, if legislation passed in seventeenth-century Virginia is any indication of public attitudes toward sex and sexuality, then it is clear that sexual mores were extremely conservative. Fornication, for example, had been a criminal offense from the earliest days of English settlement at Jamestown. Yet, in 1662, legislators in Virginia were compelled to stipulate additional penalties for fornicators who sinned across color lines. In 1691, Virginia legislators took this hostility to interracial sexual congress a step further and passed a statute criminalizing formal marriage across the color line and stipulating that violators of the prohibition be subject to banishment from the colony.[9]

According to historian George M. Fredrickson, the majority of Virginia's anti-miscegenation laws seemed to fixate on the problem of white women and black men marrying. This is not to say that such laws did not include prohibitions on sexual relations between white men and African and Indian women, however. On the contrary, the more generalized (and directly stated) purpose of these statutes was to prevent "that abominable mixture and spurious issue, which hereafter may increase in this dominion, as well by negroes, mulattoes and Indians intermarrying with English or other white women, as by their unlawful accompanying with one another." Far from promoting admixture and hybridity, the Anglo-American context was actively opposed to it: not only were English colonials in North America not creole, but also they were actively anti-creole.[10]

Louisiana was an immense expanse that bridged the profoundly different worlds of French Canada and the Gulf Coast. Louisiana is often viewed in pan-Caribbean contexts, in part due to the social, cultural, and political connections between Louisiana and Cuba and Haiti in the late eighteenth century and throughout the nineteenth century. However, the origins of Louisiana and of the Creole people of Louisiana, are in Québec. Historian Jennifer Spear even goes so far as to describe Louisiana as a colony of a colony to indicate the relationship between Louisiana and New

France, observing that "many of lower Louisiana's earliest colonizers were Canadian-born," rather than French.[11] It should be no surprise then that créolité in Louisiana was informed by the culture of métissage that had existed in French Canada for a century prior to New Orleans's founding.

Samuel de Champlain established Québec City in 1608, establishing the Habitation de Québec as a trading post from which the French forged alliances with the Algonquin and Huron nations. It is there, in Québec, that the origins of Louisiana créolité are to be found, according to historian Jerah Johnson. Jean-Baptiste Colbert, the controller-general of finances and minister to New France under Louis XIV from 1665 to 1683, demanded that French colonists, in cooperation with the Roman Catholic Church, "civilize the . . . savages who have embraced Christianity, and dispose them to come and settle them in the community with the French, live with them, and bring up their children in their manner and customs . . . in order that, having one law and one master, they may form only one people and one blood." This policy was embodied and exemplified by the French coureurs-des-bois and voyageurs and ultimately found their pinnacle expression in the Canadian First Nation of the Métis people. Johnson finds similar sensibilities articulated by Louisiana's first Roman Catholic vicar-general, Henri Rouleaux de La Vente, who proclaimed that "the blood of the savages does no harm to the blood of the French" and who defended the choices of those "Euro-Louisianians" who wished to intermarry with "sauvagesses" so long as those women were willing to convert to Catholicism. There was never an Anglo-American equivalent to the assimilationist "one blood" policies of the French in North America.[12]

The French presence in Saint-Domingue began with a pirate outpost on the small island of Tortuga that was repeatedly attacked by the Spanish, destroyed, abandoned, and refortified between 1625 and 1630. Recognized formally as a French colony in 1659, Tortuga was home to French, English, Dutch, and African corsairs who were eventually known commonly as "buccaneers." Upon relocating to Grande Terre (the main island of Saint-Domingue), the economy of the colony changed from piracy and plundering to plantation agriculture. Initially, colonial entrepreneurs experimented with crops like indigo and cocoa, but eventually sugar and coffee would emerge as the primary cash crops that made Saint-Domingue, at its height, the wealthiest of all of France's colonies. Of course, none of this wealth would have been possible were it not for a brutal and murderous regime of racial slavery, the likes of which never existed in French Canada and exactly the likes of which the French hoped to replicate in Louisiana.[13]

Louisiana was claimed for France and named for its monarchs by René-Robert Cavelier, Sieur de La Salle, in 1682, but the French did not expend resources to develop the territory for almost twenty years; the first permanent settlement was not established until 1699. The founder of the first permanent settlement in Louisiana, Forth Maurepas, was Pierre Le Moyne, Sieur d'Iberville. Iberville was an adventurer who had made a name for himself when he, along with his brother Jacques and their Mohawk, Ojibwé, and Algonquin allies, massacred sixty British colonists in the village of Corlaer (Schenectady), New York, in 1690. Following a successful naval campaign against the English in Hudson Bay, Iberville was tasked with establishing a French presence at the bottom of the Mississippi River Valley to ward off Spanish encroachment in Louisiana and to guard the mouth of the Mississippi River itself. Under Iberville's guidance, French diplomatic efforts in Louisiana were aimed at establishing friendly relations with local Amerindian nations, and French military efforts were focused on organizing buccaneers to prey upon the Spanish and English in the Caribbean.[14]

Iberville's younger brother, Jean-Baptiste Le Moyne de Bienville, established the city of New Orleans in 1718. In 1722, despite being little more than a barracks and a few decrepit warehouses and hovels, New Orleans was declared the capital of Louisiana. Census numbers of that time indicate nearly 300 white people, roughly 200 enslaved Africans and Amerindians living in New Orleans (presumably behind the rampart), with roughly another 800 people "of all castes nearby."[15] It is critical to understanding métissage in Louisiana and the ethnogenesis of Creole people there, that between the founding of the city and 1721, of the 7,020 white people brought to Louisiana, only 1,215 were women.[16] Historian Thomas Ingersoll describes French immigration to Louisiana after 1721 as "minimal," accounting for fewer than 1,000 people between 1721 and the end of the early French period in 1763.[17] As late as 1730, the French colonial presence in Louisiana amounted to no more than 2,000 settlers and an estimated 4,000 enslaved people in a territory spanning more than 523,000,000 acres

that was inhabited by tens of thousands of Amerindian people. By the time
the Spanish came into possession of Louisiana, New Orleans was already
home to a distinct Creole population, the result of three or more generations of miscegenation between Europeans, Africans, and Amerindians.[18]

Under Spanish authority, Louisiana developed a tripartite caste system
based on a principle of "limpieza de sangre," or "cleanliness of blood."
Jennifer Spear argues that the Spanish notion of "blood purity" was "initially defined by religious criteria, which named Jews, Muslims, heretics
and their descendants as those whose blood was unclean." However, "in
the Spanish-American colonies, the list of those who did not possess pure
blood had expanded to include all those with Indian or African ancestry."
This was problematic for many Creoles as the lack of European women
in New Orleans's earliest days as a military outpost led to mixed-race
children even among Creole elites. Sacramental records were changed
to reflect this new racial order, with parents occasionally (and sometimes
retroactively) omitted or listed as "unknown" so as to safeguard claims to
white privilege. Indeed, Creole elites proved remarkably adept in revising
documentation to establish "pure white" ancestry which was often more
myth than fact. Other Creoles utilized the gaps and spaces of Spanish
racial classification to "pass into" the elite (that is, white) caste over time,
a process which was not overly difficult in Spanish Louisiana, particularly
if the individual in question was phenotypically European and affluent.[19]

To regulate slavery in Louisiana, the Spanish would appropriate much
of the French Code Noir of 1724. However, the Spanish also introduced las
Siete Partidas to Louisiana, which established the most important provision
to the growth of the free colored population in Louisiana aside from concubinage. That provision was "coartación," or the right of the enslaved to
purchase him/herself. Coartación "demonstrated in concrete terms the
Spanish attitude that slavery was an unfortunate but temporary condition that could be overcome." It also allowed incoming Spanish colonial
authorities a tool with which to undermine planter autonomy and economic power. Coupled with a provision that guaranteed the enslaved person a right to work for him/herself to gather the funds for self-purchase,
the Spanish gave enslaved Africans and enslaved Creoles (and their free
relatives) an incentive to support the Spanish colonial regime that did

not exist during the early French period. In this way, the Spanish sought to divide the interests of Creole slaveholding elites from the interests of Creoles of the marginalized and servile castes.[20]

During the Spanish period, the status of free people of color became more defined, but the malleable nature of their position within the social hierarchy contributed to an instability of its own. Free people of color existed as an "in-between" group situated "below" Whites and "above" the enslaved, a group that in 1763 was comprised mostly of Afro-Creoles, and Creole Indians, the latter of whom were often reclassified as Blacks or "mulatres," especially after the Spanish made it illegal to enslave Amerindians. This hierarchical social order imposed by the Spanish was an attempt to position free Creoles of color in such a way as to divide their interests; yet, perhaps inevitably, such attempts were not able to eliminate overlap between the interests of free Creoles of color and that of both the dominant "white" caste and the enslaved caste, the latter of which became increasingly, visibly, Africanized during the Spanish period as a result of the Spanish's increased importation of African bondsmen.[21]

Although the French had used colored troops at times, colonial militias of free Creoles of color became a foundational institution of Spanish Louisiana. These militias were a check on the power of elite Creole planters as they were comprised of men whose claim to legal privilege—to honor—rested on the support of Spanish authorities. Even though these free Creoles of color were intimately connected to elite white (French) Creoles by language, custom and more often than not by blood, these militias were used by colonial Spanish administrators to limit the influence of white Creoles who were still making "secret overtures to the French minister in Philadelphia asking that France recover the province" ten years after O'Reilly's bloody demonstration of Spanish authority.[22] These militias were also used by the Spanish to prevent, and potentially suppress, slave rebellions even though these free men of color were intimately connected to enslaved Creoles in exactly the same ways that they were connected to white Creole elites. Indeed, free colored militias were often tasked with capturing runaways and assaulting runaway slave ("maroon") communities. These militias would become a cornerstone of the political and social identity of free Creoles of color during the Spanish period.[23]

Historian Gwendolyn Midlo Hall argues that the strong family connections and shared identity between free Creoles of color, enslaved Creoles, and Creole maroons rendered attempts to use the free colored militia to apprehend maroons "useless." Hall rejects the idea that "there was a deep conflict and hostility between the slave and emancipated black and mixed-black population or between mixed-blood and black." However, when she expounds on those strong family ties which contributed to militia ineffectiveness, she does not refer to the ties between free people of color and the maroons (most of whom were also Creoles), but the ties between the maroons and the enslaved which Hall suggests were "so numerous that free blacks and coloreds were afraid that the relatives of the maroons that they might capture or kill would seek vengeance and retaliate against them." It is not clear, for Hall, whether or not familial affection and a sense of African solidarity or a more cynical and self-interested fear of violent retribution for their collaboration with the slave system was at the root of the free colored militia's ineffectiveness in addressing runaways. It would seem, in keeping with the emerging in-between identity of Creoles of color during this period, that both considerations—conditional solidarity with the enslaved and conditional cooperation with the colonial slave society—manifested, circumstantially. Ultimately, the lack of clarity in Hall's account can be forgiven insofar as it is a reflection of the murkiness of the actual circumstances.[24]

For free Creoles of color in Spanish Louisiana, there were many opportunities for conditional solidarity across ethno-racial and caste lines. These opportunities existed between themselves and enslaved Creoles and between themselves and enslaved Africans. However, opportunities also existed between free Creoles of color and white French Creoles, between free Creoles of color and white Spaniards, and, eventually, between free Creoles of color and Spanish Creoles, too. Because of this apparent fluidity of allegiance and because their ties of community and kinship often transcended the racialized caste identities imposed on them by colonial authorities, free Creoles of color were often perceived as holding dangerously divided loyalties. However, there is little to indicate that these Creoles' actual loyalties were so questionable or ambiguous. In fact, it seems that free Creoles of color were consistently loyal, at least to one group: themselves.

Political upheaval at the end of the eighteenth century in Saint-Domingue had profound effects on Louisiana, particularly in New Orleans's community of free Creoles of color. Refugees from Saint-Domingue of all colors and castes fled to Havana, Kingston, St. Augustine, Mobile, Charleston, Baltimore, Norfolk, Philadelphia, and other ports along the Eastern Seaboard of the United States where some reestablished themselves permanently. For many, however, these places were temporary destinations en route to New Orleans where more than ten thousand refugees from Saint-Domingue permanently settled between 1791 and 1810, doubling the population of the city. New Orleans was seen as a favorable destination due to the shared language, religion, and, as Nathalie Dessens observes, a "real proximity in 'ethos and class structure' between the two societies" which included a shared tripartite caste system.[25]

The free colored refugees of Saint-Domingue assimilated into the existing free Creole community in New Orleans but changed it in significant ways. In Saint-Domingue, Africans outnumbered Europeans and mixed-race people by a margin of at least seven to one, and the Creole culture of Saint-Domingue was distinctly African. Many of the free people of color who arrived in New Orleans in the wake of the Haitian Revolution were skilled tradesmen and relatively affluent; some were even slaveholders. In Saint-Domingue, Creoles of color, mixed-race and otherwise, were not only free but also citizens of France after 1794 and thus had a greater vested interest in maintaining the French colonial order. This reality contributed to a qualitatively different, in many ways more sophisticated, political culture among Saint-Domingue refugees from that of free Creoles of color in New Orleans. That qualitatively different political culture became integral to an emergent Afro-Creole protest tradition which would pose challenges to governing authorities in Louisiana, especially after the Louisiana Purchase of 1803.

Louisiana experienced profound changes under the American regime. A rush for land in Louisiana brought thousands of settlers into the territory. These settlers carried their language (English), their religion (which was overwhelmingly Protestant), and their republican political sensibilities into a land populated by people who spoke many different languages (French, Spanish, Creole, and various Amerindian and African languages as well), who were officially Catholic and who had no experience of representative government whatsoever. A viable plantation economy, that most elusive of goals for the French, had emerged in Louisiana under Spanish rule but, with the arrival of American settlers, this economy would expand dramatically, which led, inevitably, to the expansion of chattel slavery and a hardening of racial lines in Louisiana.

Steeped in a history of black-white categorization, American settlers arrived in Louisiana with a set of racial expectations that stipulated black bondage as a necessary counterpoint to white liberty, and although pockets of racial liberalism existed during this same period in the Anglo-American states (notably with the rise of abolitionist sentiment and activism in the north), those Anglo-American settlers who migrated to the slaveholding South were thoroughly invested in, and utterly riveted to, a brutally oppressive language of race and slavery. As Adam Rothman makes clear, the Americans who moved west from Virginia and the Carolinas to settle the fertile lands of the Lower Mississippi River Valley took their values with them as they sought to transmute the wild frontier of Louisiana into "slave country" and all that that term implied. Their attempts to create this slave society were largely successful, in no small part due to the economic dividends paid by this new racial order. Sugar and cotton nurtured by the blood, sweat, and tears of enslaved people, transformed Louisiana from a colonial backwater into the forefront of an Atlantic economy where slavery and commercial success were axiomatic. For Louisiana's Creoles of color, who were themselves products of racial and cultural hybridity, this hardening of racial lines and the arrival of thousands of white settlers and African American slaves from the United States presented new, uncomfortable, and unwelcome challenges. Not only did these new settlers visibly represent a new and vastly different, racially defined social order, but the rigidity and characteristic severity associated with the rise of American slavery in Louisiana proved particularly troubling for those people (particularly free Creoles of color) who had historically navigated between (and sometimes across) racial boundaries. In particular, the stark black-white divide of race/caste relations had little room for Creoles of color who had existed in between the color lines of French and Spanish rule.[26]

Between 1820 and 1850, New Orleans became the largest slave market in the Deep South. Not only did this accentuate the visibility of the black-white racial divide but the arrival of tens of thousands of Anglophone African Americans (mostly from the Chesapeake Bay area and the Carolinas) considerably altered the ethno-cultural milieu of south Louisiana. Their arrival further exposed the position of free Creoles of color who were powerless to prevent the erosion of their peculiar "in-between status" once authorities began to dismantle the relatively liberal policies that had defined the rights of people of color, enslaved and free, under the Spanish.

In 1828, the Louisiana Code was changed to prohibit the legitimization of mixed-race children under any circumstances. In 1834, the free black militia was de-authorized by the Louisiana state legislature, eliminating a key organ of upward mobility for free Creoles of color. Between 1825 and 1842, the freedom of movement of free people of color was severely restricted with a number of laws crafted to either forbid free people of color from entering Louisiana or demanding that emancipated slaves leave Louisiana upon attaining their freedom under penalty of re-enslavement. As Caryn Cossé Bell observes, for free people of color in Louisiana in 1850, the "struggle to remain free often proved as challenging as the struggle to become free." Free people of color certainly had more extensive legal protections than did slaves, yet as Judith Kelleher Schafer observed, "Any white person, not just the civil authorities, could and did force free Blacks to prove their freedom." Though Creoles of color still enjoyed remnants of their old privilege insofar as "Louisiana law presumed that light-skinned persons of African descent were free" and "dark skinned 'Negroes,' as the law termed them, were presumed to be slaves," that particularly American sensibility articulated in the Supreme Court's *Dred Scott* case in 1857 defined the reality of Creoles of color in antebellum Louisiana: nonwhite people in the United States of America had no "rights" that existed beyond the convenience of the white majority.[27]

Despite their common social and political position of subordination to the dominant white caste, there were significant barriers to solidarity between free Creoles of color and the enslaved. The glorification of phenotypical European features and the corresponding degradation of phenotypical African features, or put simply, "colorism," was one such barrier. John Blassingame observed that this "separation was encouraged by the whites as a means of dividing the Negroes and making it easier to control them."[28] Yet, it is important to understand that this intra-caste hostility had its origins in a very real class division between free Creoles of color who enjoyed the benefits of education, and in some cases wealth and property, which inhibited solidarity with poorer Blacks who lacked access to such privilege.

As the enslaved population of Louisiana had become more "American" (that is, Anglophone and Protestant) between 1820 and 1860, cultural dissimilarities between free Creoles of color and Louisiana's enslaved population contributed to even greater emotional and psychological distance between the two groups. The differences in language between Francophone (and Creolophone) Creoles and Anglophone African Americans presented obvious challenges to solidarity: they literally did not speak the same language. However, not only did Creoles speak a language that was unintelligible to African Americans, but it was also a language that Creoles of color shared with Francophone and Creolophone Whites. This linguistic heritage reinforced Creoles' "in-betweenness" and would significantly impact Creole–African American relations well into the twentieth century.

The practical effect of religious differences between Roman Catholic Creoles and Protestant (particularly Calvinist) African Americans is also particularly significant. Indeed, part of the eighteenth-century French ethos transplanted to colonial New Orleans was the Roman Catholic belief in "extra Ecclesiam nulla salus" ("outside of the Church is no salvation"). Indeed, prior to the American period, there was no guarantee of religious freedom in Louisiana, and under France and Spain the state religion was that of the Roman Catholic Church. In *Dominus Iesus,* published in August of 2000 by the Congregation for the Doctrine of the Faith (the institution formerly known as the Holy Office of the Inquisition), Cardinal Joseph Ratzinger (later Pope Benedict XVI) reaffirmed the Church's centuries-old position on the inherent spiritual defectiveness of "ecclesial communities which have not preserved the valid Episcopate and the genuine and integral substance of the Eucharistic mystery" in a manner consistent with the Roman Catholic and Eastern Orthodox traditions. As the Roman Catholic Church does not regard them as "Churches in the proper sense," such ecclesial communities were formed, and exist contemporarily, in dogmatic error and hold no doctrinally whole or complete means to salvation. Such "ecclesial communities" include all Protestant Christian denominations and thus, in addition to class, caste, and linguistic differences, African Americans (like all Protestants) were, according to Catholic doctrine, almost certainly guaranteed a separate (and qualitatively inferior) afterlife from Roman Catholic Creoles, as well.[29]

This intra-caste hostility presents a dilemma to those who seek to identify a unified commitment to a progressive Afro-Creole agenda of social equality and racial liberation in Louisiana in the nineteenth century. Indeed, Creoles of color were embedded in the broader antebellum slave economy, and some were propertied, owning real estate and even slaves. Despite legal restrictions enacted by the Louisiana legislature in the 1830s to restrict the right of free people of color to inherit property, the property holdings of Creoles in New Orleans were significant by 1861. For example, according to Kimberly Hanger, free people of color had owned more than a quarter of all New Orleans's Third Ward since 1800. By the time Louisiana voted to secede from the Union in January of 1861, this property in the Third Ward included many homes occupied by immigrant Whites who paid their rent to free women of color. To suggest that free people of color in 1860 who occupied positions of power and authority over Whites (as landlords, for example) were able to somehow transcend that vantage of class privilege to declare unconditional solidarity with black slaves in the name of liberté, égalité, et fraternité overstates the case.

Still, whether they were wealthy and *passé blanc* (that is, "able to pass for white") or "low brown" (with skin that was a dark, brown color) and working class, Creoles of color in Louisiana were still subjected to racist repression and discrimination. These "in-between" people were a problematic group for Anglo-Americans whose notions of race/caste struggled to come to terms with Creoles who were neither slaves nor citizens and who were, often in the same instance, both indigenous and foreign. The American response to this problematic population was to promote white supremacist legislation and amplify racial repression. Many Creoles responded to this by leaving Louisiana altogether for Mexico, Haiti, France, and elsewhere.

The loss of skilled Creole labor in New Orleans did not go unnoticed by the white majority. By 1859, even the conservative *New Orleans Daily Picayune* was compelled to mute its typically Negro-baiting editorial tone to publish a flattering homage to New Orleans's community of free Creoles of color, proclaiming:

> Our free colored population forms a distinct class from those elsewhere in the United States. Far from being antipathetic to whites, they have followed in their footsteps, and progressed with them, with a commendable spirit of emulation, in the various branches of industry most adopted to their sphere. Some of our best mechanics and artisans are to be found among the free colored men. They form the great majority of our regular, settled masons, bricklayers, builders, carpenters, tailors, shoemakers etc whose sudden emigration from this community would certainly be attended with some degree of annoyance . . . whilst we count among them in no small numbers, excellent musicians, jewelers, goldsmiths, tradesmen and merchants. As a general rule, the free colored people of Louisiana, and especially of New Orleans—the "Creole colored people," as they style themselves—are a sober, industrious and moral class, far advanced in education and civilization.[30]

Sweet words from the editorial desk of the *Daily Picayune* did little to assuage Creoles' anxiety. In 1859, they may have formed the "great majority" of bricklayers, masons, and no few of them may have made their livings as tailors, jewelers, and merchants, but waves of immigrants from northern states, as well as from Europe, were pouring into the city during this time. The arrival of these Irish, Germans, and Italians contributed to increased social pressure on Creoles, as the character of New Orleans became increasingly Anglophone and as the influx of immigrant labor threatened Creole control of trades that they had traditionally dominated as a part of "their sphere." By 1860, the position of Creoles in New Orleans—politically, socially, and economically—had become precarious, indeed.

On the eve of secession, the city of New Orleans was just as divided as the rest of the country. The Anglo-American community, fortified by Irish and German immigrants to the city who had arrived between 1830 and 1860, was largely based in uptown New Orleans "above" Canal Street.

"White" Creoles predominated in downtown New Orleans, "below" Canal Street, along with "those other parts of the community which seemed to fuse with them into a kind of Latin solidarity" including "the foreign-born French and Mediterranean stock" and free people of color, most of whom were "natives closely allied with white creole culture and, indeed, equally entitled to the name *creole*." These divisions in the white community had often provided opportunities for Creoles of color to seek advantage for themselves, but those opportunities became fewer and farther in-between after the Civil War.[31]

Slaveholding elites and their proxies in the state legislature removed Louisiana from the Union on January 26, 1861. Louisiana Governor Thomas Overton Moore called for five thousand volunteers on April 21, 1861, and more than a few Creoles of color, in keeping with the tradition of the old Native Guards, mustered to form a Confederate regiment comprised of free men of color in response to that call. According to nineteenth-century Creole historian Rodolphe Lucien Desdunes, some of these men "could have been misled and so believed that it was their duty to remain faithful to the Confederacy," and though Desdunes is hardly an objective source, there is no reason to doubt his dismissal of those men as insignificant in number. In the end, the Confederate Louisiana Native Guard existed as little more than an article of secessionist propaganda. The Confederates never intended the unit to be fielded, and so there were no funds allocated for equipping the guardsmen; each soldier was responsible for supplying his own uniform and his own weapon. In the end, the Native Guard's duties were restricted to little more than parading as Whites balked at the prospect of arming people of color, free or no. Due to the racism of their white "comrades," most Creole officers resigned their commissions long before the fall of New Orleans.[32]

By April of 1862, Union forces occupied New Orleans with relatively little bloodshed, bringing Confederate Louisiana's direct, official involvement in the Civil War to an end. African American "contraband slaves" began pouring into the city from surrounding rural areas and gathered around Camp Parapet, a Union base established by Brigadier General J. W. Phelps near the river bend in Jefferson Parish. Phelps sought to form a regiment of colored soldiers out of these men, and so he articulated his appeal in terms of patriotism and manly honor, accompanied with promises of compensation (including land) in a fashion reminiscent of Andrew Jackson's exhortation to Louisiana's free colored population prior to the Battle of New Orleans. Some Creoles, sensing an opportunity, answered the call, and roughly one week after the fall of New Orleans, a delegation referred by Phelps representing New Orleans's colored Creole community, comprised of Edgar Davis, Eugéne Rapp, and the brothers Henry and Octave Rey, approached General Benjamin F. Butler to address the possibility of mustering a colored regiment. None of the Creoles spoke English, and Butler spoke no French, but through an interpreter, Mr. St. Albain Sauvinet, the former guardsmen claimed to have been coerced into taking up arms with the rebels amidst threats to their property and lives and assured Butler of their support and loyalty to the federal cause. Butler hoped to fortify his position in New Orleans in light of rumors of a Confederate counterattack and saw an opportunity in "re-commissioning" a Confederate unit of free colored troops and so allowed for the formation of a colored Union regiment, the First Louisiana Native Guard.[33]

Historian Stephen J. Ochs observed that Creole mutual aid societies and fraternal organizations "formed the basis of the individual companies" of the Native Guard and that the officers of these organizations, "having already won the trust and respect of their men, were often elected as officers of their companies." According to Ochs, Company C of the First Louisiana Native Guard was composed almost exclusively of men who "lived as neighbors in a nine-by-twelve block area . . . just downriver from the Vieux Carré." Indeed, the ties that bound these men spanned generations and included kinship relationships of both blood and marriage. Some were descended from free men of color who fought at the Battle of New Orleans at the end of the War of 1812; some few were, in fact, veterans of that battle. In a testament to the clannishness and insularity of New Orleans Creole society, it is worth noting that, from the War of 1812 to the Civil War, the families of Creoles of color who bore arms together remained largely the same: Barthé, Bertonneau (Bertonniere), Decuir, Glapion, Porée, Rochon, Rey, St. Cyr, and Thibaut (Thibault), among others, including Cailloux.[34]

André Cailloux was a free Creole who claimed to be of unmixed African lineage. He was an accomplished boxer, equestrian, and marksman and was invariably described as an imposing and inspiring presence who was capable of reconciling "both slave and free, black and mulatto." For Ochs, the phenomenon of the Afro-Creole war hero André Cailloux and his ability to unite people of color in New Orleans testifies to the efficacy of the "cauldron of war" to reducing "barriers between slave and free and American and Creole." The prospect of universal emancipation and full enfranchisement "encouraged increased cooperation among them [African Americans and Creoles of color] in pursuit of a common goal" of liberation, according to Ochs. Cailloux became a martyr to that cause when he died in a hail of bullets while storming Confederate fortifications at Port Hudson on May 27, 1863, almost two months before the more celebrated Fifty-Fourth Regiment Massachusetts Volunteer Infantry's gloriously doomed assault on Fort Wagner in South Carolina. The gallantry of Cailloux became a potent and unifying symbol for people of color in Louisiana, freemen and freedmen alike.[35]

Unfortunately, Archbishop Jean Marie Odin of New Orleans did not understand the significance of Cailloux's memory and thus chose not to honor it. The archdiocese's reaction to the occasion of Cailloux's funeral would create a crisis in New Orleans's Creole community, negatively affecting relations between the Roman Catholic Church and the city's colored Creole community for the next fifty years. Pro-Confederate Catholic clergy in New Orleans had enacted interdictions against Creoles of color who bore arms against the Confederates, refusing them access to the sacraments and to Christian burial. The notable exception to this policy of interdictions was the founding pastor of St. Rose de Lima Catholic Church on Bayou Road near Esplanade Avenue in New Orleans's Seventh Ward, Father Claude Paschal Maistre. For his efforts, Maistre was accused of antiwhite incitement and, at the insistence of Odin, was censured by the Vatican, which threatened formal excommunication of any who attended services he officiated. Regardless, Maistre persisted in his ministry, and in the end, it was he who performed the Requiem Mass of André Cailloux.[36]

Maistre's congregation would operate as a schismatic group within the Roman Catholic Church in New Orleans until he was forcibly removed from St. Rose de Lima by a detachment of Union soldiers sent by General Nathaniel P. Banks, who sought to soothe relations between the Union and the Archdiocese of New Orleans (which had remained staunchly pro-Confederate). This was accomplished by silencing Maistre, who had been accused of enflaming racial tensions through his ministry. Prior to the Civil War, this sort of intervention would have had dire repercussions for the colored Creole community as by law it was exceedingly difficult for people of color to create formal organized institutions outside of the Catholic Church. However, that prohibition was lifted after the fall of Confederate Louisiana. As a result of Bishop Odin's interdiction, Cailloux's funeral services were held at the meeting hall of the Friends of the Order, a Creole fraternal organization and benevolent society.[37]

One effect of the diminishing influence of the Catholic Church on the Creole community was that Creoles began to cohere around new social sodalities, voluntary associations, and fraternal orders. Some of these groups, like the Comité Central des Natifs, functioned as employment bureaus and were organized specifically to benefit liberated slaves. Others, however, were more political in nature, and, particularly with regard to pro-Union organizations that agitated for black rights, these associations became the foci for much of the anxiety and rage of conquered Confederates in Louisiana.

Alienated from the Catholic Church, many Creoles turned to alternative faith traditions. Much of the evidence suggests that they favored Spiritualist circles and freemasonry to voodoo and other Afro-Latin syncretic traditions. Other (though fewer) Creoles abandoned the Catholic Church for (Anglophone) Protestant congregations, a process facilitated and accelerated by Creole patronage of educational institutions like Straight University, a private college established by an interracial abolitionist group from New York called the American Missionary Association, which was affiliated with the Methodist Church.[38]

Despite its antagonism to Creole aspirations for social equality, the Catholic Church still played a major role in the Creole community by providing resources for the education of Creole children. Educational opportunities for Creoles in New Orleans in the antebellum period were extremely limited outside of the umbrella of the Roman Catholic Church, and the Civil War did not change that. In compiling a report on the state of "colored" education in New Orleans in 1864, Major General S. A. Hurlbut noted the "'Creoles,' generally of French or Spanish extraction, when not educated abroad, or at the North, or from fairness of complexion, by occasional admission to the white schools, were quietly instructed at home, or in a very few private schools."[39] More often than not, those private schools were parochial.

The Couvent School, organized by the Société Catholique pour l'Instruction des Orphelins dans l'Indigence, provided classes for "orphaned" children of color ("orphan," in this case, often referring to children of color whose white fathers had abandoned them) without charge and demanded a modest tuition fee from those who could afford to pay. The Sisters of the Holy Family, a Catholic order founded by a New Orleans Creole of color, Mother Henriette Delille, circumvented the law to instruct people of color both free and enslaved. These institutions were largely protected by their affiliation with the Church and financed by wealthy Creoles like Thomy Lafon, whom Marcus Christian described as the "first negro banker" in the United States and who, according to A. P. Tureaud, made his fortune by fencing pirated Baratarian contraband through his storefront in the Vieux Carré. Higher education was unavailable for those without wealth, but for those with the means, these schools served as preparation for further instruction, often abroad.[40]

The existence of segregated public schools that colored Creoles were taxed to maintain (but which would not serve their children) had been a point of contention before the Civil War, and it was not long after the fall of New Orleans that colored Creoles set about the task of desegregating New Orleans public schools. This would prove to be the first in a long line of battles for civil rights and social equality in New Orleans. Ironically, that first battle would be fought, not against a racist southern oligarch, or against an unrepentant Confederate, but against Union General Butler, who "personally quashed" desegregation efforts in 1862. Creoles were struck with a second defeat at the hands of Union "allies" in December of 1863 when President Abraham Lincoln made it clear that federal guidelines for Reconstruction would not include an extension of universal black (male) suffrage. The Civil War had provided an opportunity for people of color to enjoy expanded liberty, but on New Year's Day 1864 public education was still reserved for Whites only in Louisiana.[41]

During the gubernatorial election and selection of delegates to the constitutional convention of spring 1864, the issue of school integration would come again to the fore. Opponents of integration, like constitutional delegate Edmund Abell of New Orleans, for example, were clear in their intention to "fight every proposition that looks to the commingling of the colored with the white race," but in the end, Abell and his supporters were rebuked (though only mildly), and the Louisiana Constitution of 1864 passed, abolishing slavery in the state and providing for public education of children of Louisiana from age six to eighteen without regard to race/caste. Changing the laws did not change the attitudes of Louisiana Whites, however, and practically, segregation remained the rule in New Orleans public schools. Still, in all of the United States, Louisiana was the only state to undergo school desegregation in both the nineteenth century and the twentieth century, and this was largely due to the efforts of an economically empowered and politically aware Creole community that pressed the case for full social and political equality after the Civil War.[42]

In November of 1864, some Whites in Louisiana sought to isolate this Creole community from the freedmen community through legislation that became known as the "Quadroon Bill." Playing on the ethnic differences (often marked by phenotypical differences) between Creoles and African Americans as a means of dividing their interests, Louisiana Senator Charles Smith wrote that he "thought the time had arrived when persons having a large proportion of Caucasian blood in their veins, residing in the state of Louisiana, should be recognized as white and entitled to all the privileges of white men." The bill, which would have allowed any person with one-fourth or less African "blood" to identify as "white" was defeated in the Louisiana Senate, finding little support among Creoles of color.[43]

It is very possible that, prior to the Civil War, Creoles might have responded very differently to a "Quadroon Bill." In antebellum Louisiana, the realization of revolutionary aspirations of equality with Whites was impossible, and in that environment, Creoles of color fought to maintain their distinction from enslaved Blacks. Yet, in the chaos of the Civil War and its immediate aftermath, the political environment in Louisiana had changed dramatically, and partly as a result of this new political environment, the response of Paul Trévigne, Creole editor of pro-Union journal *l'Union*, and its replacement, *The Tribune*, was withering. Trévigne noted that there "may be a handful of selfish men that would accept the privilege provided by Mr. Smith's bill, but they are not numerous" and that the Creole community could not and should not support legislation that, in Trévigne's words, "would have created three castes . . . when it is bad enough to have two."[44] The social order of antebellum Louisiana had been disrupted by the Civil War; the slave country created by Anglo-American settlers had been occupied, and its armies routed by federal troops. In this new political environment, Creoles of color perceived their interests as bound to that of the freedmen. Indeed, one free man of color (presumably Creole) articulated that exact sensibility to Whitelaw Reid in 1865, suggesting that "we see that our future is indissolubly bound up with that of the negro race in this country; and we have resolved to make common cause, and rise or fall with them. We have no rights which we can reckon safe while the same are denied to the field-hands on the sugar plantations." Creoles of color declared solidarity with African American freedmen, yet theirs was a solidarity largely void of fraternity and, as a result, the "common cause of the negro race" in New Orleans was perpetually contested and continually compromised.[45]

In the immediate aftermath of Confederate Louisiana's fall, the political and social position of freedmen was precarious and ill-defined. During this same period, Creoles positioned themselves as leaders of a, theoretically, united black community. Looking to the experience of the French Antilles in 1848, where all enslaved persons in Guadeloupe and Martinique were emancipated and granted universal male suffrage, Creole radicals in New Orleans exhorted the people of Louisiana and of the United States to make people of color "honored citizens" and to "model [its] fundamental principles on those of France, and like her, reach the heights of civilization." The political agenda of Creoles in Louisiana during the 1860s included the dismantling of Louisiana's caste system, which would benefit all people of color, and so Creoles articulated that agenda using the language of race, and used racial affinity as a means of pursuing political equality, not only for themselves, but also for African American freedmen.[46]

In fact, there was a significant gap between theory and practice with regard to Creole and African American racial solidarity. David C. Rankin's

1974 study on "black" leadership during Reconstruction concluded that the overwhelming number of "black" delegates to the 1868 Louisiana Constitutional Convention were of mixed heritage and often roughly, inaccurately and, often to their sensibilities, offensively, classified as "mulattos." Unlike the African American freedmen they claimed to represent, many Creole delegates were phenotypically European, and most spoke French. When directly questioned about their racial background, it was not uncommon for Creoles to respond indecisively or ambiguously. Nevertheless, a generalized opposition to white supremacy was enough to bring Creole and freedmen interests together in 1868, and the Louisiana Constitution which was ratified that year still stands as an example of revolutionary republicanism and a philosophical and political commitment to social equality that could only be described as radical.[47]

Rankin's demographic survey of the people of color that served in the Louisiana legislature, and who were responsible for ratifying the Constitution of 1868, also offers insight into the class stratification that separated the interests of many Creoles and African Americans. The colored delegates to the 1868 Louisiana Constitutional Convention were overwhelmingly from the middle class, the vast majority being skilled artisans, businessmen, and professionals before the war. Most of them possessed wealth valued between $1,000 and $25,000. The vast majority of them were free before the war, and of those, the majority had been born to free parents. Most of them lived on the downtown side of Canal Street in Creole New Orleans, as opposed to the American Quarter of the city "above" Canal Street, in residences clustered in and around the Vieux Carré. Materially, the circumstances of Creoles and Freedmen could not have been more disparate. Still, for Creoles and African Americans in New Orleans who were marginalized by the white majority, there was no way forward, politically, outside of racial solidarity.

Confronted with the prospect of fully enfranchised Blacks and racially integrated public accommodations, particularly racially integrated public schools, conservative Whites in Louisiana united behind what they perceived as common racial interests. Former slaveholding Whites particularly, whether Creole or Anglo, found it particularly difficult to shed themselves of the language and practices of slavery and white paternalism.

Though people of color vigorously challenged them, white conservatives busily worked to restore the social privileges of whiteness: to "redeem" Louisiana for white rule. In this reworking of the racial order, American Whites and white Creoles abandoned old points of ethnic contention in favor of a unifying investment in "whiteness."

In order to guard their own positions of privilege, white Creoles invested in a mythology that proclaimed their racial purity. Historian Jay Gitlin suggests, convincingly, that white Creoles' choice to invest in the ideology of white supremacy was, at least in part, due to "the tendency of Anglos increasingly to view all French people in racialized terms, as being nonwhite" since "the French in the United States were thought to be more inclined than Anglo-Saxons to racial mixing . . . with both Indians and blacks."[48] Historian David Roediger observed a similar assertion of whiteness by Irish immigrants to the United States in the mid-nineteenth century who were "eagerly, militantly, and loudly white, even and especially when not broadly accepted as such."[49] Just as Creoles had scrambled to revise their ancestral histories to reflect "blood purity" after the Spanish had taken possession of Louisiana in the 1760s and 1770s, white Creoles a little over a century later scrambled to revise the history of Creole ethnogenesis in Louisiana to accommodate nineteenth-century concepts of white racial "purity." Scholars like Charles Gayarré produced revisionist histories that whitewashed the multiracial origins of Creole Louisiana, proclaiming that a Creole was a "person of pure white blood" and that the wives of the original French soldiers who founded Louisiana "were not, as has been generally stated and believed, house of correction women, but industrious and virtuous girls of the same rank as their husbands." This was, of course, absurdly transparent revisionism, but in the polarized racial environment of Reconstruction, this convenient lie was infinitely preferable to the alternative choice of admitting nonwhite ancestry and opening themselves up to the risks associated with white American racial hatred and bigotry.[50]

Still, as historian Justin A. Nystrom observes, "as late at the mid-1870s . . . white New Orleanians remained divided in their attitudes toward the status of the city's substantial population of mixed-race citizens," and "[b]lood ties across the color line could and often did feed both liberal and reactionary impulses." Nowhere was this more apparent than in the Unification movement, a political alliance between white elites and their colored Creole cousins (literally, in at least one instance) in early 1873. Although they had assailed the Republican carpetbagger Warmoth, the Roudanez brothers, the Creole publishers of the *Tribune,* stood shoulder to shoulder with former Confederate General Pierre Gustave Toutant Beauregard in Unification. White Creole Michel Musson would join the movement with his first cousin, Edmund Rillieux, who was the younger brother of colored Creole inventor Norbert Rillieux; ironically, Michel Musson was also a White Leaguer who was chosen as "presiding officer of the occasion" of a white supremacist coup d'état in 1874. Nystrom notes that the Unification manifesto "bore a remarkable resemblance to the Civil Rights Act of 1964," but it seems that very few of the Whites who joined the movement took seriously notions of affording people of color social equality. Less than a month after Unification published its manifesto, it seems many Whites (including both Beauregard and Musson) had abandoned the effort. Racial identity and commitment to white supremacy had trumped both bonds of cultural affinity and familial loyalty.[51]

The effort to safeguard their claims to white privilege divided families along color lines in a dynamic described by George Washington Cable in his story "Belles Demoiselles Plantation," originally published in 1874. In Cables's story, two Creole cousins—one white, one mixed-race—engage one another with less than familial amity until they are brought together in the end in a tearful, deathbed reconciliation. Cable's story called into question the "pure whiteness" of all New Orleans Creoles and earned him the enmity of no few white Creoles, including Gayarré himself, who dismissed Cable as "a malevolent, ignorant dwarf."[52]

Marcus Christian noted the diligence with which white Creoles "assiduously pruned away the dark-skinned branches from their family trees, erased or destroyed public records, and in several celebrated court cases resorted to high-priced lawyers to keep them ever-pure."[53] As they "passed over" fully into a "white American" identity, white Creoles' connections with their cousins (often literally) in the colored Creole community were typically severed, at least publicly. Ultimately, this contributed to the waning of Creole influence in the city and, as historian Joy Jackson notes, "from the 1880s on, the [white] Creoles were a declining ethnic group and no longer a vital factor in politics as they had been before the Civil War." Tregle agrees, observing "that by the 1890s what might be called [white] 'creole society' was already an anachronism in the city where once it had been the vital present." To successfully confront the radical Republicanism of colored Creoles and their allies in the legislature, to undo the gains afforded people of color under the 1868 Constitution, and to reassert a regime of white supremacy in Louisiana, white Creoles divorced themselves from Creole identity. It is for this reason that references to "Creoles" or "Creoles in New Orleans" or the "Creole community" in this study, from this point on, should be understood as references to Creoles of color. In the end, it was impossible to deny the multicultural, multiracial origins of Louisiana's Creole people, and so for many, including most contemporary scholarship of "black New Orleans," the identity of the "New Orleans Creoles" became largely synonymous with New Orleans "Blacks," or "African Americans."[54]

The Unification movement failed as conservatives in Louisiana responded to the radical efforts of black legislators during Reconstruction with ideological extremism, murder, and terror. Sometimes this extremism manifested as night riders like the Ku Klux Klan and the Knights of the White Camellia, organizations dedicated to suppressing colored suffrage. However, the cause of white supremacy in Louisiana was not an unpopular one, and other white supremacist organizations, like the Crescent City White League, for example, operated openly. Indeed, White Leaguers did not attempt to obscure their identities, and some of the most affluent men in the city were members. Working closely with the Democratic Party and championing the disputed Democratic regime of John McEnery, the Crescent City White League represented the fruition of the efforts of white Americans and white Creoles in New Orleans to make a stand against Republicans, carpetbaggers, and freed Blacks. In September of 1874, after a bloody gunfight which would be later referred to as the Battle of Liberty Place, Crescent City White League insurgents took control of the statehouse and held the government for three days until federal troops returned to re-occupy New Orleans and restore federal control over the city.[55]

The chicanery associated with the contested 1876 election provided the backdrop to the restoration of white political power in Louisiana, and the Democrats wasted little time in gutting the progressive aspects of the preceding Republican administrations. Emboldened by extremism, white supremacists attempted to silence the black vote and to elect Democrats who would undo the gains of the 1868 Constitution. The result of their efforts, the Louisiana Constitution of 1877, was arguably the most radically oppressive and racist legal code the state had ever been governed under.

The introduction of formal racial segregation in the 1880s forced Creoles and freedmen into one subordinate caste position beneath Whites, a situation that Creoles deeply resented. Whereas Creoles had vigorously and vehemently opposed racial segregation, African American community leaders had adopted a more accommodationist stance to racial separation. Creoles created a new social order in Louisiana in 1868, characterized by equality before the law and the dismantling of the legal structures of caste. However, African American freedmen were not as interested in Creole aspirations of liberté, égalité, et fraternité as they were in being, as one freedman put it, "rid forever of MASTERISM."[56] Historian Joel Williamson notes that, throughout the South, it was often the case that segregation and racial separation often were "the Negro's answer to discrimination" as much as it was the Whites' answer to the reality of black emancipation, and as Louisiana Whites "redeemed" their state, Creoles in New Orleans found themselves caught in between a great mass of Whites and Blacks, few of whom seemed to wish to participate in the same society together.[57]

As racial separation became the order of the day, some Creoles in New Orleans would protest this new social order by circumstantially "passing" into whiteness when possible, thereby "defrauding" white society of privileges reserved for the dominant caste. Other Creoles chose to flee the state permanently and passed completely into white identities once removed from their social context in Louisiana. As a community, however, it seems that Creoles responded by withdrawing and separating themselves from African Americans, socially. Marcus Christian observed that, after the failure of their radical agenda, Creoles "drew themselves into a clannish group, and in pride and self protection, refrained from all possible social intercourse with full-blooded negroes." Indeed, one cannot help but detect a tone of underlying contempt in Desdunes's articulation of what he perceived as the essential differences between Creoles (or "Latin Negroes") and African Americans (or "Anglo-Saxon Negroes"): "One hopes, and the other doubts. Thus we often perceive that one makes every effort to acquire merits, the other to gain advantages. One aspires to equality, the other to identity. One will forget that he is a Negro in order to think that he is a man; the other will forget that he is a man to think that he is a Negro. These radical differences act on the feelings of both in direct harmony with these characteristics. One is a philosophical Negro, the other practical."[58]

The choice Creoles made to withdraw from the African American community was ideological and cultural. However, Marcus Christian put it most succinctly when he suggested that the value attached to fair skin by black people in New Orleans could not be overstated given that they lived in a society where "color [was] everything and everything else [was] secondary." The antebellum connection between free status, free lineage, and European features reinforced colorism and antiblack prejudice among Creoles after Reconstruction, and this attitude created dissonant relations with (typically dark-skinned) African American freedmen who eventually came to denounce these Creole attitudes as bigotry and racial self-hatred.[59]

Throughout the nineteenth century, Creoles were structurally compelled to obsess over their social status. Sometimes, tiny slips of paper confirming free status was all that stood between a man (or woman) and a life of bonded servility.[60] Even then, their "freedom" was extended as a privilege by Whites; it was not enjoyed as an inalienable right, and so being able to prove status, often through lineage, became a necessity. That necessity created an extremely status-conscious people who, Marcus Christian maintains, "became almost painfully historically minded" and who, after their constitutional revolution of 1868 had been defeated, desperately grasped after the tattered remnants of antebellum class and caste privilege as they "did not intend to be relegated to the great mass of ignorant Negro freedmen." As in antebellum times in Louisiana, the realization of revolutionary Creole aspirations of equality with Whites was impossible, and so, once again, Creoles fought to maintain their distinction from (formerly enslaved) Blacks. Just as it had been in antebellum times, that distinction was often constructed in terms of phenotypical appearance as status-obsessed Creoles understood both the practical value of fair skin and "good hair," that is, hair that was in texture "nearest to a white man's" as well as the relative devaluation of dark skin and "nappy" or "bad hair," or "that which most closely approximated that of the pure Negro's." Still, colorist sensibilities among Creoles did not prevent them from acting collectively to challenge white supremacist rule.[61]

It was a cohort of Creoles and their allies who came together as le Comité des Citoyens and brought the issue of racial segregation to the highest court in the land in 1896. In 1890, the Louisiana legislature passed the Separate Car Act, which demanded "separate but equal" accommodations in intrastate train transportation for Whites and people of color. The committee immediately mobilized against this law and orchestrated a dramatic challenge to it on June 17, 1892, when Homer Plessy, a passé blanc Creole "octoroon," refused to relinquish his seat in the "Whites Only" section of a train bound for Covington, Louisiana, a small suburb of New Orleans on the North Shore of Lake Pontchartrain. The resulting case, *Plessy v. Ferguson,* was the first to draw upon the equal protection clause of the Fourteenth Amendment as justification for dismantling the legal basis for a caste system that had always been enforced by law and custom but which was forced to rearticulate itself in the face of the civil rights amendments to the Constitution that accompanied the aftermath of the Civil War. Reconstruction-era legislation had not changed custom, and white advocates of racial segregation articulated the desire to be separate from colored people as a matter of personal freedom and individual liberty. The majority opinion of the Supreme Court concurred with white separatists, arguing that individuals ought to have the right to free association and furthermore, that if the desires of Whites to be separated from Blacks imposed a feeling of inferiority upon black people, then this was due to black people projecting a sense of inferiority upon themselves that was altogether unrelated to white people or white people's wishes to be segregated from them.[62]

Curiously, although the Supreme Court refused to acknowledge an imposition of inferiority through segregationist legislation, it did affirm that in a white supremacist society, whiteness, indeed the "reputation" of being white, was itself property "in the same sense that a right of action or of inheritance is property." This, a definitive articulation of the basis for

America's racialized caste system ("whiteness as property"), was an important element of the case as Plessy argued that the notoriety of the case had deprived him of his "reputation as a white man." Plessy was denied, despite his appearance, because by law he was not in fact entitled to the property of a reputation as a white man.[63]

In the end, Plessy did not prevail. Perhaps in recognition of the absurdity of the circumstances, though, the majority opinion of the court advised Homer Plessy to challenge his "blackness" under the law in Louisiana.[64] As historians David Brown and Clive Webb have observed, although passing for white may have "improved the status of individual African Americans, it represented a tacit acceptance on their part of the southern caste system."[65] Plessy never bothered to challenge his "blackness" in court because, for Homer Plessy, "blackness" was not the issue. It was not colorism, or Negrophobia, or a desire to become white that drove Plessy's struggle to the Supreme Court. On the contrary, he pursued his case all the way to Washington, DC, as a challenge to white supremacy. That challenge did not originate in the cane fields of southern Louisiana, nor did it originate in the working-class, African American neighborhoods of New Orleans, or on the waterfront. Homer Plessy's challenge originated in Creole New Orleans, where petite-bourgeoisie, often white-looking, people of color challenged racial oppression from a precarious vantage point that existed in between the color lines of Jim Crow America.

2

STRANGERS IN THEIR OWN LAND

The reification of a modern caste system in the United States was not confined to an event but was the end result of a historical process. That process was rooted in an explicit history of legal white supremacy most concisely articulated in the Dred Scott case where, in the majority opinion of the court, the social inferiority of people of African descent in the United States was the "universally recognized . . . natural position and real status of the negro" and, moreover, "no legal decision can be found in all America based on any other assumption."[1] Though the Fourteenth Amendment to the Constitution would reverse the legal implications of this decision, granting (at least in theory) the protections of citizenship to all people born in the United States, regardless of racial designation, the culture of white supremacy, particularly in the southern states, would not be undone by any act of Congress.

At the turn of the twentieth century, Creole people in New Orleans experienced a more radical, nationalist Americanization that articulated itself in a vocabulary of race that was utterly foreign to them, but that they were absolutely beholden to. These experiences forced Creoles to see themselves in ways that they were not accustomed to; they were forced to see themselves as Americans saw them.

Complicating the narrative, Americans saw all sorts of things when they set their gaze on the Creole people of Louisiana; sometimes they saw "Whites," sometimes "Blacks," and sometimes "Indians." Still, by the early twentieth century, certain tropes had been established in both literature and popular media. Examining some of these tropes promises insight into the ways that Creoles were portrayed in the popular (English-language) American media at the turn of the twentieth century, how the image of "Creoles" was constructed in the popular American consciousness, and, conversely, how Creoles perceived themselves in relation to the Anglo-American majority (both Whites and Blacks).

The explicit adoption of southern paradigms of white supremacy by the US government as represented by the *Plessy* verdict was coupled with a surge of American nationalism between 1898 and 1918. This ideological commitment to racism and nationalism constituted two key components of a modern social and cultural movement of Americanization that had a profound effect on New Orleans and particularly on the New Orleans Creole community.

Theodore Roosevelt, president of the United States from 1901 until 1908, an ardent proponent of a progressive "New Nationalism," and, in the words of historian Robert Wiebe, "a man of unlovely traits" who "nursed harsh personal prejudices" and who "relished killing human beings,"[2] articulated the position of the American hegemon in a letter to his acquaintance Richard Hurd, dated just three days before his death in January of 1919:

> There must be no sagging back in the fight for Americanism merely because the war is over. There are plenty of persons who have already made the assertion that they believe the American people have a short memory and that they intend to revive all the foreign associations which most directly interfere with the complete Americanization of our people. . . . There can be no divided allegiance here. . . . We have but room for one flag, the American flag. . . . We have but room for one language here and that is the English language, for we intend to see that the crucible turns our people out as Americans, of American nationality, and not as a polyglot boarding house.[3]

Roosevelt's comments were directed at European immigrants who, if willing to assimilate and become "American," could expect to be "treated on an exact equality with every one else, for it is an outrage to discriminate against any such man because of creed, or birthplace or origin."[4] Of course, the lesson of the *Plessy* verdict was that people of color (including Creoles specifically) were not included in this social contract. After all, what European immigrant braved the Atlantic crossing in hopes of being escorted to jail by policemen for having a seat in a train car reserved for Whites only? New Orleans's Creoles were not immigrants, but they still had no legal claim to the "exact equality with every one" available to foreign-born (white European) immigrants that Roosevelt mentioned in his missive. Creoles in New Orleans at the beginning of the twentieth century were foreigners in their own country. Rendered politically powerless as a community, they were disenfranchised and at the mercy of white men who, for the most part, did not speak their language and who resented Creoles for not speaking English.

Creoles in Louisiana had always been a part of a transnational dialogue with the Francophone world, yet, at the turn of the twentieth century, that legacy was not necessarily perceived as a cultural asset. Anglo-Americans in Louisiana had determined, like Roosevelt, that there was only room for the English language in the United States, and although the existence of Francophone and Creolophone people in Louisiana complicated that determination, it did not dissuade or undermine the white Anglo-American majority's commitment to "English only" as a political principle in the state. There is no doubt that Creoles intuitively grasped this dynamic: the Creole word for "English," when referring to the language, is not "Anglais" but "'Mericain."

Turning Creoles into Americans was a traumatic process for many, but that did not dissuade Anglo-Americans in Louisiana from prosecuting that agenda. A 1916 legislative act mandated public education in Louisiana. This was followed up with a 1921 Louisiana Constitution which demanded that mandatory education be administered in English, exclusively. The prohibition on the use of French in school by the students themselves was often enforced through the application of corporal punishment. Beating Francophone/Creolophone children for speaking their native languages in school and forcing them to kneel on corn kernels or rice were common methods of enforcing linguistic "discipline" in the classroom and on the schoolyard.[5]

Roosevelt had argued that infusing political action and consciousness with nationalized identities in the United States was not conducive to the public good. He railed against the use of the hyphen to divide people into

"Italian-Americans," "German-Americans," "Irish-Americans," and so on. Speaking at a Columbus Day celebration at Carnegie Hall in 1915, Roosevelt was direct and unambiguous:

> There is no place here for the hyphenated American . . . and the sooner he returns to the country of his allegiance, the better. . . . The one absolutely certain way of bringing this nation to ruin, of preventing all possibility of it continuing to be a nation at all, would be to permit it to become a tangle of squabbling nationalities, an intricate knot of German-Americans, Irish-Americans, English-Americans, French-Americans, Scandinavian-Americans, or Italian-Americans each preserving its separet [sic] nationality, each at heart feeling more sympathy with Europeans of that nationality than with the other citizens of the American Republic.[6]

Roosevelt's inclusion of "English-Americans" among the list of unacceptable hyphenated identities must have seemed like a magnanimous courtesy to the predominately Irish Catholic crowd of Knights of Columbus gathered at Carnegie Hall that evening. Yet, for all his magnanimity, it is doubtful that anyone in the crowd took those flattering words at face value. It was the privilege of Anglo-American elites, like Roosevelt, to imagine their own context and perspective as "the norm" to which other prospective Americans ought to conform, as Robert Wiebe observed: "Few found it possible to deny that somehow the United States was caught up with Britain in a common destiny, a vague yet compelling belief that the American Negro soldier captured with grim unintentional humor when he spoke proudly about 'us angry Saxons.' Even the citizens accused of being 'German-American' or 'Irish-American' never thought to retaliate with 'British-American,' for fundamentally 'British-American' was the norm by which one calculated deviations. 'Anglophile,' the closest counterpart, carried none of the hyphen's divisive, disloyal connotations."[7]

It is telling that Roosevelt's musing on prospective citizens included no "Japanese-Americans" or "Chinese-Americans." Nowhere in Roosevelt's nationalist diatribe was there any mention of "Native/Indigenous-Americans" much less "African-Americans" and, certainly, there was no mention of Creoles. These omissions reflect that sensibility which did not perceive people of color as citizens in the sense that white Europeans, even foreign-born white Europeans, could be citizens of the United States. Though people of Chinese, Japanese, Amerindian, and African descent resided within the country, they were, nevertheless, excluded from the larger civil dialogue. At the same time that these people experienced exclusion and marginalization, however, they were all still subject to similar pressures to assimilate and conform to Anglo-American norms as European immigrants were. Most often, for those who were not white, those pressures were even more severe.

In the end, the difference between Roosevelt's concept of the public good of the United States and Anglo-American hegemony in North America was semantic. Anglo-American hegemony *was* Roosevelt's public good, and it was in Roosevelt that this ideology found its greatest and most passionate advocate. Yet, where Roosevelt exhorted those unwilling to Americanize to return to their countries of allegiance, Creoles in New Orleans had nowhere to go. Creoles had not come from any other country; the country had come to them, and after a little more than one hundred years, the Anglo-Americans had finally established themselves as the dominant ethnic group in Louisiana, in general, but also in New Orleans, specifically.

At the turn of the twentieth century, the Creoles of Louisiana were largely regarded as foreign and exotic "others" by Anglo-Americans, white and black alike. Some Creoles bristled at this objectification, complaining that "Northern People come here to New Orleans to study us as curiosities. They walk up and down Royal street with 'Dr. Sevier' in one pocket, 'The Grandissimes' in another and "Old Creole Days' in their hands trying to identify the localities and types of person."[8] Indeed, the success of George Washington Cable's fiction contributed to a popular perception which was described by the editor of the *Indianapolis Freeman* in 1901 as the "perversity which causes some Northerners to insist that the term 'creole' signifies an admixture of Negro blood."[9] White Creoles in Louisiana continued to protest the practice of associating the Creole identity with people of color well into the twentieth century, repeating the distortions of Gayarré, but their efforts were feckless. Though they were white, white Creoles still lacked the structural power to control the way they were perceived by the Anglo-American majority, and the Anglo-American majority perceived them as foreign curiosities and the products of French race-mixing.

In *The Black Image in the White Mind: The Debate on Afro-American Character and Destiny, 1817–1914,* historian George Fredrickson suggested that at the turn of the twentieth century, "mulattos"—shorthand for any mixed-race people—were constructed as a degenerate species of humanity by white racists. Mulatto women were thought to be emotionally fragile, prone to hysteria, jealous, and sexually perverse. Mulatto men were constructed as natural-born rapists and insatiable sexual predators who had too much "white blood" to accept a life of passive servility but too little to avoid behaving like animalistic savages. All said, these views echo earlier Anglo-American commentary on mixed-race Francophone and Creolophone people dating at least as far back as Washington Irving's tour of the Missouri Territory. Just as Beatte was constructed as a contrast to the civilized Irving and his European companions, and just as Tonish was the only one of his companions for whom Irving details a sexual history, at the turn of the twentieth century, mixed-race people were still constructed as antithetical to a harmonious, civilized, white society, and as being predisposed to sexual deviance.[10]

Stereotypes based on these ideas were writ large on the silver screen in D. W. Griffith's 1915 film, *The Birth of a Nation.* Based on Thomas Dixon's 1905 novel, *The Clansman,* Griffith's Civil War film depicts a white, carpetbagger politician, Austin Stoneman, manipulated into acting against his own (that is, white) people after falling under the influence of a sultry (mulatto) maid, Lydia Brown. His mulatto lieutenant, Silas Lynch, leads a clique of black Reconstruction-era politicians who feast on chicken and wine while legislating their right to marry white women. The Ku Klux Klan is introduced as a civic-minded group of patriots who cannot abide this state of affairs and who resist the mulatto tyranny of Reconstruction. Through the Klan, southern Whites and northern Whites find reconciliation in their common struggle against Lynch and in "common defense of their Aryan birthright."[11]

The impact of *The Birth of a Nation* cannot be understated. The normalization of the Ku Klux Klan and of white southern racial sensibilities in general cannot be seriously discussed without mentioning this film, which remained the largest-grossing motion picture for more than two decades after its release.[12] The imagery of the minstrel show was taken from the vaudeville stage and bawdy houses and presented to mainstream American audiences as history. Silent images of mulatto rapists chasing white women to their deaths over cliffs spoke thousands upon thousands of ugly, ignorant, bigoted words, and all of those words warned of the dangers of a society based on racial equality and integration. In Griffith's portrayal of Reconstruction, white actors in blackface portrayed uppity Blacks pursuing an agenda of Black supremacy which, apparently, consisted mostly of bullying defenseless white people and pushing them off of public sidewalks.

Writing in the 1920s and 1930s, Marcus Christian recalled a "legend" of a white lawyer who deserted his white family for the Creole family that he maintained in New Orleans. By Christian's account, "one day the colored wife met the white wife and pushed her from the sidewalk. When the white wife remonstrated and added . . . that she was 'Mrs. So-and-so' the colored common law wife retaliated, 'Well, I am Mrs. So-and-so, too!'"[13] Perhaps Christian's tale recalls, with added detail, the story contained in an angry letter to the *Louisiana Gazette* in 1825 from a "Mother of a Family" complaining of insolent Creole women driving her from the city's walkways and threatening the racial purity of Louisiana's best families through their dalliances with wealthy white men. However, it is equally possible that Christian's tale originates in the sensationalized stories of Creoles—particularly of Creole women—published in Anglo-American newspapers at the turn of the twentieth century.[14]

Editorialist William M. Lewis in a column titled "Pencilings" for the *Freeman* newspaper of Indianapolis observed in 1902 that in Louisiana "microscopes are called into requisition in order to tell who is who and what is what" and that "Negro blood, 'tis said, has percolated in many of the grand old Creole families, and it requires eternal vigilance in keeping these sun-kissed beauties from capturing the very citadel of society."[15] Whether or not microscopes were truly requisitioned in cases to determine blood quantum, what was undeniable was the presence of old Louisiana family trees with branches that breached the color line. To explain this, stories of the dazzling glamour of sun-kissed Creole women overwhelming the better sensibilities of otherwise reasonable white men became as ubiquitous as the legends of Marie Laveau, the nineteenth-century "Voodoo Queen of New Orleans" (and hairstylist), who was said to concoct love potions for her wealthy clients.[16]

Another example was "How He Liked It," a piece of creative fiction about Creoles by an author identified only as N. Y. Ledger, published in the *Detroit Plaindealer* in June of 1890. The story begins with a conversation between the "old Major," Gerald l'Estrange (literally, "the foreign"), and Dolores, the wife of his nephew who is a Creole woman from New Orleans. Upon meeting Dolores for the first time, the old major wonders to himself, "is this the girl my nephew Paul has married? . . . She is nothing but a child, and a lovely child too. . . . She was only 16, but she belonged to the beautiful creole race, who blossom so early into womanhood . . . with her jet black hair gathered into a net of gleaming gold." As the story proceeds, the elder l'Estrange is compelled to humiliate his nephew, threatening to cut off his monetary support. This attack is launched in defense of Dolores, the New Orleans Creole girl whose charms have forced the old major into action. The resolution of the story entails Uncle Gerald l'Estrange providing a monthly cash allowance to his nephew on the condition that he allow his wife unfettered access to her rightful portion of it without having to seek his permission to spend it. After Uncle Gerald guarantees Dolores's financial emancipation from her husband's authority, he asks her: "'And you are sure you are quite happy now?' 'Oh yes, quite,' declared Dolores with emphasis." It is then left to the reader to imagine Uncle Gerald as either a benevolent, fatherly, Kris Kringle–type figure, or as a lecherous hebephiliac. Similarly, the reader is free to imagine Dolores as a mostly clueless, unquestionably virtuous belle, or as a dark-haired Creole enchantress with a savage sexuality simmering just beneath the surface of her milky-white skin that even the most refined southern gentlemen found impossible to completely resist.[17]

"How He Liked It," though an extremely short composition, provides a wealth of insight into the way Creole identity, particularly the identity of a Creole woman, was constructed in the popular Anglo-American imagination. Although Dolores's virtue is uncompromised, it is clearly her beauty, the shapeliness of her form, and the power of her unconscious sexuality which compels old Major l'Estrange to provide her with the means to assert her independence from her husband; it is a sanitized allusion to the history of free women of color in New Orleans who lived as concubines and who inherited large swaths of property for themselves, and for the children they bore to their white paramours.[18] The sexual tension between the old Uncle Gerald and the pubescent Dolores hints at the illicit liaisons between the Creole girls who "blossomed so early into womanhood" and the old colonial history of French planters and Spanish dons who were responsible for the abundance of nonwhite people in Louisiana bearing names like Trepagnier, Charbonnet, Martinez (pronounced MAWt-in-ehZ), and Pappas. Dolores's "jet black hair" certainly suggests perhaps a touch of the tarbrush (that is, generationally removed and remote non-white ancestry), which was, itself, no barrier to a claim to whiteness in 1900 New Orleans as long as it was impossible to prove in court.

One true-life Creole story, ripe for fictionalization, was the case of Mary Belle Tardy who, in March of 1890, took Dr. Maurice B. Early to court for $25,000 for breach of promise. The story of Mary Belle Tardy's litigation was run in the *Brooklyn Daily Standard-Union*, the *Marion* (New York) *Enterprise*, the *St. Paul Appeal*, and the *Roanoke Daily Times*. One week later, a reprint of the *Appeal* article was published in the *Cleveland Gazette*. Tardy is described variously as a "Negro woman," "a good-looking mulatto girl" and, in the *Standard-Union*, as a "good-looking octoroon . . . who is said to be so white that she would be readily taken for a Caucasian." Tardy, who claimed that her father was white and that her mother was a Creole, charged Early with turning her out into the street "in a delicate condition" after promising to marry her. She and Dr. Early, who was white, already had three children together and, although they lived in New York, where Early worked, they were both natives of Lynchburg, Virginia.[19]

The fullest picture of the drama between Mary Belle Tardy and Dr. Maurice B. Early was in the account offered by the Brooklyn paper, which begins by describing the entire situation as "a funny story." Early did not deny turning Tardy out into the street, but instead offered as explanation that Tardy's mother was not a Creole, but a "full-blooded African." If the reader has difficulty in imagining the humor in a pregnant woman with three children being thrown out into the street for having a mother of arguably nonwhite ancestry, the story proceeds from there to identify Tardy as the daughter of Maurice Early's cousin. However, if the reader still experiences difficulty in identifying the humor, the *Daily Standard-Union* delivered the punch line at the end: "the paradox here appears that, though prompt to make love to the plaintiff, he was a tardy wooer. His early promises are tardy of fulfillment and she hopes to bring about a tardy settlement of his alleged promise of marriage. . . . What would have been thought a few years ago of the daughter of a quadroon bringing suit . . . for breach of marriage especially?"[20] Such a convoluted tale of love across the color line in the South played into the cliché of the "tragic mulatto," a recurring literary trope that emerged in abolitionist propaganda in the middle of the nineteenth century but which was also used often in cautionary tales meant to dissuade miscegenation.

There is a general agreement that the earliest example of the "tragic mulatto" in literature was Lydia Maria Child's 1842 short story, "The Quadroons." However, it was an 1856 novel by Thomas Mayne Reid titled *The Quadroon, or, A Lover's Adventure in Louisiana* that would extend the reach of the trope into the modern era. The plot of *The Quadroon* revolves around an Englishman who arrives in New Orleans and falls in love with a quadroon woman. Although she had lived her life under the impression that she was free, through the novel's course of events she discovers that she is actually a slave. Eventually, the protagonist succeeds in liberating her, and the two elope, being unable to marry in Louisiana due to the constraints of the caste system there. Reid claimed that the events and characters he described were real and that the "book was 'founded' upon actual experience" though he maintained that all names had been changed to protect the identities of those involved. All of the narrative components of the "tragic mulatto" are represented in *The Quadroon,* including commentary on racial in-betweenness, the uncomfortable phenomenon of "white" slaves, and the allegedly inevitable self-hatred that people of mixed race were forced to deal with as a result of their status.[21] *The Quadroon* was adapted for the stage by Dion Boucicault and debuted at the Winter Garden Theater in New York City in 1859 as *The Octoroon.*[22] In 1913, Boucicault's play was adapted by Bartley Campbell for a film titled *The White*

Slave or The Octoroon directed by James Young and starring his wife, Clara Kimball Young, a white woman from Chicago whose career was marked by her willingness to take on sexually risqué roles.[23]

Ultimately, the media accounts of Mary Belle Tardy and Maurice B. Early were not unique. The national press carried multiple accounts of illicit relations across the color line that enhanced the prototypical concept of Creole deviance. In May of 1890, the *Cleveland Gazette* published a story titled "A Southern Romance" about Dr. Charles H. M'Callister of Chicago. M'Callister had sued his stepmother and cousin for $20,000 that had been left to him by his father, a wealthy southern planter who owned a two-thousand-acre plantation on the banks of the Ohio River. According to the *Gazette*, his mother was a quadroon who had moved to New Orleans where, it was reported, "the pretty young girl passed for a Creole, after learning to speak French." M'Callister was raised with his half-brother and half-sister, who were both white, but had survived them both. So, M'Callister brought his father's second wife (who was white) to court after she refused his claim to money his father had set aside for him in his will. Despite the story's headline, it is difficult to discern exactly what it is about a bitter intrafamilial fight over money and inheritances that might be described as originating in the excitement associated with love. However, the story does mention Creole people, and contemporary audience expectations of stories involving Creole people in 1890 demanded romance, and if that romance was sordid and/or ended in tragedy, so much the better.[24]

On June 21, 1890, the *Cleveland Gazette* ran a prominent page-two article titled "Elopes With a Creole, Colored William McKay Jilts an Older Sister for a Younger." William McKay, a thirty-five-year-old African American man living in Plainfield, New Jersey, and working as a coachman, stole away with sixteen-year-old Laura Robinson, the daughter of a Baptist deacon, after having been engaged to marry her older sister. The *Gazette* reported, "Miss Robinson is said to be a creole. She was a pupil in the high school, and is a handsome girl," yet the paper did nothing to qualify Robinson's claim to a Creole identity and thus left readers with a number of unanswered questions.[25] For example, Robinson is not a French or Spanish name, which was often a reliable (though not universal) indicator of Creole heritage. Robinson's father was a deacon of a Baptist congregation, not a

Roman Catholic like most Creoles in Louisiana; was he a Creole (and a Protestant convert), or was her claim to a Creole identity through her mother? Indeed, perhaps most problematic is that the reader is left to wonder if Laura Robinson's sister was somehow less Creole given her inability to enchant Mr. McKay sufficiently to prevent his abandoning her. In the final analysis, there is actually nothing at all in the *Gazette* story to indicate that Robinson was a Creole yet, given the journalistic tropes of the time and audience expectations, one must consider the possibility that Ms. Robinson was only ever "said to be a Creole" because she was a "handsome girl" who had apparently blossomed fully into womanhood by sixteen and who was involved in a sordid romance with her sister's thirty-five-year-old fiancé.

On July 15, 1890, the editor of the *Cleveland Gazette* was posed with a dilemma. The *Gazette* reported that the *New Orleans Crusader*, the print publication of le Comité des Citoyens, was owned by a stock company composed of both "white and colored men, but the editor is a Negro." Yet it also reported that "Ex-Editor Albert of the New Orleans (La.) S.W.C. Advocate, says Editor Martinet is a Frenchmen. Which is right; neither?" Perhaps the confusion was due to the African American editors of the *Gazette* being unable to imagine a person being a "Frenchman" and a "negro." Or perhaps it was because Martinet was, as they go on to clarify, "a very light Creole."[26]

Louis André Martinet was an important figure in New Orleans's Creole community. He operated a notarial practice on Exchange Alley between St. Louis and Conti streets in the Vieux Carré from 1888 until his death in 1917. His mother was a free woman of color, Marie Louisa Benoit from De Sainte-Claire, Louisiana; his father was Pierre Hippolyte Martinet, a carpenter who was born in Petanque, Belgium. Louis was one of eight children, but his parents were not married until only a few days before his twentieth birthday in December of 1869. From 1872 to 1875, he served as a state representative to the Reconstruction Louisiana legislature. In 1876, he marched in the first graduating class of the Law School of Straight University. In 1877, Louis Martinet served on the Orleans Parish School Board, the first of many government positions he would fulfill throughout his career. Martinet began publishing the *Crusader* in 1889. Of all the things Louis André Martinet was, he was not a Frenchman. Yet, in a context where "'Mericain" meant "one who speaks English," perhaps Martinet was more of a Frenchman than an American.[27] Or perhaps it is was because of Creoles' propensity to describe themselves as Frenchmen, in Creole, "mo Francé."

Alan Lomax's published interviews with Ferdinand Joseph LaMothe, *Mister Jelly Roll*, begins with "My Folks Was All Frenchmens." Jelly Roll Morton (LaMothe) describes his ancestors arriving in New Orleans "directly from the shores of France, that is across the world in the other world, and they landed in the new world years ago." Of his grandparents and great-grandparents, Morton recalled "they was never able to speak a word in American or English."[28] The veracity of Morton's account of all of his ancestors arriving in New Orleans from France is on par with his claim to have single-handedly invented jazz in 1902. Yet, this emphasis on French origins—an emphasis that was complemented by Anglo tendencies to associate French identity in America with nonwhite people—was common among Creoles in Louisiana and in New Orleans specifically.[29]

The city of New Orleans and its Creole community were constructed as sites of an alien, foreign, cultural production where deviance and exoticization merged into one. In 1902, the *Indianapolis Freeman* ran a two-part special series on New Orleans called "The Gay Paris of America." The series, written by J. D. Howard, promised "Facts Gleaned of Its Mongrel Population, Habits and Ways." The author explained over the course of five sentences that in writing the article he was "brought into closer touch with the strangest people, the strangest customs and the strangest city" in America. From this sensationally exotic introduction, the author plunged headlong, deeply, and passionately into the mandatory account of the "beautiful Creole girl whose dainty French accent, studied mannerisms, and cosmopolitan affections puzzle you for the moment just what category in which to correctly place her, as regards the scale of nations."[30] The *Freeman* correspondent did not mention whether the research for the article was accomplished with or without copies of *The Grandissimes* in one hand and *Old Creole Days* in the other, but the focus of the article was definitely on identifying and attempting to understand the "Creole Negro," in part, through contrast with New Orleans's African American community which, being Anglophone, represented the regional norm from which Creoles signified deviation. That said, Howard's *Freeman* piece on Creoles in New Orleans in 1902 was a serious journalistic effort that has been unfortunately overlooked.

Howard notes that even the "typical old 'black mammy'" who lived on the north side of Canal Street (Creole New Orleans) spoke "broken French and butchered English" and that everyone born downtown "is classed a Creole."[31] This view of a relatively uninformed, Anglophone outsider confirms A. P. Tureaud's description of the downtown New Orleans neighborhood where he spent his childhood. In interviews conducted between 1969 and 1970, Tureaud recalled to Joseph Logsdon:

> The neighborhood in which we lived was a neighborhood of whites and some Negroes and Filipinos. The whites were of mixed background. They were Italian . . . and there were some Spanish people from some of the Central American countries. . . . Esplanade Avenue was a very popular avenue for Creoles. Some of the famous people in the government of Louisiana lived there. Governor W. C. C. Claiborne and his descendants, for example, lived just a block from me. . . . Then there were other families with French names that represented the social elite of the city of New Orleans just along Esplanade Avenue where I played many a day on the neutral ground. Negroes also called themselves Creoles and others called them Creoles. In fact, in the section of the city where I lived, the 7th ward, we had a large number [of] so-called Creoles. Their ethnic background was a mixture of French, or Spanish, or Indian or West Indian.[32]

In 1832, Washington Irving had observed "half-breeds, creoles, negroes of every hue; and all that other rabble rout of nondescript beings" that lived on the frontier. By 1900, that frontier context had become markedly urban. In addition to the aforementioned twilight folk who would "hover about the confines of light and darkness" like bats in the colonial era, there were recently immigrated populations of Hispanophone Latin Americans, Filipinos, Italians (all of whom were considered "Whites"), and indeed the occasional American (both Blacks and Whites) as well. All of these people came together in Creole New Orleans, intermarried with one another, and added to the mélange.[33]

In many ways the social context of downtown New Orleans was very different from uptown New Orleans, "the American Quarter." Uptown, there were more Europeans than Latin Americans, and those Europeans tended to be northern Europeans, not southern Europeans. New Orleans's Irish Channel was situated beyond the Faubourg Ste. Marie, between First Street and Toledano and Magazine Street and the Mississippi River, uptown. Carrollton, near the Riverbend, was settled primarily by German immigrants. There were small pockets of Creoles in uptown New Orleans, but the colored community of Uptown was mostly Protestant African Americans. Uptown, for the most part, was an Anglophone community, in Creole, "ye té parl 'Merican-la." Uptown was the New Orleans of the Americans.

Gilbert E. Martin Sr., a native of the Seventh Ward, was an author and the founder of the International French Creole Cultural Society. In an article referencing the anti-American sentiment of the New Orleans Creole community of his youth in the 1920s, Martin described the prevailing attitudes of his parents' and grandparents' generation: "an undercurrent of resentment against the Americans flowed throughout the Creole community. And that resentment did not begin to abate until after World War II. Prior to that war, the older Creoles did not refer to themselves as Americans. They considered it an offense should anyone else referred [sic] to them as Americans. I saw many older Creoles spit on the ground after mentioning the word 'Merican.' As a young Creole . . . I didn't know why my elders hated Americans so much."[34]

To understand Creole perspectives on Americans in the early twentieth century, it is perhaps best to begin with Rodolphe Lucien Desdunes. Desdunes, born in New Orleans to a Haitian father and a Cuban mother, was sixty years old in 1911, the year that he published *Nos Hommes et Notre Histoire*. Desdunes was a Creole radical in the spirit of the 1868 Louisiana Constitution, and as the editor of the *Crusader*, his editorial voice was an important one in the early battles against segregation in New Orleans. Indeed, Desdunes reserved the right to take to task the foremost African American intellectual of his time, W. E. B. Du Bois, when the founder of the National Association for the Advancement of Colored People (NAACP) suggested that "the southern Negro lacked book learning and industrial skills." Desdunes, who categorically rejected any flight from "blackness" or a "Negro" identity, took exception to Du Bois's failure to appreciate Creole academic and artistic achievements. Desdunes also decried Du Bois for his poor attention to the ideologies of black liberation beyond the Anglophone sphere. According to historian Charles O'Neill, Desdunes called attention to Du Bois's misunderstanding of the context of the Haitian Revolution, chiding Du Bois for uncritically accepting Toussaint Louverture "as the greatest black hero of the Saint-Domingue revolution, whereas, in actuality, he argued . . . Toussaint l'Overture was the Booker T. Washington of Haiti." It was a bold and characteristically Gallic slap in the face, and *Nos Hommes et Notre Histoire* was Desdunes's follow-through.[35]

Nos Hommes et Notre Histoire is a short work, mostly of biographical vignettes and poetry. Rather than a true history, it is more of a tribute to the Creoles, or in Desdunes's terms, the "Latin Negro" people, of Louisiana. It begins by recounting the betrayal of free Creoles of color who were promised citizenship and an honoring of their rights as per the Louisiana Purchase Treaty in return for their service at the Battle of New Orleans by General Andrew Jackson. His account of this initial betrayal sets the tone for what amounts to a century's worth of struggle. The rest of the work presents a variety of biographical sketches of Creole authors and poets, professionals, Reconstruction-era politicians, musicians, and philanthropists. No matter where Desdunes meanders, however, he always returns to the central theme of his people's ongoing struggle against what he perceives to be a racist and unjust American regime. Desdunes's work was not a challenge to Du Bois's "Talented Tenth," but rather it was his insistence that Creole heroes be counted among them.[36]

Nos Hommes et Notre Histoire has often been cited by scholars of Creoles in Louisiana including Caryn Cossé Bell, Joseph Logsdon, and Rebecca Scott as a representative articulation of the ideological sympathy of the Creole community in New Orleans. The fact of the matter, however, is that Desdunes's voice was just one of many, and though he stands out as a champion of radical racial egalitarianism, there is little cause to infer that his views were shared by the majority of Creoles in New Orleans. Desdunes advocated solidarity between Creoles and "Anglo-Saxon Negroes"

(African Americans) for civil rights, but if such attitudes had been more widespread, one would expect that that conviction would be reflected in the membership of representative Creole organizations and social sodalities in New Orleans during Desdunes's time. The exact opposite is true, however. Radical Creole Republicanism had been defeated in the US Supreme Court, and in its place emerged a conservatism informed by colorist bigotry that distanced Creole interests from those of African Americans and, in some cases, even from other Creoles. Where Desdunes's generation demanded representation among the "Talented Tenth" of the "Negro race," many Creoles who came after him preferred not to be associated with anything to do with the "Negro race."[37]

From time to time, white Creoles would assert their right to call themselves Creole, restating the contentions of Gayarré that "true Creoles" were white. As late as 1926, one article published in the *Harrisburg Evening News* proclaimed that "the ire of many a 'Creole' has been provoked because the innocent tourist thinks the word means 'of colored blood.'"[38] It was to little avail, however: white Creoles were spitting into the wind as they desperately, yet unsuccessfully, offered their counter-narrative. George Washington Cable had done permanent damage to the Creole "brand" by associating it with race mixing and people of color, and so, fearful that their own racial purity would be called into question, white Creoles in New Orleans abandoned the Creole identity.

Creoles of color faced a different, and in many ways opposite, dilemma from that faced by white Creoles. The antebellum nomenclature of *gens de couleur libres* was obsolete since all people of color were nominally free in 1900. However, by embracing the Creole identity, Creoles were able to fortify a preexisting emotional and psychological distance from African Americans by emphasizing their cultural differences and fortifying the sense of "otherness" that Americans, black and white, ascribed to them. This emotional and psychological distance allowed some middle-class Creoles, particularly those who fostered bourgeois aspirations and pretensions, to extend the life of the antebellum tripartite caste division in the city by identifying themselves as an in-between "colored" caste that was neither white nor black and by conflating that caste position with a Creole ethnic identity.

In 1864, Paul Trévigne had scoffed at the attempts of Whites to divide the interests of Creoles and African Americans, but by the early twentieth century, Creole historians like Alice Moore Dunbar-Nelson (her own family names curiously absent of any trace of Latin influence) took delight in Grace King's misrepresentations concerning the supposed historical distinction between the "pure-blooded African" and the "colored" in Louisiana, positing the spurious notion that the "gens de couleur, colored people, were always . . . separated from and superior to the Negroes, ennobled were it only by one drop of white blood in their veins."[39] It did not matter that such a proposition was easily disproved by the prominence of free black (dark-skinned) Creoles like André Cailloux. Such myths served to infuse the realities of Creoles' social separation from African Americans with a spurious racial logic, in the same way that white racial mythologies served to legitimize white separation from non-Whites. Unsurprisingly, this spurious racial logic that separated "negros" from (mixed-race) "colored people" was reinforced through the power of the courts in Louisiana. Homer Plessy may have balked at challenging his blackness in court in Louisiana, but there were certainly other Creoles who did not.

In 1900, the state of Louisiana concurred with Creoles' self-assessment as an "in-between" racial group, at least for those Creoles of mixed ancestry. In 1894, the Louisiana legislature criminalized interracial marriage. In light of the failure of that 1894 law to prevent interracial sex, the Louisiana legislature passed another law in 1908 that prohibited a person of the "Caucasian race" from cohabitating or otherwise engaging a person of the "negro race" in a state of "concubinage." In 1910, Octave Treadaway was indicted for felony violation of the 1908 law for maintaining an "octoroon" paramour. However, the Louisiana Supreme Court found in Treadaway's favor and concluded that his companion, while "colored," was not a "negro." A "negro," the court maintained, was a designation that was only "properly applied to a race or variety of the human species inhabiting the central portion of Africa. . . . Their characteristics are skin black, hair wooly, lips thick, nose depressed, jaws protruding, forehead retiring, proportions of the extremities abnormal." Furthermore, the court clarified that there "are no negroes who are not persons of color; but there are persons of color who are not negroes." It was in response to the Louisiana Supreme Court's decision to acquit Octave Treadaway of the crime of miscegenation in the *State of Louisiana v. Treadaway* that the state would close the racial gap between "coloreds" and "negros," but the Treadaway decision had affirmed that among those persons of color who were not considered Negroes were mulattoes, quadroons, and octoroons.[40]

Many New Orleans Creoles self-consciously identified themselves as mixed race, and eventually the construction of Creoles as racially in-between, or "mixed," would become as much of a basis for inclusion in the city's Creole community as either ancestry or language. This sensibility was often articulated as a vicious colorism that not only manifested in strained Creole relations with (typically dark-skinned) African Americans but also contributed to strained relations within the Creole community. For example, there were rivalries between Creoles from the Seventh and Eighth wards, who saw themselves as "real" Creoles from "way back," and Creoles who lived across Elysian Fields Avenue, in the Ninth Ward. According to Creole jazzman Paul Dominguez, Ninth Ward Creoles spoke French and were apt to "call themselves Creole," but were nevertheless dismissed as "black" by "real Creoles" (that is, those from the Seventh and Eighth wards) because of their African features, including their "bad hair."[41] Still, to the extent that Creoles practiced a colorist elitism among themselves, those attitudes were practically benign when compared to Creole exclusion of African Americans.

Contemporary scholars of critical mixed-race theory have observed a number of ways that mixed-race people have approached the process of forming identities. In 2008, Kerry Ann Rockquemore and David Brunsma noted the four most common approaches to identity formation among several hundred mixed-race (that is, with one "black" parent and one "white" parent) people surveyed. The first approach, reported by almost 60 percent of all respondents, they describe as the "border" identity wherein the individual perceived their identity as separate from either parent (that is, not black and not white but biracial). The second most common approach was that of "singular" identity (that is, either black or white exclusively). The third most common approach was the "transcendent" identity that rejected racial categorization altogether. The last, and least common, was what Rockquemore and Brunsma described as the "protean" identity, which allowed the individual to assume different racial identities from context to context. Understanding these approaches is useful in understanding both how Creoles saw themselves and how they engaged with the larger community of New Orleans. While there were certainly individuals who identified themselves as "black/negro" and "white," and though there were some who rejected racial classification on principle, it seems that many Creoles adopted a "protean" approach to self-identification that allowed them to situationally pass for white or colored as their need arose.[42]

Sometimes Creoles identified themselves as Creoles, but sometimes they didn't. Depending on their phenotypical appearance, sometimes they identified themselves as white, sometimes they identified as black, and sometimes they identified as colored. Sometimes, Creoles were Americans and sometimes they were not; sometimes they were Acadian or French or Spanish or German. Sometimes Creoles identified themselves as Amerindians.

Sometimes, one person might identify him/herself as white, black, or colored all in the same day as they moved from one social (and/or physical) context to another. During the Jim Crow era in New Orleans, this phenomenon amounted to a culture of "situational passing" in which people of color who appeared to be white would assume a white identity for convenience without forsaking their nonwhite identity. This is in contrast to the more dramatic and absolute instances of racial passing which entailed people denying any and all nonwhite familial connections. For example, A. P. Tureaud, in recalling his first experience with racial discrimination to Joseph Logsdon, described the experience of working as a child at a job in his neighborhood where he situationally passed for white. His job was to deliver bread, but he was fired after six months once one of the partners in the business learned that he was not white.[43]

In New Orleans in 1900, Creoles understood the power they wielded in their racial ambiguity, and they capitalized on it when the opportunity to do so presented itself. New Orleans was no sprawling metropolis in 1900, but as small as the city was, Tureaud was able to work for six months at a local bread business before his employers discovered he was not white. Tureaud does not indicate, nor imply, that his employers learned this fact from himself, and so barring some outside interference, it seems that he could take home a (white) wage as long as he did his job and kept his mouth shut about his ancestry. This gave Creoles like Tureaud a marked advantage over those with dark skin and phenotypically African features, whether Creole or African American. Especially after the imposition of Jim Crow segregation, there was little incentive for Creoles to challenge their racial in-betweenness; on the contrary, there was an overabundance of cause for them to promote it.

Situational passing was possible because some Creoles, like Tureaud for example, looked white. However, situational passing would still have been a more difficult proposition if not for an unspoken agreement among people in New Orleans akin to "don't ask, don't tell." This unspoken agreement allowed people of ambiguous racial background access to white privileges just as long as they did not openly proclaim themselves to be nonwhite people. It was this unspoken agreement that allowed Homer Plessy to purchase a ticket for a "Whites Only" seat on the train to begin with, and it was this unspoken agreement that Plessy's attorney referred to as the "property" of the "reputation" of being white.[44]

Creoles understood the value of the reputation of being white, and many passé blanc Creoles were adept at exploiting their phenotypical whiteness for profit, a proposition that was actually much easier for passé blanc Creoles who left New Orleans during the Great Migration. Tureaud recalled moving to Chicago as a young man in search of job opportunities: "They were advertising for whites. They wouldn't take Negroes, even in a job like elevator attendant. . . . In every case where there was an opportunity for [passé blanc Creoles] to do so, they would take these jobs. Normally some of those people were too dark to be white in New Orleans; they would be easily identifiable as colored. But in Chicago they wouldn't know that much difference between them. In cases where the hair was the determinant, they'd cut their hair short. Or sometimes, they would use an accent."[45]

When the workday was done, these passé blanc Creoles in Chicago would go home to their families and their transplanted communities and resume their lives as people of color, enjoying "dinner and gumbos" with other Creoles who had also made the journey to the Windy City.[46] This history of Creole con men pilfering the privileges of whiteness, by its nature, does not lend itself to an abundance of case studies. Again, because the order of the day was "don't ask, don't tell," many chose not to ever speak of such things. Still, there are certainly a few high-profile stories demonstrating this dynamic that Tureaud describes, and perhaps the most compelling of them is that of the creator of the syndicated comic strip *Krazy Kat,* George Joseph Herriman.

George Joseph Herriman's paternal family origins in North America extend to the early seventeenth century and a man named John Harriman from Uldale, Cumberland, England, who settled in Massachusetts. His great-grandfather, Stephen Herriman, was born in Jamaica, Queens, in New York but moved to New Orleans in the 1850s with his wife, Jeannette Spencer, also from New York.[47] His grandfather George Herriman Sr. married a Creole woman named Justine Olivier who appears in the 1850 census as a "mulatto" born in Louisiana in 1797.[48] Both George Herriman Sr. and his son, George Herriman Jr., were members of the seminal New Orleans Creole fraternal society, the Fraternité No. 20 Masonic Lodge.[49] Herriman Jr. married Clara Morel, both of whom appear in the 1880 US Census as "mulatto" and both of whom reported having been born in Louisiana.[50]

According to the most comprehensive biography of George Joseph Herriman, *Krazy Kat: The Comic Art of George Herriman,* Herriman identified himself to his friends as a Creole and ascribed his "kinky hair" to what he suspected was his "Negro blood."[51] It is unlikely that he shared these suspicions with his colleagues, however, which led some of his contemporaries to invent ethnic biographies for him. Comics journalist Jeet Heer said it best in a 2011 article, noting that "Herriman . . . didn't just pass for white, rather he became an ethnic chameleon. His colleagues and friends at various times referred to him as Greek, French, Irish, and Turkish, and he himself dreamed of returning to life as a Navajo: he was of all races and of no race."[52] George Joseph Herriman never claimed his African heritage publicly and thus forged a career for himself in a profession where people of color had no representation at all. Like Tureaud's job at the bakery, Herriman's livelihood rested on the assumption that he was white. Unlike Tureaud's bosses at the bread store, Herriman's employer, William Randolph Hearst, was never appraised of his nonwhite ancestry and so, since willing to remain silent as to the details of his ancestry, he kept his job.

At the time of the 1900 US Census, George Herriman Jr.'s family lived in Los Angeles, where they were listed as "white."[53] While it is possible that the Herrimans identified themselves as white, the responsibility of recording the race of respondents fell to census workers who were directed to record respondents' race as they perceived it, not necessarily as respondents identified themselves. In the 1900 Census, George Herriman Jr.'s parents' birthplace is listed as "France," but if he were asked "where were your parents from," it is not unlikely that he would respond "yé Francé" or, in English, "they [are/were] French" which is how many Creoles referred to themselves (again, "mo Francé"). All said, there is enough gray area to obscure a clear narrative, which speaks to a larger point that, even in the early twentieth century, some Creoles still managed to "hover about the confines of lightness and darkness," or rather the margins of whiteness and blackness, in ways that were not so dissimilar to those employed by their ancestors in colonial Louisiana.

In "Autocrats and All Saints," Wendy Ann Gaudin recounts a story related to her by one member of the Autocrat Club, a prominent Creole social organization in the Seventh Ward, who explained how requiring voter registration for membership to the club created a controversy. A key point of the controversy was that voter registration required one to declare one's race. For many Creoles, this was a problematic proposition for many reasons and, as Gaudin indicates, not least among those reasons were the inconsistent definitions of "white" with which Creoles operated. Many Creoles experienced anxiety in declaring themselves black, yet they were not white, or at least not white in the sense that the law required one to demonstrate whiteness. A declaration of race, one way or the other, would eliminate an ambiguity and in-betweenness that many Creoles preferred to maintain.[54]

In giving the majority opinion of the court in the *Plessy* case, Justice Brown defended the constitutionality of "separate but equal" railway cars for white and colored patrons. However, Brown also affirmed the liability of individual employees of the railroad (for example, ticket sellers, conductors) for racially categorizing someone incorrectly. Whites may have been empowered to discriminate against non-Whites, but only if the non-Whites they were discriminating against were indeed not white, by law.[55] If employers "learned" that a white-looking employee or customer was not white and acted to discriminate, then they could pat themselves on the back, secure in the satisfaction that they had done their part to secure the existence of white people and a segregated future for white children. However, if an employer guessed incorrectly and mistakenly discriminated against a white person who they thought was not white, then there were consequences. Their discrimination could be construed as depriving the individual of the property of their "whiteness," which would expose them to the possibility of punitive legal action. In a country like the United States, where fortunes have been both made and lost in litigation proceedings, racists were inclined to err on the side of caution when it came to ascribing racial identities. Indeed, the only thing that could undermine the efforts of some passé blanc Creoles to pass fully into a white identity was a paper trail identifying them, in any way, as "colored." Given the sort of financial success enjoyed by passé blanc Creoles like George Joseph Herriman, it is not hard to imagine that, for passé blanc members of the Autocrat Club, there was more value in being perceived as white men than in having the right to vote.

As the nineteenth century rolled into the twentieth, Creoles acquired the cultural language of the Americans. They had little choice after white Anglo-Americans made it illegal for them to acquire education in their own language. The transition to English-only education in Louisiana reflected a new, national political and economic order which included Jim Crow, which was deeply resented by Creoles, as well as an abundance of opportunities for English speakers in such faraway places as Chicago and Los Angeles.

The contrasting cultural processes of creolization and Americanization had resulted in very different cultural contexts in the Anglo-American states and Louisiana in the early nineteenth century. That difference was articulated in American popular media in very consistent ways throughout the 1800s and into the 1900s. For Americans, Creoles were the exoticized, deviant, racial "other," emerging as a result of the sexual proclivities of race-mixing Frenchmen. Creoles' self-perception varied, but, as a general rule, Creole self-perception and self-identification rarely conformed to Anglo-American norms. Words like "white" and "black" and even "Frenchman" often had very different (and inconsistent) meanings in Creole Louisiana, and Creoles were adept at finding and exploiting the spaces that existed between those identifiers.

To say Creoles were color-conscious would be a gross understatement as there was certainly a culture of colorist bigotry among Creoles in New Orleans. Yet, many Creoles were ambivalent when it came to Anglo-American conceptions of race and went back and forth across the color line at will. Diasporic Creoles in the North and West were far removed from their context in Louisiana racially and recreated themselves as "white" (and, perhaps more significantly, as "Americans") in their new contexts, bringing about economic opportunities and a freedom impossible for them to enjoy back home. For those Creoles who remained in Louisiana, a different (though not entirely unrelated) story unfolded. Back home, where Whites with keen eyes for racial markers did their best to maintain color lines, Creole attitudes toward color and race would evolve to accommodate a new, American, racial order.

3

CLIQUISH, CLANNISH, ORGANIZATION MINDED

Jelly Roll Morton described the New Orleans of his youth as a collection of cliques. He played the chords of "Flee as a Bird to the Mountain" to Alan Lomax as he explained:

> Of course, everybody in the city of New Orleans was always organization-minded, which, I guess, the world knows. And, a, a dead man always belonged to several organizations, such as clubs, and, er, we'll say, secret order, and those so forth and so on. And every time one died, why, nine out of ten, there was always a big band turned out, when the day that he was supposed to be buried—never buried at night, always in the day. And, of course, a lot of times right in the heart of the city, the burial would take place. . . . when the band would start, why, we'd know that the man was fixing to be buried. So, you could hear the band come up the street, before they would get to the, er, to the place where the gentleman was to be taken in for his last rites. And they would play different dead marches.[1]

Morton was known for colorful turns of phrase. "Organization-minded" is a phrase, in particular, that stands out as a way to characterize the city of New Orleans at the turn of the twentieth century. Indeed, the proliferation of voluntary associations and fraternal organizations at the turn of the century was a common response to modernism, and New Orleans was not exceptional in this regard. Ferdinand Tönnies had already described the transformation of small, family-oriented, western "communities" into large, impersonal western "societies" in *Gemeinschaft und Gesellschaft,* published in 1887. Social sodalities entered for mutual benefit and professional advancement were not rare in these new, increasingly urban, modern societies forming in Germany, France, England, and the United States.[2] In fact, in the United States, these mutual aid and benevolent societies often facilitated the process of Americanization in minority ethnic communities from New York to San Francisco and scores of towns and cities in between. What is curious, however, is the extent to which ostensibly Gesellschaft social sodalities in Creole New Orleans at the turn of the twentieth century retained a distinctly Gemeinschaft character. Unlike the impersonal, professional associations or the immigrant fraternal societies of New York, Chicago, or San Francisco, these Creole organizations' memberships were often comprised of people with kinship relations—through blood, marriage, or both—that extended back in time, across multiple generations in Louisiana, often in the city itself.

Marcus Christian described the insularity of New Orleans's Creole community, noting that "the average Creole" was "clannish, usually Catholic," and had "too many personal factors involved in their business, social and environmental relations."[3] Adam Fairclough referenced that same insularity when he observed that, in the early 1900s, "the Creoles of the Seventh Ward still resembled a clannish elite" in their exclusivity.[4] In fact, a survey of the membership of representative New Orleans Creole institutions of the period bears out both of these observations. Creoles in New Orleans cohered around fraternal organizations and benevolent societies in much the same way that other ethnic communities did in the United States at the turn of the twentieth century. However, while maintaining the form of modern, Gesellschaft sodalities, Creole organizations were typically populated by people with Gemeinschaft social connections. Demonstrating that dynamic, New Orleans Creoles maintained the boundaries between their community and the larger African American community through processes of institutional inclusion and exclusion.

Though Jim Crow thrust the descendants of the city's gens de couleur libres into the same caste position as the descendants of the enslaved, by 1900 there was little left of the post–Civil War solidarity that had flourished between Creoles and African Americans. When an African American man named Robert Charles chose to defend himself from police violence one night as he waited on the steps of a friend's house on Dryads Street in uptown New Orleans, his act of defiance inspired an orgy of white mob violence that lasted for four days. The two communities' differing responses to the violence speaks directly to the gulf that had emerged between them.

Although the sympathies of Creoles in New Orleans certainly did not lie with the Whites who were murdering Blacks indiscriminately on the streets of New Orleans and who threatened "to set fire to an entire block of Negro homes, then shoot all the inhabitants when they ran out,"[5] it is equally certain that their sympathies did not lie with the poor African American community of uptown New Orleans. Indeed, some Creoles (just as some middle-class African Americans did) saw Robert Charles not as a hero, but instead as a "'demon,' 'devil in embryo,' 'lawless brute only in the form of human,' and 'hideous monster.'" According to William Ivy Hair, middle-class Creoles were "said to be more gratified at Charles' death than were the whites since their fear of racial retaliation had grown with each day he remained at large."[6] Jelly Roll Morton recalled to Alan Lomax that Robert Charles had been memorialized in a popular song in New Orleans that he once knew but that he found "best for me to forget . . . in order to go along with the world on the peaceful side," a sentiment that well serves as an apropos metaphor for the New Orleans Creole community's collective reaction to the racial violence of July of 1900.[7]

One of the few places where Creoles regularly mixed with African Americans in New Orleans was, predictably, a place that Whites also regularly mixed with people of color in the city: downtown New Orleans's famous red-light district. Established in 1897 due to the efforts of City Councilman Sidney Story, it was known variously as "Storyville," "the Tenderloin," or simply "the District. "It was bounded by Iberville, Basin, St. Louis, and North Robertson streets in a predominantly black neighborhood on the Creole side of Canal Street, abutting the Vieux Carré and the Faubourg Tremé. Although Herbert Asbury's pop-history account of New Orleans is laden with inaccuracies, there is no reason to doubt his assessment of Storyville at the turn of the twentieth century as "the most celebrated red-light district in the United States." After all, Asbury himself dedicated more than 450 pages (sometimes accurate, though often not) to celebration of the "city that care forgot," where the native population's joie de vivre was such that it led them to proclaim "laissez les bon temps rouler" in "the District" every night until the federal government declared the party over in 1917.[8]

Most recently, Alecia P. Long investigates the sex trade in Storyville in *The Great Southern Babylon* and draws on an extensive body of court cases and legal history to investigate the trade in New Orleans. Long reviews one case study after the other documenting the intricacies of commercializing sexuality in New Orleans and specifically the fetishization of interracial sex, which brought in sexual tourists from all over the United States. According to Long, the institutionalization of a district for commercialized, often interracial, sex in what had been a historically black neighborhood (the Tremé) was the culmination of the efforts of Anglo-American Whites who sought to safeguard public morality by regulating prostitution. Through these efforts, Long argues, New Orleans was brought into the fold, as it were, of the Redeemed South where the old Latin paradigms of racialization (for example, quadroons, griffes) would be replaced with standardized American racial classifications (that is, "Whites" and "Coloreds"). The city's lax approach to vice and the decriminalization of prostitution would complicate matters in new ways as the sex trade, and the profit that came along with it, would provide a vehicle of economic empowerment not only for the people of color who ran the brothels and serviced the Johns, but also for entertainers and musicians like Jelly Roll Morton, Buddy Bolden, Sidney Bechet, and others, who provided music and other diversions for brothel patrons.[9]

The Creole community's relationship with Storyville was anything but straightforward. Obviously, Storyville provided economic opportunity for some, serving the interests of Creoles who aspired to upward social mobility, whether through playing music or whoring. At the same time, conservative, and often religiously motivated, Creoles deeply resented the red-light district established in their downtown New Orleans enclave, decrying its corrupting influence. Jelly Roll Morton's grandmother went so far as to evict him and forbade him from associating with his sisters when he confessed to playing music in the brothels and sporting houses of Storyville.[10]

Of course, there were other perils for Creoles in the District aside from the corrupting influence of women, whiskey, and jazz, not the least of which was the presence of (white) Americans from all over the country, intent on behaving badly. Although Storyville was certainly the venue for much interracial contact, it would be foolish to suggest that that interracial contact was somehow removed from the racist violence that characterized Jim Crow New Orleans at the turn of the twentieth century: Storyville was only a short walk from the scene of Robert Charles's last stand, after all. Despite the attempt to market Storyville as a relatively tame tourist attraction, and despite the pretentions of the Storyville Blue Books inscribed with the credo of the Order of the Garter, "Honi Soit Qui Mal y Pense," the city's red-light district could be an exceedingly dangerous place, especially for people of color.

In Al Rose's collection of interviews with musicians and sex workers from the Storyville era is an account from a woman named Carrie, "of very dark pigmentation," who had been a prostitute in Storyville. Carrie offers an account that is illuminating in a number of ways. Although her last name (which Rose does not record) was French, Carrie did not identify herself as Creole, but as black, or in her words as a "nigguh," and she apparently "took a perverse pride in the fact that both of her parents had been born slaves." Although her parents spoke Creole, Carrie herself did not although she knew "some Creole words and expressions." Indeed, Carrie was "completely illiterate," and her thickly accented English was, according to Rose, "almost an unbroken stream of obscenity, scatology, and blasphemy." Rose notes that she "grew up in a poor neighborhood near Perdido Street on the uptown side of Canal Street" and lived within a block of Louis Armstrong's birthplace. She did not live downtown in the Vieux Carré, Faubourg Marigny, or the Faubourg Tremé. Despite her "very dark pigmentation," Carrie may still have been only of partial African descent and in any case had an undeniable claim to Creole culture and heritage through language. However, as a working-class woman with dark skin in Jim Crow New Orleans, her ties to the culture of colonial French Louisiana brought absolutely no added value to her lived day-to-day experience. She did not count herself among those illustrious personalities of Desdunes's *Our People* any more than Desdunes counted himself among Carrie's people, whom she referred to as "us nigguhs."[11]

The prostitute Carrie is not a romantic, sensuous, high-yellow "Creole Lady Marmalade" staring out from the brothel windows at white "Southern Gentlemen" seeking to indulge their fantasies of "white" women possessed of the mythically visceral and primitive sexuality of African people. On the contrary, Carrie is a completely powerless victim of American white supremacy and misogynoir, as evidenced in her account of her assault by a "jolly" group of American Whites:

> One time on d'Fo'th of July, a bunch of white pricks grab me outten ma crib and c'ay me t'd' cohnuh. Dey taken off all ma clo'es and dey tie ma han's an' feet t'd' light pole. Den one of 'em stick a big salute [firecracker] up my cunt an' anothan one up ma ass an' he light both a dem! Shit! I *done* some holla'in'! A fuckin' police, he standin' right deah an' he laughin'. . . . D'em t'ings din' go off. . . . Dey wuzn' loaded. It was ju' one a dem jokes, *you* know. . . . Den dey tells me to blow 'em all an' dey says dey ain't gon' gimme a cent an dey tells me lucky dey din' blow up ma cunt. . . . So, I shet up and sucked 'em all off. When I got done, one of d'mens gimme twenny dolluh an' say Carrie is a good spo't. Den dey all sings dat song. "Fo' She a Jolly Good Fella," you knows dat song.[12]

As bound as some New Orleans Creoles were to Storyville, or at least to the economy of Storyville, it was still not "theirs." White men could have sex with women of color in Storyville, but men of color were still not allowed to have sex with white women, at least not as a matter of official policy.[13] The music of Storyville was ragtime and jazz, and as Creole jazzman Dr. Sidney Bechet observed, when "the settled Creole folks first heard this jazz, they passed the opinion that it sounded like the rough Negro element. . . . they had the same kind of feeling that some white people have, who don't understand jazz and don't *want* to understand it."[14] Although those musical idioms were adopted, refined, and expounded upon by Creoles like Bechet and Morton, in origin they were African American, not Creole. "For She's a Jolly Good Fellow" is definitely not a Creole song.

Americans flocked to Storyville in search of "hot music" and the promise of illicit (and interracial) carnal delights until the federal government brought the curtain down on the show during World War I. However, by 1917, Storyville had already provided an opportunity for African Americans to assert their equality with Creoles through the capitalization of their music. As Lomax observed, "these black Americans had no music lessons, no family name and no stable community life to support them. . . . If they became professional musicians, it was only by virtue of exceptional talent and drive."[15] As more Creoles benefited from their association with these exceptionally talented and driven African American musicians, the cultural capital of the African American community among Creoles appreciated: African Americans had taught Creoles how to empower themselves through music in Jim Crow America. Creoles would, nevertheless, exclude African Americans from some of their key community institutions for decades after World War I. Marcus Christian understood this as clannish and prideful Creoles withdrawing from social intercourse with "full-blooded negroes," but it was not "negroes" that Creoles were protecting themselves from but "'Méricains," some of whom were "negro," but the vast majority of whom were white.[16]

Martin Behrman was a Jewish man, born in New York City, who moved to New Orleans as a child, but he could nevertheless praise the white supremacists' struggle in the 1870s that "broke the power of the carpet baggers and routed the Metropolitan police force"[17] and compared the suffering of the Ladies of the Confederate Southern Memorial Association during that "dark and trying period . . . of Reconstruction" to the "trials and tribulations of the women of Sparta" without the faintest trace of irony.[18] A complicated person and a keen politician, he understood the interests of his constituents so well that, after replacing the city's last native Francophone mayor, Paul Capdeville, Behrman proved to be the longest-serving mayor in the history of the city. First elected in December of 1904, Behrman served as mayor continuously until December of 1920. He was reelected one final time in May of 1925 before dying in office in 1926. Despite the city's considerable native Francophone/Creolophone population, Behrman neither wrote nor spoke French (much less Louisiana Creole) and. to the extent that he celebrated New Orleans's French past, it was still understood that the city's present and future belonged to America and would be written in English. Indeed, the legacy of Martin

Behrman, the New Yorker, is that on his watch New Orleans became a thoroughly American city.[19]

The power of racist white oligarchs had reemerged stronger than before the Civil War in Louisiana, and in New Orleans the face of that racist, white, oligarchical regime belonged to Martin Behrman. Prior to his term as mayor, Behrman served as a delegate to the 1898 Louisiana Constitutional Convention, which oversaw the disenfranchisement of more than 120,000 colored voters, an agenda that Behrman pursued because, in his own words, he "saw that the fact that the negroes were able to vote was at the bottom of a great deal of trouble."[20] In Behrman's estimation, Whites in New Orleans had given "the negroes a great deal" through their disenfranchisement and, as proof of this assertion, he offered the comparatively low incidence of race riots and public lynchings in New Orleans as evidence.[21] In his memoir, Behrman reminisced on the relative improvement of race relations over the course of his term and articulated his own belief in the role that black disenfranchisement played in that improvement:

> I remember the murder of two police officers in a negro church called the "Council of God." . . . There was no danger of a riot. The murderers were arrested, tried and hung without the least sign of a riot. Had the two officers been deliberately murdered by negroes in my youth, anywhere from two to twenty negroes would have been killed. Perhaps more than that. . . . The negroes no doubt are better treated and enjoy more peace in New Orleans than in any other large city. A majority of them appreciate this. . . . In Chicago on the other hand a serious riot occurred immediately after the war [World War I]. The negroes vote in Chicago.[22]

It would seem that, in Behrman's estimation, enfranchisement sent the wrong message to Negroes, and that message was that they had the right to self-government and equality in the United States. Linking enfranchisement of Negroes to social disorder, white supremacists like Martin Behrman saw only two solutions to the problem of Negroes in American society: absolute white domination or annihilation. All other things being equal, it is better for two murderers of white policemen to be arrested, tried, and hanged than for "anywhere from two to twenty," possibly un-involved bystanders, to be murdered by Whites in acts of terror abetted by the New Orleans Police Department, as was the case between July 23 and July 27 of 1900. It is in this sense that Negroes in New Orleans had been extended a "great deal" through disenfranchisement and Jim Crow. Indeed, life with segregation seems like quite a bargain if the alternative was to be murdered by a white mob the way Robert Charles was.

Even Behrman's most strident opposition, the reform-minded and nominally nonpartisan Citizens' League, was just another faction of the Democratic Party which was committed to racial oppression as a matter of principle. The gains of Radical Reconstruction had completely disap-peared by 1900 and, for people of color, there was no recourse from white domination. Indeed, some Whites in the city had begun to revisit their Confederate history with nostalgic fondness, and accompanying that nos-talgia, seemingly, was a renewed commitment to racial hatred. Historian Eric Arnesen noted that, by "the end of the century, disenfranchisement had eliminated the need to make even a gesture toward accommodating" the needs of people of color in New Orleans, and so the status of people of color, despite the Reconstruction-era amendments to the Constitution, had been relegated to a de facto state akin to that articulated by the Su-preme Court in the Dred Scott case almost a half-century earlier in which Chief Justice Roger B. Taney, in the majority opinion, made it clear that a "free negro of the African race . . . whether emancipated or not, yet remained subject to [white] authority, and had no rights or privileges but such as those who held the power and the government [that is, whites] might choose to grant them." People of color may have been nominally free in Louisiana, but were nevertheless a subjugated population.[23]

After the Louisiana legislature's decision to close the legal distance between "colored" people and "negroes" following the Octave Treadaway case in 1910, Creoles were mostly ignored by City Hall as they no lon-ger had the voting numbers to represent any significant threat to white power, or to lobby for the interests of people of color.[24] A. P. Tureaud Jr., in an interview with Wendy Ann Gaudin in 2002, observed that the ra-cialization of Creoles as "negroes" was primarily "an economic manipu-lation . . . to keep the Creoles out of the growing strength and political action and that's why they disenfranchised all those people of color. . . . So [Whites thought], take them out of there. Make them all black. Take the vote away from them."[25] Gaudin notes that, in her research, "absent from many Creoles' notion of manliness is political action or protest; absent from the many family and individual histories . . . is political participation or resistance to colored people's disenfranchisement,"[26] but it is unclear whether she connects that phenomenon to the absolute marginalization from political power that people of color experienced in Jim Crow New Orleans.

A. P. Tureaud Sr. noted to Joe Logsdon that the average Creole in the New Orleans Creole community of his youth "was satisfied to live his own life in the community with his accustomed social attainments."[27] This informs Gaudin's earlier observation on the absence of political activism among Creoles and her argument that the dominant Creole ethos in the face of segregation was "apolitical and apathetic."[28] Yet, it is unclear what sort of activism the Creole community might be expected to bring to bear in a context where the prevailing wisdom of the governing authorities was that even allowing people of color the vague impression of a political voice would inevitably result in violence. Perhaps, as Tureaud himself concluded when his and his contemporaries' activism was called into question, Creoles during the Behrman era were "as aggressive as the times permitted."[29]

If he truly believed his own spin on colored disenfranchisement, then Martin Behrman must have thought that he was doing the Creole community a favor by refusing it the dignity of an audience. The Seventh Ward Improvement Association that Behrman corresponded with included members W. Bagert, N. A. Dana, L. Reeder, M. Vandenboore, W. Richards, J. W. Engelhardt Jr., E. Becker, and Phil Daly, but with the single exception of A. E. Arnoult, who was listed in the US Federal Census of 1910 as "white," the association had no member with a recognizable French or Creole name.[30] The St. Bernard Avenue Improvement Association that Behrman corresponded with was similarly absent of any nonwhite members in September 1911, even though the Seventh Ward had the highest concentration of Creoles in the entire city. It is the equivalent of a Harlem neighborhood association in upper Manhattan that included no one of

African American heritage, or a civic improvement organization in San Francisco's North Beach that included no one of Italian heritage.[31]

Creoles were not openly hostile to the "Old Regular" Democratic Party machine of Martin Behrman in New Orleans, despite their disenfranchisement. This was not a product of apathy, it was a calculated political concession. In return, the Behrman administration was, though neglectful, not actively hostile to the Creole community in the city. Just so long as Creoles in New Orleans did not, in Behrman's words, "try to be treated as equals by the white men," he was even content to make token appointees from the colored community (African American and Creole, though mostly Creole it seems) to various (low-level) positions in city government, including patrolman positions with the New Orleans Police Department.[32] Given the racist culture of the Jim Crow–era department, as evidenced by the Robert Charles affair, it was no trivial privilege for Creoles to have their neighborhoods patrolled by Creole policemen.

Historian Howard Rabinowitz noted that "blacks served on [New Orleans's] metropolitan police until the overthrow of the Radicals in 1877," after which point he asserts that, like other cities in the South after Reconstruction, New Orleans fortified its municipal police "as the first line of defense against the blacks." Rabinowitz, however, is mistaken. Between 1878 and 1913, there were ten colored officers on the New Orleans police force, including Arthur Boisdoré, Etienne "Stephen" Broyard, Henry LeBeaud, Louis Joseph Therence, and George Doyle, all of whom were Creoles. According to Vanessa Flores-Robert, Creole officers were treated to comparable disciplinary standards as their white colleagues and were empowered to wield their constabulary authority over Whites.[33]

In 1923 the superintendent of police, Guy R. Molony, rejected the African American community's demand for the right to police their own neighborhoods, recalling that the "experiment" of Negro policemen had "occasioned much trouble" since it was "impossible to limit the activities of negro policemen to their own race."[34] This suggests that not only were Creole officers empowered to wield their authority over Whites but that they actually exercised that power, too! It was an arrangement that echoed colonial-era privileges enjoyed by their forebears who bore arms in the Native Militias in service to French and Spanish regimes that had also rejected the right of Creoles to participate in their own governance. It was also an arrangement that Whites rejected as race/caste relations became more antagonistic.

In February of 1929, three years after Behrman's death, former NOPD officer George Doyle would present to the Craig School, one of New Orleans's Jim Crow–era public schools established for Negroes, a life-size bust of Martin Behrman sculpted by Italian artist Romeo Celli, presumably in honor of Behrman's decision to provide resources for Negro education in the city.[35] Although Desdunes had scorned Booker T. Washington for his servility, the Creole ethos in Jim Crow New Orleans was strikingly Washingtonian given the extent to which the Creole community was willing to accept white (Anglo-American) domination in exchange for the paternalistic support of the white community. Although, willing or not, it is hard to perceive another choice available to people of color in New Orleans during this time, aside from that of white domination or exile.

Even the perception of colored influence on politics incited a resentment among Whites that was, according to Martin Behrman, as volatile as gunpowder in that "[a]ll it needed was the match of some small trouble to light it and produce a considerable explosion."[36] In an era rife with considerable racial explosions, there is no reason to assume Behrman was speaking hyperbolically. On the contrary, all the evidence suggests that he was deadly serious.

The Creole political ethos of the early twentieth century was accommodationist because it faced an ever-present threat of annihilation from white mobs who were willing to set Creoles' homes ablaze and gun them down if they tried to flee the fire. It is arguable that Martin Behrman gave Creoles a "great deal." It is more certain, however, that when compared to the horrific episodes of white violence endured by people of color in places like Chicago and Elaine, Arkansas, in 1919 or Tulsa in 1921, things could have been a lot worse—a lot bloodier, in fact—for Creoles in New Orleans than they were during the Behrman years.[37]

Wendy Gaudin observed that in her research, which incorporated many interviews and oral histories, there was a striking absence of political action or protest "from many Creoles' notion of manliness" and that "absent from the many family and individual histories that [she] recorded or scribbled notes from is political participation or resistance to colored people's disenfranchisement."[38] Obviously, Gaudin is aware of the Creole contributions to the civil rights movement in New Orleans: A. P. Tureaud Jr. was one of her interviewees. However, Gaudin is correct in questioning the significance of the role that Creoles played in the struggle for African American civil rights in New Orleans as the Creole community's relationship to that struggle was just as complicated and problematic as their relationship to the African American community, in general, during the early twentieth century.

Fairclough's understanding of Creole participation in the civil rights movement represents, in some ways, an exact opposite tendency from Gaudin's. Fairclough offers the example of A. P. Tureaud as a Creole who "led the civil rights struggle."[39] Fairclough dismisses the claims that "Creoles thought and acted as if they were a superior caste" as a "gross exaggeration." He points to the Dejoie family, founders of the *Louisiana Weekly*, as egalitarian-minded Creoles "whose eloquent editorials flayed the hypocrisies of racism."[40] In Fairclough's narrative, it is culture, not colorism or caste bigotry, at the root of common perceptions of Creole exclusivity. Fairclough meticulously crafts the narrative of an emerging consciousness of class in the Creole community that is reinforced through racial solidarity with African Americans over the course of the twentieth century. His argument is nuanced and compelling, but it overstates the case for progressive Creole racial sensibilities in the early twentieth century.

Adam Fairclough notes that, in the early twentieth century, "visitors to New Orleans frequently commented that the cultural divide between Creoles of color and the 'American' Negroes was an obstacle to black unity and progress," and though much of the disharmony between the two communities can be ascribed to cultural dissimilarities, as Fairclough suggests, not all of it was. Some Creoles at the turn of the century in New Orleans nurtured deep, antiblack bigotry. Fairclough lauds A. P. Tureaud, suggesting that there "was no more dedicated servant of the NAACP and foe of racial discrimination" than he. At the same time, Tureaud didn't want either of his daughters to "marry a black man," according to his son, A. P. Tureaud Jr.[41] For many Creoles, a shared commitment with African Americans to the struggle for black civil rights did not necessitate a belief in ethno-racial unity with African Americans, nor did it entail a tolerance for African Americans in Creole social spaces. Creoles decried white racism and, at the same time, it is not a gross exaggeration to say that many Creoles nurtured vicious bigotries that were rooted in a two-hundred-year-old culture of caste elitism inseparable, even if distinct, from white racism. These contradictory tendencies among many Creoles, tendencies that were universally despised by African Americans, were at the root of much distrust, disharmony, and dysfunction. Nowhere was this unfortunate circumstance more obvious than in the New Orleans branch of the NAACP.

The NAACP was founded in 1909 in New York City as an interracial organization dedicated to ensuring "the political, educational, social, and economic equality of minority group citizens in the United States."[42] Its ideology was bourgeois and liberal, which set it apart from the Communist Party, which demanded absolute racial equality, as well as Garveyism, which promoted black empowerment through segregation and separatism. Its founding membership was predominately composed of white liberals, socialists, and Republican abolitionists, and only seven out of sixty of its original signatories were African American (including both W. E. B. Du Bois and Ida B. Wells-Barnett).[43] The New Orleans branch of the NAACP received its official charter in 1915, though in 1911 a group of local activists began organizing themselves as a branch, without official sanction from the national organization.[44]

From its inception, the New Orleans branch of the NAACP was dominated by African Americans. The Rev. Eugene W. White of Tulane Avenue Baptist Church led the organization from 1915 until it experienced a reorganization in 1924. In 1924, the organization was headed by Dr. George Lucas, an African American from Mississippi who would serve as president until 1931. The first Creole president of the NAACP, George Labat, was not elected until 1932 and served only one year in that position before being replaced by former branch president, Rev. Eugene W. White.[45]

Most historians who have seriously engaged the subject very generally agree that the NAACP provided one of the earliest and most successful vehicles for joint Creole–African American activism in New Orleans. All of them acknowledge problems associated with the ethno-cultural divide between Creoles and African Americans, too. Fairclough refers to the problems associated with "cultural differences" between the two peoples as "an irritant, especially before 1930." Decuir observed that, during the 1920s, Creoles and African Americans "rarely interacted" but that, by 1925, elites of both groups, through organizations like the NAACP, "came together to provide the black community in New Orleans with its first racial progressionist leaders." Emanuel and Tureaud describe the dissension in the NAACP, including A. P. Tureaud Sr.'s attempt to establish a separate branch of the NAACP in New Orleans, as a function of class and ideological difference, positing Tureaud and his allies as a younger, more aggressive generation rebelling against the old guard who represented the middle-class, accommodationist elements within the group.[46] None of these historians seriously engages the ethnic animosity between the two groups that proved far more than an "irritant" even as late as May of 1938 when NAACP Executive Secretary Walter White remarked that "Negroes and Creoles maintain a division in New Orleans that is a definite hindrance to their progress."[47]

White's comments set off a firestorm of controversy that summer as Creoles and African Americans in the city took turns hurling loud condemnations at one another. African Americans decried their exclusion from downtown Creole social sodalities and denounced Creoles as ignorant and uneducated as a result of their refusal to send their children to public schools with African Americans. Creoles retorted that they had "contributed more than a share for the betterment of the group" and that the "uptown Negroes" were agitating an "age-old assumption" (of Creole negrophobia). It is hard to reconcile Fairclough's characterization of Creole–African American antipathies after 1930 as "an irritant" when the *Sepia Socialite*, an African American magazine published weekly in New Orleans from 1937 to 1945, describes Walter White's commentary as inspiring "a threatened split-up of the N.A.A.C.P. executive committee" in New Orleans.[48]

Creoles did not explicitly deny African Americans' accusations even as they demanded that African Americans abandon those "age-old assumptions" in the interest of "mutual cooperation."[49] This is because those African American accusations were true: even as late as 1938, many Creole organizations in New Orleans remained categorically off-limits to African Americans. A survey of representative organizations in the city between the turn of the century and World War II bears out this argument.

Both Creoles and African Americans in New Orleans were "organization minded." Many joined mutual aid and benevolent societies because insurance companies refused to extend insurance policies to people of color, and colored social sodalities fulfilled a number of other vital functions as well. In fact, these groups represented the key components of late-life planning for many people of color in New Orleans well into the 1930s and 1940s. Often, an individual would belong to more than one benevolent organization to draw end-of-life benefits from more than one source. The three oldest of these colored sodalities in the city were la Société Des Artisans de Bienfaisance et d'Assistance Mutuelle (the Artisans Society, founded in 1834, composed primarily of Creole artisans and craftsmen), l'Économie (the Economy Society, founded in 1836 as an outgrowth of the Artisans' Society) and Dieu Nous Protégé Benevolent and Mutual Aid Association (founded in 1844, and dedicated to purchasing slaves for the purpose of manumitting them).[50] However, after the Civil War, these sorts of organizations proliferated and included sodalities composed primarily of African American freedmen, mixed sodalities including both African Americans and Creoles and exclusively Creole sodalities.

The Zion Benevolent Sons and Daughters of Camparapet (Camp Parapet) was one of the earliest African American organizations in New Orleans, incorporated on June 8, 1872, and, through the turn of the century, was "active among English-speaking, Protestant black Americans mostly of slave ancestry." Its stated mission was to "take care of the sick, the Widows and Orphans and to bury the dead of the association." Of the founding members— John Brown, Peter Jackson, Patrick Carter, Newton Burton, James Harrington, David Madison, Mack E. Nelson, Louis Carter, James Meyers, Ralf Everidge, Alex Jackson, James Jackson, Andrew Wilson, Alex Houston, Luchien Gregoir—only one, Gregoir, was Creole. The constitution of the organization and its bylaws in original form were notarized in Jefferson Parish by the parish recorder, Thomas McCormack, and were printed in English. This pattern—Protestant, Anglophone organizations composed primarily of members with Anglo surnames with unclear connections to one another prior to their association in the organization—is consistent among African American organizations and provides a useful benchmark for comparison to more exclusive Creole organizations in the city.[51]

Creole New Orleans was not a monolithic community. There were some Creoles like the Dejoie family, for example, who lived uptown. There were Creoles who spoke English natively and some (again, like the Dejoies) were even Protestant Christians. In the decades between Emancipation and the turn of the century, New Orleans had undergone significant physical transformation that had begun to crack the shell of insularity that the downtown enclaves had created, and the result was the "Creole American" (a concept that in previous times would have been a contradiction in terms along the lines of "dry wetness" or "violent gentleness"). These Creole Americans would be instrumental in bridging the divide between African Americans and the downtown Creoles.

The Juvenile Cooperators Fraternals Mutual Aid Association, founded in January of 1894 and incorporated in October of 1897, was a joint Creole–African American organization. The organization's records, beginning in July of 1894, are exclusively in English.[52] George Doyle, mentioned previously in connection to his job as a police officer, was a member of the Juvenile Cooperators and is an excellent example of the twentieth-century Creole American.[53]

Doyle was the product of a "mixed marriage." His mother, Eulalie Doyle (née Ducas), was from Louisiana; her father was born in France, and her mother was, at least partially, of African descent. In 1857, Eulalie married Henry Doyle from Virginia. It is unclear what Henry Doyle's mother's origins were, but his father was from Ireland according to the 1880 US Census, which identified Henry Doyle as a "mulatto." George Doyle had no claim to French or Spanish colonial–era Louisiana ancestry at all. Nevertheless, the name "Doyle" would become one of the most important in the Creole community in New Orleans at the turn of the twentieth century.[54]

George Doyle sat on the board of directors for the Marie C. Couvent Institute, which later became Holy Redeemer Catholic School in 1917 and was involved in the rebuilding process of the school when it was almost destroyed by a massive storm in 1915. He served the New Orleans Police Department for twelve years and was later appointed US federal marshal by

President Howard Taft. He also headed up efforts to keep alive the memory of the Battle of New Orleans, particularly the Creoles of color who fought at that battle, despite his own lack of ancestral connection to that event. In a time of machine politics and neighborhood bosses, George Doyle was affectionately described by the board of directors of the Couvent School as a "hustler."[55] In a way, he was to New Orleans's Creole community what Martin Behrman was to Whites in New Orleans: he was a political boss. He was the polyglot, Irish–African American, boss of Creole New Orleans.

In 1890, the *Cleveland Gazette* mentioned a woman who "passed for a Creole, after learning to speak French."[56] George Doyle's life and experience as a civic leader of New Orleans's Creole community offers a step-by-step instructional on exactly how that sort of passage into a Creole identity was accomplished. Marcus Christian describes George Doyle as "a born aristocrat" who "boasts that his paternal grandfather was an Irish immigrant and that his maternal grandfather was born in France," which speaks to his phenotypical appearance. Besides his appearance, however, the Doyle family was Catholic, spoke French natively, and lived in the Vieux Carré, which placed them solidly in the social context of Creole New Orleans. Finally, as if to seal his claim, George Doyle married Mary Coste, a New Orleans Creole woman who was descended from Captain Charles Forneret, a free man of color who commanded his own company at the Battle of New Orleans in 1815.[57] If an African American was inclined to "pass for a Creole," that is how it was done.

George Doyle was one of the earliest members of the Juvenile Cooperators with solid Anglo-American roots. However, as early as March of 1895, in addition to all the Messieurs Du Bois, Porché, Labat, Daliet, and Saloy, there were also a significant number of Misters Thomas, Watermann, Epps, Greg, and Collins.[58] The Juvenile Cooperators was a progressive organization in this respect.

Adam Fairclough describes the 1920s NAACP struggle against a municipal housing ordinance demanding residential segregation as "one of the first occasions" on which Creoles and African Americans in New Orleans "made common cause." He quotes Dr. Ernest Cherrie, who ascribed much of the difficulty of that struggle to the fact that, in Fairclough's summation, "light-skinned African-Americans were insufficiently militant."[59] Dr.

Ernest Cherrie, a Creole, was a member of the Juvenile Cooperators and a self-described "RACE man in every detail," which is to say that he believed in promoting the interests of the "Negro race" without distinction between Creoles and African Americans.[60] As Fairclough notes, Cherrie, who was also a member of the NAACP in New Orleans, complained of New Orleans's population of "Negro descent" that were so "thoroughly mixed that approximately seventy-five percent have what is termed 'white complex,'" an infirmity that apparently prevented Creoles from joining with African Americans in solidarity for collective political benefit.[61] Marcus Christian had described Creoles in New Orleans as "individually militant" in defense of their rights, even when they were unable to engage this militancy in collective action (presumably with African Americans), but Ernest Cherrie does not fit that description. Dr. Cherrie represented a prototype for the sort of fusion Creole–African American identity that prevailed in the second half of the twentieth century in New Orleans. As far as the most conservative elements of the city's Creole community were concerned, however, those sensibilities articulated by Ernest Cherrie in 1931 were decades before their time.[62]

In many ways, the typical form of the exclusively Creole sodality in New Orleans was the mirror image of the African American sodality. The membership of Creole organizations was overwhelmingly composed of people with Creole surnames, not Anglo surnames. The constitutions of Creole organizations, bylaws, and meeting minutes were typically recorded in French (until the 1910s–1920s), not English. The stated religious affiliation of the vast majority of the members of Creole organizations was Roman Catholic, not Protestant. Unlike many African American organizations in the city whose members held unclear connections to one another prior to their association in the organization, Creole sodalities were composed of people with multigenerational familial connections to one another through blood, marriage, or both.

One early example of an exclusive New Orleans Creole sodality is Fraternité No. 20, a Masonic lodge established in 1867 after Eugene Chassaignac, a white Creole composer and supreme grand commander of the Ancient and Accepted Scottish Rite of Freemasonry in Louisiana, opened membership to people of color.[63] Caryn Cossé Bell collected names culled from minutes books of the lodge from the year 1867 until 1873 and even provided superficial biographical data on the membership of the lodge.[64] Cross-referencing Bell's list of members of Fraternité No. 20 with the roster of the Battalions of Free Men of Color who fielded at the Battle of New Orleans, there is an interesting correspondence.[65] Of 163 total members over the six-year period that Bell provides data for, 155 of those members were people of color. Of those, 33 were people of color whose families were among those who fought at the Battle of New Orleans in 1815 at the close of the War of 1812 between the United States and Britain. Of those 33 families of veterans of 1812, 26 of them could trace their families to the same unit: the First Battalion (a unit of roughly 300 men), commanded by Lieutenant Colonel Michel Fortier and Major Pierre Lacoste. There were no members with English names besides one named Joseph Taylor, who had to have at least been Francophone since all of the business of the lodge was conducted in French.[66]

Some of the most prominent and influential Creole politicians of the Reconstruction period were affiliated with Fraternité No. 20. The Rey brothers, Henry and Octave, who had negotiated with General Benjamin F. Butler for Creole support for the Union in 1862, and who had commanded the Metropolitan Police force that did battle with the White League, were members of Fraternité No. 20. Charles St. Albain Sauvinet, the interpreter who facilitated that meeting between the Rey brothers and General Butler, was also a member. Fraternité No. 20 and its successor lodge, l'Amite No. 27, would serve as seminal organizations for a number of other fraternal orders and benevolent societies in the city, but certainly one of the most notable organizations to grow out of l'Amite was the Société des Jeunes Amis.

Originally chartered by Legislative Act 103 of 1874, the Jeunes Amis represented a core institution of Creole New Orleans whose membership, in one capacity or another, had a tremendous impact on the city. Its founding members were almost all cigar makers, with a few other assorted tradesmen and celebrated personalities besides, including Creole financier Thomy Lafon. Of approximately 217 members in 1887, all but 4 had Latin surnames. All deliberations of the organization were in French, as were the minutes taken of meetings. When Louis Martinet notarized the amended charter of the organization in 1899, the officers were President

C. Joinville Staes and Secretary Samuel J. Perrault. The Jeunes Amis is a perfect example of an exclusive New Orleans Creole social sodality.[67]

The Jeunes Amis was not an overtly political organization, it was a social organization. Yet, it was a social organization composed of no few individuals who held radical views on caste and racial egalitarianism (again, as Marcus Christian noted: many Creoles may have been individually radical, but not always so collectively). Some members were certainly ideologically representative of Caryn Cossé Bell's "Afro-Creole Protest Tradition." Louis A. Martinet, editor of the *New Orleans Crusader*, the print publication of le Comité des Citoyens, was employed to notarize the charter of the Jeunes Amis, although he was not listed as a member at its founding in 1874 nor in 1899. However, Martinet's Comité des Citoyens comrades, Alcee Labat and Numa E. Mansion, were members. Comité secretary Firmin Christophe was a member, as well.[68]

The Société des Jeunes Amis owned a hall at 1321 Dumaine Street in the Tremé between North Villere Street and Marais Street.[69] Many benevolent societies had such halls: the 1912 *Wood's Directory* lists at least twenty.[70] These halls would become important foci for cultural production and exchange, especially between Creoles and African Americans during the incubation of jazz in the early 1900s. The Jeunes Amis hall was used for many occasions. It was a clubhouse for socializing and a place for members to host meetings. It was a dance hall and a venue for private parties and functions. When members died, it was a place to hold the repast after the funeral.

One block away from the Jeunes Amis hall in New Orleans, on St. Anthony Street between North Villere and Robertson, stood the meeting hall of the Francs Amis.[71] The Société des Francs Amis, or "True Friends Society" (literally "French Friends"), was a statewide Creole benevolent organization. It seems the earliest branch was founded in 1876 in St. Martin Parish by a group of Creoles, all one generation removed from New Orleans, who bought land in St. Martinville and built a benevolent hall there.[72]

All of the observations made previously regarding the membership of the Jeunes Amis are borne out in an analysis of the membership of the Francs Amis. In fact, there is significant crossover and intersection between the two organizations. Thomy Lafon, for example, was a member of the Francs

Amis as well as the Jeunes Amis. The membership lists of the Francs Amis are overwhelmingly composed of Creole family names, and many of those family names are also represented in the old Creole Masonic lodges, Civil War Native Guard, and the Native Militia that fielded at the Battle of New Orleans in 1815: Armand, Auguste, Augustine, Barthé, Blanchard, Charbonet, Decou, Dessales, Dominguez, Dolliole, Duplessis, Duconge, Derbigny, Forestal, Frederick, Labat, Louis, Mary, Pichon, Petite, Populus, Porée, Plessy (as in Homer Plessy of the Comité des Citoyens), Raphael, Rey, and Roudanez.[73]

Just as the Jeunes Amis hall provided sources of income for that organization, the Francs Amis also derived revenue from renting out its society hall. During the Carnival season in New Orleans, the Francs Amis hall was rented out to a variety of other organizations for seasonal balls. At other times, the Francs Amis hall was rented for dances and social functions for young adults.[74]

Studying the financial records left by the New Orleans branch of the Francs Amis offers insight into the way these Creole benevolent societies in the city were able to marshal financial strength through the collective efforts of the membership. Meetings of the Francs Amis were held monthly, and every month a member was expected to contribute $1.00 in dues. The earliest records of fees and assessments available for the group in New Orleans is 1907, and dues remained consistent from that time until 1927. During that period, the membership of the organization was never lower than 80 and hit a high point in 1922 at 106 members. Petitioning for membership to the society cost $1.10. Missing a monthly meeting cost ten cents. Missing the funeral of a fellow member incurred a fine of 50 cents. The officers of the Francs Amis were paid modest salaries every month (a total cost of $21.20 in 1907) to manage the financial affairs of the organization, which was no small task. Monthly account balances of the organization in the same period between 1907 and 1927 never dipped much lower than $20.00 and were as high as $460.60 in 1907.[75] Using data compiled by Robert Sahr at Oregon State University, it is possible to convert the relative value of the Francs Amis' 1907 US dollars into 2013 US dollars at an approximate value of 1 to 25 which, in contemporary figures, would have given the Francs Amis more than $11,500 (in 2013 US dollars) in 1907 at the high point of its financial power but would have still left it with between $250 and $500 (in 2013 US dollars) every month after all of its financial obligations were met for the entire period between 1907 and 1927. At no point was the organization ever in debt during this time.[76] Certainly these are small numbers, but they do suggest a committed membership that was dedicated and vigorously engaged.

At its founding, the Francs Amis was an exclusive Francophone organization. In fact, in New Orleans all business of the Francs Amis was conducted exclusively in French until 1919. However, a careful reading of its cashbook and meeting notes reveals a fascinating evolution of the use of language in the Creole community in New Orleans that begs attention. Until October of 1912, all entries in the cashbook and meeting notes are in French. From October of 1912 until September of 1916, all entries were written mostly in French except that the words are devoid of diacritics that would accompany text written by someone literate in French and, from time to time, Financial Secretary J. J. Mary would interject single words or expressions in English. By October of 1916, the Francs Amis records are in English, evidence of the process of Americanization that was well underway by the 1910s.[77]

Wendy Gaudin characterizes Creole clannishness and propensity to exclusivity as "separatism" and goes on to suggest that because of "anti-black racism, and [Creoles'] own determination to be seen as different, [Creoles] came to a shared conclusion that their especial history of sameness with the white population made them exceptional."[78] Yet, for whatever role race and colorism played in Creole hostility to African Americans (and it definitely played a role), Creoles didn't need any artificial mechanism like race or colorism to experience a psychological and emotional distance from people who didn't share their religion (and, by extension, the same spiritual and moral values) and who didn't speak the same language they did. Creoles were determined to be seen as different because they were different. It is no coincidence that relations between Creoles and African Americans tended to warm as time went on and more Creoles began to speak English as their primary language.

Many of the Francs Amis were, no doubt, fair-skinned Creoles who existed in between the color lines of Jim Crow. The Francs Amis financial secretary from 1912 to 1916, J. J. (listed variably as Joseph John and John Joseph) Mary, is a perfect example of the racially ambiguous Creole who so confounded attempts to impose rigid concepts of race in downtown New Orleans. In 1910, J. J. Mary, who was born about 1879, married to Alda Mary and the son of Mathilde Johnson, was listed as a mulatto in the US Census. In 1920, the exact same J. J. Mary is listed as white. In 1930, J. J. Mary was listed in the US Census as a negro.[79] However, it would be a mistake to assume that all the members of the Francs Amis were passé blanc Creoles.

In *Louis Armstrong's New Orleans*, Thomas Brothers recounts the story of Baby Dodds, an African American who gained an invitation to a dance at the Francs Amis hall after befriending a Creole in his youth: "The friend's skin was darker than Dodds' but he was able to gain admission for both of them by speaking French. The girls refused to dance with Dodds until, once again, his friend spoke to them in French and asked them to be nice."[80] This story offers a more nuanced understanding of Creole attitudes toward dark-skinned people, particularly dark-skinned African Americans, than is often represented. Creoles were exclusive, and many nursed colorist prejudices, but Creole exclusivity was never a product of colorism alone.

Brothers goes on to observe that the "differences between uptown Negroes and downtown Creoles were in some ways, at some times, as marked as those between Negroes and whites," but therein lies a problem of translations: "Negroes" and "Creoles" are not necessarily exclusive categories the way that "Negroes" and "Whites" were racially constructed as oppositional categories.[81] This imprecision of language plays out further in the commentary of older Creoles, like the "old Jeunes Amis member" who vehemently demanded that the "Jeunes Amis was not a *black* organization! Thommy Lafon [the founder] was not *black*! I am not black. Thommy Lafon would rise up from his grave in sheer anger if he ever knew that you called us *black*!"[82] On the surface, this elderly person's rant could be easily understood as colorism. However, Edmond Dédé, described by Desdunes as a "black man born in New Orleans about 1829," was a violin prodigy, a composer, and a celebrated personality of the New Orleans Creole community whose dark skin and kinky hair were no barrier to his being invited into the fellowship of the Jeunes Amis.[83]

If the Jeunes Amis is viewed as an organization composed of color-ist bigots, a "brown bag club" where skin color determined eligibility for entry,[84] it is difficult to explain a letter from Dédé to Monsieur A. M. L. Perrault, the Jeunes Amis' secretary, wherein Dédé writes: "I have received the communication of the mission you were charged and the eulogistic terms with which you made me known flattered me." Dédé continues, writing "yes, I accept your fellowship. Please, sir, accept for yourself and all of the 'young friends' my warmest regards."[85] Given the dark skin and African features of Edmond Dédé, it would seem that Gaudin's tendency is to overstate the case for colorism as much as Fairclough tends to overstate the case for Creole racial progressivism.

Edmond Dédé's father, Francois Dédé, and his uncle, Basile Dédé, both served in the Louisiana Native Guard under the Confederacy. When the unit was reconstituted as a Union regiment, the Dédé brothers served in Company E, First Regiment, Louisiana Native Guards, under Captain André Cailloux and First Lieutenant Paul Poreé. Thomas Brothers notes that "traditional markers that we consider ethnic were vividly in play" in the relations of Creoles and "Uptown Negroes," and the case of Edmond Dédé is a perfect example: even in the most exclusive Creole sodalities in New Orleans, dark skin and African features were no barrier to inclusion as long as the individual in question spoke French and was from a family with multigenerational connections to the Creole community in the city. Edmond Dédé had dark skin; Edmond Dédé had coarse and kinky hair; Edmond Dédé was not African American, however. He spoke French and hailed from an established and recognized New Orleans Creole family, and that is why he was invited into the fellowship of the Jeunes Amis. Gemeinschaft social connections prevailed.[86]

Historian Nikki Dugar cites the overwhelming pressure of Jim Crow as a primary inspiration for Creoles "to establish institutions in their neigh-borhoods that allowed them to separate themselves not only from Whites but also from non-Creole Blacks."[87] Dugar notes that, in part, this urge to separate themselves was also motivated by self-protection. Gaudin argues that these "separatist" Creoles employed a "pragmatic vision of race as a tool to distance and differentiate themselves from African Americans while drawing themselves closer, theoretically, to whites," but that ignores the reality of the sometimes murderous hostility that existed between Creoles and African Americans, independently of Whites.[88]

The cultural differences between Creoles and African Americans manifested in many ways. Some of those manifestations were terribly violent. A. P. Tureaud Jr. recalls "unprovoked attacks on people," including stabbings of Creoles "by African American kids." Tureaud was not attempting to construct a narrative of victimization, however. "Creoles would do their share, too," he said, indicating clearly that vicious antipathy and a willingness to spill blood was in abundant supply on both sides of Canal Street.[89] Tureaud's comments echo his father's account to Joe Logsdon in a 1970 interview when A. P. Tureaud Sr. recalled the circumstances of his own youth:

> The Creoles of the 7th Ward had a society almost exclusively of their own. Back in those days there wasn't too much mingling between the Creole Negroes and what we used to call the American Negroes, those who lived above Canal Street. . . . There had been occasions when a Creole would go above Canal Street to socialize, go to some parties, etc. That could result in his being beaten by some of the young people up there who resented him coming into their territory. Sometimes this also worked in reverse when the uptown American Negro came down into what was called the Creole section; he would probably find himself in the same situation.[90]

A. P. Tureaud Sr. grew up in the 1910s whereas A. P. Tureaud Jr. grew up in the 1930s and early 1940s, but from one generation to the next, this reality of ethnic animosity endured in New Orleans. It would be a grave error to misunderstand the significance of the testimony of these men, or to underestimate its importance in a context like New Orleans, a city with an extremely problematic culture of murderous street violence for most of its history. As a point of reference, one would do well to consider that in 1926 (a midpoint in the era covered in this study), there were only four cities in the entire United States with higher murder rates than New Orleans (where the murder rate was 33.7 per 100,000 people). One might also consider that, in 1926, the murder rate for Chicago was 16.7 and New York

City's murder rate was 5.7.[91] New Orleans in 1926 was one of the most dangerous cities in the United States, and it is in that context that one must consider the accounts of the Tureauds regarding the potential for violence associated with Creoles and African Americans violating the borders of their respective enclaves: New Orleans was a place where people regularly killed other people on the street. Creoles and African Americans risked their lives in wandering into one another's respective ethnic enclaves.

It should not be inferred from any of this that African Americans were passive recipients of Creole scorn, desperate for Creole acceptance. On the contrary, the African American community had its own separatist element at the beginning of the twentieth century. The best example of this ideological tendency was articulated through Garveyism and the Universal Negro Improvement Association (UNIA), which had three chapters in New Orleans founded between 1920 and 1933.[92] Mary G. Rolinson notes that racial segregation and a virulent opposition to miscegenation (in particular, white male sexual aggression against black women) were integral to Garveyism, and "preventing miscegenation through violence became the salient and compelling feature of Garveyism on which the movement could take hold and have purpose in local communities in the South." Rolinson observed that, informed by Garveyism, "racial separatism was an assertive act on the part of black communities, a way to promote the dignity of the community."[93] Of course, this militant opposition to race mixing represented a mirror image of the opposition to race mixing that white supremacists articulated, a point that remains problematic when taken in the context of Garvey's dalliances with the Ku Klux Klan.[94]

Predictably, the historically mixed-race Creole community of New Orleans demonstrated little if any sympathy for Garveyism. On the contrary, Garveyism was primarily an uptown New Orleans, African American, phenomenon. On July 14 and 15 of 1921, Marcus Garvey visited New Orleans and spoke to his followers there. Rene Grandjean, a friend of Henry Rey and highly regarded Creole spiritualist, recounted Garvey's visit in a letter to a friend identified only as "Mr. B."

> We have also been honored, a few weeks ago, on the 14th & 15th of July to
> be precise, with a visit of the Hon. Marcus Garvey in New Orleans. For 2

consecutive days a monster meeting of colored & black (but *mostly black,* I have been told, a few people of color having so far identified themselves with it in N.O., although persons of color in our city mostly equal, if they do not outnumber, pure black Africans) people was organized at the National Park, 3rd & Williams St, uptown, in which place the Black Moses harangued *"his people"* and received a tremendous ovation from them. . . . Like Cap. Gipsy Pat Smith, the Hon. Marcus Garvey is a spiritual revelation unto himself, & like the Celebrated Revivalist, The Black Demosthenes is working to hasten a spiritual upheaval, but quite in another direction.—One is preaching Love, or rather Love for money; and the other may or may not be preaching for money, but has for gospel that of Hatred.[95]

Whatever message of black empowerment Garvey had for African Americans was lost on Creoles who, for the most part, ignored Garvey when he came to speak in New Orleans and who did not participate in the UNIA in any appreciable numbers. Creoles had a difficult enough time negotiating common political cause with African Americans in the comparatively conservative and petit-bourgeois NAACP. Given the hostility Garvey expressed for mixed-race people like W. E. B. Du Bois, whom Garvey dismissed as a "monstrosity" due to the fact that his ancestors were "Dutch" and "French" in addition to "Negro," the lack of Creole interest in the UNIA in New Orleans comes as no surprise at all.[96] Steven Hahn described New Orleans as "a hotbed of UNIA organizing," but none of that organizing happened below Canal Street.[97]

The Creole community of New Orleans in the early twentieth century was cliquish and insular, although it became less so as time marched on. In part this is because, no matter how much Creoles tried to insulate themselves from the larger society in their enclave in downtown New Orleans, they could not escape the overwhelming pressure of Americanization. The twentieth century was, without question, going to be the American century in New Orleans.

America came to Creole New Orleans and turned it into a venue for whoring and hot music, much to the chagrin of conservative Creoles with elitist class pretensions (and caste prejudices). African Americans invaded these downtown venues, created the most important art form to ever emerge from the United States, and in the process struck Creoles with awe. Some Creoles, like Jelly Roll Morton, appropriated this African American musical art form, added a layer of technical sophistication to it, and marketed it as jazz.

It is unfortunate that the beautiful music that African Americans and Creoles were capable of making together was not matched by a comparable harmony of political interests. The Jim Crow regime of Martin Behrman made no distinction between the Creoles of color and the uptown American Negroes, especially after 1912. Creoles and African Americans tried to come together in organizations like the NAACP and Juvenile Cooperators but, prior to World War II especially, such efforts were always fraught with conflict, mostly due to ethnic tensions.

Traditional Creole sodalities in New Orleans, like the oldest African American sodalities, tended to be ethnically homogenous with few (though sometimes notable) exceptions. Though the form of these organizations resembled the sort of Gesellschaft voluntary associations that emerged in cities all over the country during the modern era, traditional Creole organizations like the Jeunes Amis and the Francs Amis were mostly comprised of people with multigenerational, Gemeinschaft, social connections with one another. In short, traditional Creole social sodalities in the city tended to be clannish. This tendency to clannishness did not end with Creole fraternal societies and benevolent organizations, though.

4

THE AMERICAN LABOR MOVEMENT
IN CREOLE NEW ORLEANS

While trade unions are, in the end, just another form of social sodality, it is necessary to consider Creole participation in unions in New Orleans separately from participation in other benevolent societies and fraternal organizations. Organizations like the Jeunes Amis and Francs Amis sequestered themselves downtown and closed ranks around parents and children, siblings and cousins, and in-laws, creating a separate, Creole, social space. However, the purpose and function of trade unions was to protect workers from exploitation in the marketplace, and the marketplace in the city was not confined to downtown. To make a living in twentieth-century New Orleans, Creoles had no choice but to venture out of their insular faubourgs and form economic alliances with European immigrants, African Americans, Irish Americans, and also with American Whites. Thus, there were no "exclusively Creole" trade unions in New Orleans in the same sense that the Jeunes Amis was an "exclusively Creole" fraternal society. The only trade union in twentieth-century New Orleans that was truly dominated by Creoles, the Plasterers' Union Local 93, was founded by a group of Creoles and Irish Americans.[1]

Gemeinschaft social connections prevailed in New Orleans's Plasterers' Union Local 93 just as they did in Creole social sodalities like the Jeunes Amis. Local 93's Creole membership, like the membership of the Jeunes Amis, or the Francs Amis, or Fraternité No. 20, was composed of families with multigenerational kinship connections through blood, marriage, or both. In fact, Local 93's Creole membership demonstrates significant crossover with all of those aforementioned organizations, yet Local 93 was different from those traditional Creole sodalities in its primary function as a protective labor union. As such, the history of Local 93 offers an opportunity for unique insights into the Creole community's response to the pressures of industrialization and the modernization of New Orleans's economy through a mainstream, American, organized labor movement.

It is not always a simple task to identify the Creole presence in a racialized landscape that has often rendered Creoles indistinct in an ocean of "colored people," "negroes," Blacks, and African Americans in much of the contemporary literature on US labor history, and specifically on the history of race and labor in New Orleans. However, there are as many distinctions as similarities between the Creole experience and the African American experience in the larger context of the culture of work and labor in Louisiana (and in the United States more generally) in the early twentieth century. Creoles experienced economic marginalization as a result of Jim Crow, but often Creoles had more resources to draw from, including but not limited to conscious, multigenerational transferences of intellectual capital and extended familial connections (sometimes across the color line, too). Segregated syndicates of organized labor, dominated by white Americans, in New Orleans at the turn of the twentieth century excluded Creoles in much the same fashion as they excluded African Americans. However, in New Orleans, there were labor unions that were dominated and controlled by Creoles, and those served as vehicles through which Creoles challenged and resisted their economic and political marginalization.

The extent to which the patterns of inclusion and exclusion in New Orleans Plasterers' Union Local 93 are consistent with such patterns in the city's Creole benevolent societies like the Jeunes Amis is demonstrable. Local 93 was, above all else, a sodality of artisanal clans, along the same lines as traditional nineteenth-century Creole social sodalities, which is to say it was a collection of families with multigenerational ties to one another that extended as far back as the eighteenth century, in some instances. Just as language was utilized to create a separate Creole space below Canal Street in the halls of Creole benevolent societies, the use of Louisiana Creole and French allowed Creoles to create a space within the union that was as impenetrable as the canvas screens erected by master craftsmen on the job site, to protect their intellectual property from the eyes of those without the proper pedigree to partake in the sharing of family trade secrets.

Finally, it would be a mistake to underestimate the extent to which the struggle entailed in the organized labor movement functioned as an assimilative instrument for the Creole community. Participation in the American labor movement facilitated a transition into an American identity over the course of the first half of the twentieth century. Local 93, and indeed the other unions that Creoles would join and support in New Orleans, thrust clannish and insular Creoles into a larger, American, political movement, and demanded Creoles engage a new language of fraternity (as opposed to "fraternité"). For a community often derided for its lack of political engagement and, worse, for its willingness to accommodate white-supremacist racial expectations, Creole participation in Local 93 offers a faint glimpse of Caryn Cossé Bell's nineteenth-century Afro-Creole protest tradition as articulated by Creoles in the twentieth century. Often, these were not protests intended to influence electoral politics but rather, in the traditional idiom of organized labor, the protests of Local 93 took the form of direct action against employers, city government, and even other racially segregated unions in the city. Through union mobilization, Creoles in Local 93 agitated for workplace equality for people of color and not only for plasterers, but through their engagement with the influential New Orleans Building Trades Council, for workers throughout the city across a number of trades and professions, regardless of caste.

The abolition of private slave labor had a profound impact on the economy of New Orleans. New Orleans labor historian and organizer for the Industrial Workers of the World (IWW), Covington Hall noted that, until the 1840s, Louisiana statutes governing labor relations rarely used the term "laborer." Instead, workers were divided between "slaves" and "mechanics," with the latter term designating "skilled workers, that is machinists, carpenters, engineers and even dentists . . . today styled 'professional workers.'"[2] Regardless of the real skills of enslaved people, to be a slave was to be relegated to a unit of brute labor; the slave could not truly be considered a "crafts-man" or "trades-man" in the same way that a free person could be because the caste sensibilities of white racists, to a larger degree than not, prevented them from admitting that the slave was a man at all.

After Emancipation, and in light of the narrow legal acknowledgments of citizenship afforded to people of color by the Thirteenth, Fourteenth, and Fifteenth amendments to the US Constitution, adopted between 1865 and 1870, people of color were no longer commodities to be traded in contracts of private enslavement, but conservative white racists still experienced difficulty viewing them as men and women.

As Blassingame observed, many of those enslaved in New Orleans "worked as draymen, porters, carpenters, masons, bricklayers, painters, plasterers, tinners, coopers, wheelwrights, cabinetmakers, blacksmiths. . . . Most, however, were unskilled laborers often owned by brickyards, iron foundries, hospitals, distilleries, railroad companies, and Catholic convents."[3] Lorenzo J. Greene and Carter G. Woodson observed in 1930 that, after the Civil War, almost all of these workers found their economic position diminished regardless of skill, in part due to increased competition from immigrant workers, but also because of the "unwillingness of employers to hire Negro mechanics, and the keen competition for jobs, in which the white workmen were usually given the preference" for hiring in all but the most distasteful or dangerous jobs.[4] This imposition of a racialized caste sensibility upon the nature of labor itself manifested in the characterization of the most undesirable jobs, often requiring the least skill, as "nigger work." Historian Robin Kelley deconstructs the concept of "nigger work" thoroughly, observing that "in some cases white workers obtained very real material benefit by institutionalizing their strength through white-controlled unions which used their power to enforce ceilings on black mobility and wages. Black workers had to perform 'nigger work.' Without the existence of 'nigger work' and 'nigger labor,' to white workers whiteness would be meaningless. Determining the social and political character of 'nigger work' remains essential for an understanding of black working-class infrapolitics."[5]

The institutionalized occupational subordination of "nigger work" created the material foundation for caste differentiation between Whites and people of color everywhere in the southern United States. However, in New Orleans, where Creoles of color had long occupied an in-between artisanal caste, and where they were not easily dislodged from their position of domination and economic control over a few key trades, the institutionalization of "nigger work" also created the material foundation for a rearticulated caste distinction between the descendants of freedmen and the descendants of the city's gens de couleur libres.

Allyson Hobbs observed that, in the US slave society of the nineteenth century, acquiring the intellectual capital of a skilled trade was often enough to obscure the line between free people of color and enslaved people of color even when those people of color could not pass for white. Hobbs argues that "passing as free," another manifestation of situational passing, was often accomplished "by identifying oneself as a tradesman or an artisan or by affiliating with a profession comprising men who were known to be free."[6] In the nineteenth century, to be a "tradesman" was a coveted achieved status that lent itself to obfuscation with the ascribed status of "freeman" for enslaved people throughout the South. Just as free Creoles of color in New Orleans had historically occupied a racialized caste position in between wealthy Whites and the enslaved, so too did a significant number of Creoles in early twentieth-century New Orleans occupy an in-between class position situated below the property-owning wealthy (mostly Whites) and above the unskilled laborer (including "conditionally white," unskilled, European immigrants like the Irish or the Sicilians).[7] That in-between class/caste position afforded by artisanal labor was a familiar one for Creoles: the occupational patterns of Creoles in New Orleans in the early twentieth century remained fairly consistent with the occupational patterns of their fathers and grandfathers, who formed the "great majority" of the city's "regular, settled masons, bricklayers, builders, carpenters, tailors, shoemakers etc."[8] Alan Lomax in recording his interviews with Creole jazz legends remarked that there was

one proudly descriptive phrase that kept ringing through [upon meeting his interviewees for the first time] "painter by trade . . . plasterer by trade . . . cigarmaker by trade." Apparently the Creole musician was also a craftsman. . . . Papa Bechet, who played flute for fun, was a shoe maker. Leonard Bechet, who played trombone in Silver Bell Band, is a maker of fine inlays. Sidney Bechet, the poet of New Orleans musicians, always followed music. Papa deLisle Nelson, was an amateur accordionist, and a butcher. Louis deLisle (Big Eye) Nelson, maybe the first "hot" clarinet, worked as a butcher's apprentice. Papa Dominguez, a fine classical bass, was a cigar-maker. Paul Dominguez, first a violinist, then ragtime fiddler, was always a professional musician. Bab Frank, led the "first hot band" with his piccolo, ran restaurants. Albert Glenny, bass-player, painter by trade. Freddie Keppard, the greatest New Orleans trumpet, was a professional musician. F. P. LaMenthe fooled with slidin' trambone, but made money as a contractor. Ferdinand Morton (LaMenthe), disdained manual labor. Manuel Perez, the favorite Creole trumpeter, also knew how to make cigars. Alphonse Picou, composer of High Society, tinsmith by trade. Piron, composer of Sister Kate, his barber shop was a musicians' center. Johnny St. Cyr, the best hot guitarist, plasterer by trade. Papa Tio, classical clarinet, cigarmaker by trade. Lorenzo Tio, son, taught clarinet, cigarmaker by trade.[9]

These names—Bechet, Dominguez, Perez, St. Cyr, Tio—all refer to old Creole families internationally associated with New Orleans jazz. In the city of New Orleans each of these surnames was also associated with families of craftsmen and artisans, and had been since the middle of the nineteenth century. From generation to generation, families passed on trade skills and specialized knowledge, bequeathing intellectual property to their children and with it a class status. It was not an elite status, but it was certainly above that of the masses consigned to "nigger work."

Industrialization represented a fundamentally new scheme of production that diminished the role of both the rural laborer and the skilled craftsman in favor of the "semiskilled machine operative," according to historian Bruce Laurie.[10] Unlike the rural laborer, the industrial worker was expected to be mobile, or at least mobile enough to access the urban locales where industrial jobs were often located. Unlike workers in the artisanal trades, there was no specialized knowledge or multigenerational intellectual capital that the individual industrial worker had to bring to bear with which to claim some measure of control over his labor and professional life. Consequently, even though the skilled worker might lay claim to an elite status in relation to the unskilled worker, the social positions of both were diminished in the new economy that had only limited use for preindustrial labor of any kind, skilled or otherwise.

New Orleans's economy was thoroughly industrialized by the early twentieth century, and industrialization fundamentally changed the economic realities of Creole New Orleans. In the first place, industrialization undermined the economic power of skilled tradesmen that their privileged status had been based on. As semiskilled industrial labor became more common, and in some instances more lucrative, much of the economic power, even if not the prestige, of the individual artisan was lost. Laurie argues that, for the most part, the "supple artisan culture of the small shop was swept to the industrial periphery" where "no one referred to the employer as a master craftsman any longer."[11] Just as modernization had contributed to social pressures that undermined traditional Creole caste in-betweenness, industrialization exerted similar, and related, pressures on Creoles by undermining the basis of their economic power, such as it was. The sole exception to this pattern, according to Laurie, was in the building trades, a view that is shared by Gunnar Myrdal.

Myrdal found that the "trowel trades," including those whose interests were guarded by the unions of "Bricklayers, Masons . . . Operative Plasterers and Cement Finishers," were particularly prestigious, and lucrative, trades for people of color who "had managed to maintain a substantial position in these occupations before the time when the unions started to become powerful in the South."[12] This was certainly true in New Orleans, where Creoles were well represented in the unions of the "trowel trades" well into the twentieth century. In the city's Bricklayers' Union Local 1, Creoles aligned themselves with African Americans (and indeed, some American Whites as well) in a single, interracial union where all members were regarded equally. In New Orleans' Operative Plasterers' and Cement Masons' International Union Local 93, Creoles allied themselves with white Americans and immigrant Whites (primarily Irish), in the only labor union in the city that could be truly described as "Creole controlled." In stark contrast to the egalitarian organizational principles evidenced in Bricklayers' Union Local 1, however, Plasterers' Union Local 93 denied membership to African Americans for almost a half-century after its founding.

Protective trade unions, typically affiliated with the American Federation of Labor (AFL), enjoyed much success in organizing workers in New

Orleans. The AFL was a deeply conservative organization that positioned itself as an alternative to more radical traditions in the organized labor movement, and this was certainly part of the formula for its organizing success. As Covington Hall observed, it "was the A.F. of L. that 'scabbed' the Knights of Labor, the American Railway Union and the Western Federation of Miners out of existence" because of a preference for organizing "a 'caste' and not a 'class' unionism" that was meant to keep unskilled and semiskilled workers unorganized and subordinate to skilled craftsmen who preferred to keep unskilled workers as "'helpers' forever," consigned to low-paid positions with no job security.[13] This concept of the protective union as a product of "caste unionism" is an indispensable interpretive device for unraveling the complexities of organized labor in New Orleans.

Caste unionism, in the mode of the AFL, rejected the sort of transracial class solidarity articulated and espoused by socialists, communists, anarcho-syndicalists, and collectivists and accommodated southern racial bigotry. According to Covington Hall, this "caste unionism" rejected any organizing principle that threatened the trades unionists' "petty special privileges as an 'aristocracy of labor.'"[14] To the extent that Creoles in New Orleans participated in the organized labor movement, their participation was almost always defined by the limitations of caste unionism and, though sometimes they challenged those limitations, their predominant mode of engagement throughout the first half of the twentieth century was accommodationist.

Eric Arnesen offers the best and most comprehensive study of the complex race/caste relations among waterfront workers in New Orleans, and his overall assessment of the period between 1863 and 1923 is as clear as it is sobering. Irrespective of cooperation across the color lines, "white workers guarded their privileged position in the city's employment hierarchy: black unskilled workers constituted a potential threat to their security, not potential allies in a larger struggle."[15] Two years after union cooperation across the color lines inspired a general strike on New Orleans's waterfront which was, according to Roger W. Shugg, the first in the history of the United States "to enlist both skilled and unskilled labor, black and whites, and to paralyze the life of a great city,"[16] the waterfront was the scene of horrific episodes of racial violence. In 1894, a British shipping company doing business in New Orleans made the decision to hire black workers who were willing to labor for lower wages than their white counterparts, sparking race riots on the docks, which were suppressed only with the intervention of the state militia.[17]

Scholars from Du Bois onwards have, of course, argued that racial phobia split black and white workers inseparably, but fewer have seriously investigated the sort of intra-racial/intra-caste hostility that existed between Creoles and African Americans. Race relations between Blacks and Whites on the waterfront were tumultuous at times, but the sort of ethnic strife that characterized Creole–African American relations in other contexts in the city were mostly absent on the waterfront, or rather, if there was ethno-racial tension between Creoles and Americans on the waterfront, that tension was not sufficient to warrant a mention by Arnesen.

On the waterfront, people of color participated in subordinate, colored, subdivisions of segregated unions controlled by American Whites in a pattern referred to as "bi-racial unionism." The New Orleans' Screwmen's Benevolent Association (SBA) was a typical example of a "biracial union." The SBA consisted of a primary syndicate controlled exclusively by white workers with an affiliated, subordinate, colored subdivision. Imperfect as this biracial union model was, it proved sufficiently powerful to support a general strike in New Orleans in 1892 that lasted for three days and that was maintained by all workers, white and colored, despite attempts by management to divide workers along racial lines.[18] According to Arnesen and others, the Screwmen represented one of the most powerful labor syndicates in the city, if not the most powerful of them all, at the turn of the twentieth century.[19]

The binary racial order implied by the term "bi-racial unionism" renders the Creole narrative impossible to discern in Arnesen's work as Creoles are subsumed in the larger category of "blacks," a racialized caste category that Arnesen does not interrogate for ethnic distinctions. Where Arnesen does engage the subject of "black Creoles" he qualifies the distinction between them and the larger mass of "free blacks," describing Creoles as an elite class. Arnesen artificially separates Creoles from the larger, non-elite, black masses who "found employment as artisans or as skilled or unskilled laborers in the building trades" even though those building trades had been controlled by Creoles throughout the nineteenth century and well into the twentieth century.[20] Arnesen's narrative on the Creole presence on the waterfront is therefore suspect since the extent of Creole identity, for Arnesen, is that of a "free black elite" before the Civil War who became, simply, the "black elite," after the war was over. It is possible that Arnesen simply lacks the interpretive framework to engage a narrative of intra-racial/intra-caste ethnic encounters on the New Orleans waterfront: it is possible that he doesn't locate a significant Creole presence because he doesn't understand what to look for.

Still, it is equally conceivable that the reason Arnesen's account lacks significant engagement with Creoles on the waterfront is because there was no significant Creole presence on the waterfront. The African American–dominated Screwmen's Benevolent Association No. 1 (Colored) was founded in 1891, and not one of its founding members was from a recognizable Creole family.[21] In remarks saturated with class pretensions, Creole jazzman Paul Dominguez denigrated the work of longshoremen and screwmen in an interview with Alan Lomax: "Downtown people, we try to be intelligent. Everybody learn a trade. Like my daddy was a cigarmaker and so was I. All us people try to get an easy job that our education qualifies us for. . . . There's a vast difference here in this town. Uptown folk all ruffians, cut up in the face and live on the river. All they know is get out on the levee and truck cotton, be longshoremen, screwmen."[22]

Dominguez clearly took pride in having never worked on the river "a day in [his] life." His reference to "Uptown folk all ruffians," is particularly striking: he could just as easily be referring to Irish immigrants and Irish Americans as to African Americans in this regard, and with little distinction between them in the measure of his contempt. In Creole New Orleans, white workers weren't the only ones who were able to capitalize on the institutionalization of deleterious and loathsome labor as "nigger work." Creoles, by disassociating themselves from grueling, arduous, waterfront work, were also able to disassociate themselves from the people doing that work, whether those people were African Americans or working-class white Americans. The fact that Dominguez associated getting "out on the levee and truck[ing] cotton" with a devalued class status despite the fact that these industrial occupations paid excellent wages is very telling.

Though A. P. Tureaud's father, Louis Tureaud, worked on the river as a young man, he eventually left his job to become a cistern maker and a building subcontractor. This decision afforded him, according to his son Alexander, "a sort of middle-class status . . . above that of the unskilled worker."[23] Certainly, that "sort of middle-class status" is manifest in the achieved status conveyed in the title of "master artisan," yet, according to A. P. Tureaud, his father wasn't even a particularly adept contractor.[24] While there is clearly nothing about construction work and building contracting that indicates bourgeois class interests, for a person of color in Jim Crow New Orleans, the sort of autonomy afforded by such an occupation allowed some Creoles to distinguish themselves from (and to assert their superiority to) the proletarian masses, black and white alike (but especially black). The "sort of middle-class status" that A. P. Tureaud describes is embedded in the self-managing nature of building contracting, which affords the builder a measure of workplace autonomy above that of those unfortunates who "slaved like niggers" (and "white niggers," too) on the waterfront.[25]

Creoles were contemptuous of the biracial model of "caste unionism" that characterized AFL-affiliated trade unions, whether on the waterfront or otherwise, especially when that model of caste unionism marginalized them as people of color. The proof of that contempt is demonstrated in their refusal to abide subordination in the unions that they had controlling interests in, like the Bricklayers' and the Plasterers' unions. With that understood, it also bears mentioning that the Bricklayers' and Plasterers' unions were clearly the exceptions to a standard rule of subordination or, in some cases, outright exclusion.

The oldest trade union in the city was the New Orleans Typographical Union No. 17, the local branch of the oldest national labor union in the United States. Founded in 1852, the Typographers' national barred people of color from membership altogether, along with women and the Irish.[26] The New Orleans local was no more inclusive than the national, and that institutional exclusion made printing and typesetting a profession that Creoles, for the most part, were structurally barred from. One exception to this rule of exclusion was a New Orleans Creole named Adolf Moret Sr., founder of the Moret Press, a major twentieth-century New Orleans Creole institution.

Adolf Moret Sr. learned the typesetter's and printer's trade at Steeg Printing Company in New Orleans, which was a family-owned business and the largest printing establishment in the city. Steeg was also a non-union shop and, with no Jim Crow union to prevent the managers from hiring colored staff, Steeg employed Adolf Moret Sr. for twenty years before he was finally made redundant. In the words of Calvin Moret, his father, Adolf, was desperate to "keep the wolf from the door" after losing his job, and yet there were no opportunities in New Orleans for a colored typographer, or rather there were no opportunities for waged labor in New Orleans for a colored typographer. Recognizing a need in his own community, and confident that he had the skill and competence to provide professional high-quality printing services, Adolf Moret Sr. secured $200 for an initial investment in his own printing business. He acquired all the equipment and machinery he needed to open his doors for business in the week between Christmas and New Year's Day 1932. The Moret Press operated under the direction of Calvin and his brother, Roy Moret, until the devastation of its office on Allen Street in the Seventh Ward caused by the levee breach that followed the storm surge of Hurricane Katrina in 2005. When the Moret Press finally closed its doors for business, it had been in operation for seventy-three years.[27]

The Moret Press printed bills and pamphlets for social organizations like the Jeunes Amis and the Autocrat Club as well as for churches, local businesses, and school functions. Even though it was not a union shop, the Moret Press enjoyed ample patronage from New Orleans's Bricklayers' and Plasterers' unions, as is evidenced by printed materials in both archival collections. While there is no paucity of archival evidence of the Plasterers and Bricklayers engaging the language of working-class fraternity and solidarity common to organized labor syndicates, Creole-dominated unions in New Orleans did not patronize printing shops controlled by Typographical Union No. 17. For Creoles in New Orleans, "Whites Only" unions that excluded them by caste made class solidarity with such unions a nonissue, even though they were all AFL affiliated by the 1910s.

Before engaging the subject of the Creole-dominated Plasterers' Union, it is necessary to first recognize that there were opportunities for true interracial solidarity in New Orleans's organized labor movement. For example, the Bricklayers, Masons, and Marble Masons' International Union No. 1 of Louisiana represented a sodality composed of European immigrants, Italian Americans, Irish Americans, African Americans, and Creoles in New Orleans. Martin Behrman, when offering commentary on race and organized labor in New Orleans, recalled that the "whites and the blacks are together in the bricklayers' union and it is probably the strongest building trades union in New Orleans."[28] This view is confirmed by a retired Creole bricklayer and lifelong union man, Earl R. Barthé, who recalled in a 2010 interview that the bricklayers' union "was always integrated from the beginning, Whites and Blacks. It didn't matter as long as you gave an honest day's work . . . and it seemed like there was always work for a bricklayer." Consequently, New Orleans Bricklayers' No. 1 became an important vehicle for interracial and intercultural solidarity not only between Whites and people of color in New Orleans, but also between Creoles and Americans.[29]

Based on a survey of union records and rosters, it is clear that Bricklayers' Local 1 was a thoroughly integrated syndicate, which rendered it immune to the sort of division of interest that segregated caste unionism promoted between white workers and workers of color. In fact, it is not an overstatement to observe that New Orleans' Bricklayers' union was unique in the city in its inclusivity, especially in the period between 1910 and 1940. Martin Behrman described the union as thoroughly interracial, but he also clarified that its membership was composed of "mostly negroes."[30] In this instance, Behrman made no distinction between Creoles and African Americans, but it is clear that Creoles occupied key roles in the union at various times in the organization's history. Clearly recognizable Creole family names like Barthé, Breaud, Broyard, Christophe, Daliet, Dugar, Duplessis, Fontenot, Gaudett, Labat, Lamothe, Landry, Marchand, Perrault, and even less obvious Creole family names like Chase, Davis, Diggs, Harris, Mitchell, and Williams appear in the archival materials of Bricklayers' No. 1 from the earliest ledger entries, dated 1908, until the last, dated 1958. Yet, among these Creole names are other names like Banks, Blanks, Blatt, Braun, Caldwell, Hargis, Porter, Jensen, Caifaro, Carey, Casey, Faulk, Hagan, Mann, McMurray, Maxwell, Richardson, Solomon, Sculley, Sterling, Thomas, and Wills.[31] Creoles participated in the Bricklayers' Union and even occupied positions of leadership in it, too. However, the Bricklayers, Masons,

and Marble Masons' International Union No. 1 was never controlled by
Creoles in the same way that New Orleans's Operative Plasterers' and Cement Masons' International Association of the United States and Canada
Local No. 93 was controlled by Creoles. If the Bricklayers represented an
"aristocracy of labor," then at least it was a truly multiracial aristocracy.

The true power of the Bricklayers' Union did not rest in its interracial nature, however. Its power rested in the financial resources that it could bring
to bear. Like other unions in the city, Bricklayers' Local 1 rented space for
its meetings, paid token salaries to its officers, and provided benefits by the
week for members with legitimate claims.[32] The union consistently managed to keep its finances in credit from 1908 through 1958 according to the
meticulously detailed cash ledgers kept by the union treasurer, William H.
Davis, who held that post for an entire half-century, which speaks to the
stability and continuity of the organization as well. By the end of the first
quarter of 1911, Bricklayers' No. 1 had a total bank balance of $191.75. By
the end of the first quarter of 1921, that balance was $399.60. By the end
of the first quarter of 1951, Bricklayers' No. 1 had a balance of $39,344.30
with one outstanding check in the amount of $443.00.[33] These numbers
should not be surprising: bricklaying was among the more lucrative of
the building trades, and the city of New Orleans saw a period of rapid
expansion of its urban footprint in the beginning of the twentieth century.

In the first four months of 1923, more than $29 million was spent on
building construction in Louisiana with $12,184,700 of that being spent
in New Orleans alone. In May of 1923, the *Times-Picayune* announced
"Rapid Development of St. Charles Street" in uptown New Orleans,
"Rampart Street Joins Building Boom," and "Algiers Take Vigorous Steps
to Become Great N.O. Residential Suburb." That same month, the Co-
operative Homestead, a group dedicated to facilitating home ownership,
reported the disbursement of five loans worth $15,050 and two building
contracts worth $6,300 each. In that same month, another group, the
Italian Homestead, reported $17,200 in loan applications, five acts of sale
totaling $22,600 with ten more acts of sale totaling $63,000, awaiting
signature. Another group called the Mutuals reported the passage of three
loans worth $10,600, $6,000, and $760 while refusing five more applica-

tions totaling $17,800. The Security Homestead reported receipt of fifteen loan applications in May of 1923 for a grand total of $63,000. The Eureka Homestead in New Orleans reported home-building loan applications in the amount of $81,600, and described the housing market in the city, noting that "demand is active and supply ample." The Eureka Homestead signed two contracts that month for projects in the Sixth Ward, one for $5,075 and the other for $4,550, while making payments amounting to $6,305 on three other sites where construction was in progress. This physical, geographical expansion of the city translated into lucrative work for professional builders, a fact acknowledged by Roger W. Babson, entrepreneur, business theorist, and founder of Babson College in Massachusetts, who observed at a gathering of the Associated Advertising Clubs of the World in 1923 that "several hundred thousand retailers in this country would be better off as plasterers or bricklayers."[34]

The building boom of the early twentieth century was accompanied by a rise in wages for professional builders. By April of 1924, the *Times-Picayune* announced that the average building costs and the average cost of labor had doubled compared to costs prior to World War I. This inflation in building costs was not an across-the-board increase, however. Changes in costs of materials varied wildly depending on the materials used. The changes in the cost of labor varied as well with slim to modest gains among the most skill-intensive professions coupled with "astonishing rises in hod-carrying and none too intellectual pursuits." Most importantly, the article states decisively that, along with plasterers, bricklayers "in general receive the highest total wage." If the Bricklayers' Union was truly an "aristocracy of labor," it was because of the economic power the members wielded, collectively.[35]

The late Earl A. Barthé (not to be confused with his cousin Earl R. Barthé) was a former president of New Orleans Plasterers' Local 93, an inductee in the Louisiana AFL-CIO Labor Hall of Fame, a fellow of the National Endowment of the Arts, and a historian of the plastering trade. Much of what is known of the founding of Local 93 is due to the oral history work produced by New Orleans folklorist Nick Spitzer while working with Earl A. Barthé, who described the founding of union in 2007:

Peter Barthé, my great-grand uncle was the organizer with Sam Ball, who was white. Barthé was working on the St. Louis Cathedral and Ball was working next door on the museum and they had a problem, I think on the museum. So, at twelve o'clock they would just talk about their problems and what-not and, to make a long story short, they realized that they had the talent. Now, I want you to remember, this is 1898. You know the racial things of that time. . . . So, they decided that they wanted to join together and put that talent together. So Peter, in 1898, he wrote to the International Union in Washington to organize the plasterers in New Orleans. . . . From 1898 to 1901, they was trying to get the Union in, and in Washington, they wouldn't let them organize because they were of two races. But Peter Barthé and Ball, they stood together and decided they would have one union or none. . . . in 1901, Peter was the President and Ball was the Vice-President. . . . There was too much talent to let it go.[36]

There are always problems associated with oral histories, and Barthé's accounts are not without their discrepancies. Indeed, there are a number of things in his account which beg clarification. The first, and most obvious, is what Earl A. Barthé meant by "they were of two races." Sam Ball, the son of Irish immigrants Simon and Jane Ball, was almost certainly considered "white." However, in 1901, there were still three caste designations (articulated as "racial identities") in New Orleans: "white," "colored," and "negro." Pierre Barthé was not considered white, despite his phenotypical appearance, but in 1901, Pierre Barthé was not considered a "negro," either.[37]

Leon Barthé, Pierre's older brother and a vocal member of the Plasterers' Protective Union (a precursor to Local 93 that operated through the 1880s in New Orleans), was the first person in the family to describe his profession as "plasterer."[38] It is not clear how he "broke into" the plastering trade, however. Plastering, especially ornamental plastering, is a demanding craft that requires extensive training and instruction, and such training was jealously guarded within families.

Martin Levine, a New Orleans Creole, recalled that "to become a plasterer you had to be related to one or to know him some kind of way to

get into the plasterers' union." His interviewer, Arthé Agnes Anthony, attempted to contextualize Levine's comments, observing that "young men
from the [Creole] community had a decided advantage in gaining acceptance" into the Plasterers' Union Local 93 when compared to the opportunities available to African Americans, but this is a gross understatement of
the case.[39] Local 93 was founded in New Orleans in 1901 but, for almost a
half-century, there were no opportunities at all for African Americans to
learn the plastering trade in the city, and union membership in Local 93
was, for all intents and purposes, closed to them. Membership patterns of
Local 93 followed the same pattern as other exclusive (and exclusionary)
Creole sodalities like the Jeunes Amis and the Francs Amis, and Local 93
membership demonstrated significant overlap with those organizations as
well as their precursors (including the Creole Masonic lodges, the Civil
War–era Native Guards, and the Native militias of the French and Spanish colonial era). In fact, before the Plasterers' Union established its own
union hall at 1419 St. Bernard Avenue, in the Seventh Ward, its meetings
were held at the Jeunes Amis Hall in Faubourg Tremé.[40] Local 93, in the
end, was another Creole Gemeinschaft social organization masquerading
as a Gesellschaft social organization.

In a survey of union membership rosters, there are many family names
that recur intergenerationally. Some Creole family names, like Barthé,
Dejean, Desvignes, Doyle, Dupont, Fleury, Ganier, Jean, Labat, LaFrance,
LaTour, Marchand, Monier, Poché, Porée, Quezerque, Rousséve, and Tio,
were all plastering families represented in the Native Guard and/or colonial militias of free people of color and/or the Creole Masonic lodges.
From one generation to the next, union control was vested in the hands
of a small group who inherited positions of prominence within the organization by virtue of familial connection. Indeed, there is no evidence to
suggest that there was any time between 1901 and 1954 where there was
not at least one Barthé, Doyle, Ball, or Ritchie (Irish American family
related to the Ball family) serving as either an officer or a sales agent of
Local 93. New Orleans's Plasterers' Union Local 93 was a vault of intellectual capital rendered completely inaccessible to those without the proper
pedigree, even within the union and even on the job site.[41]

The intellectual property of New Orleans plastering craftsmanship was carefully guarded by master plasterers who, knowing well the value of their skill, erected screens or curtains on job sites to prevent the uninitiated from learning trade secrets reserved for family. Terry Barthé, one of Earl A. Barthé's surviving daughters, completed her plasterers' apprenticeship in the early 1980s and, when speaking to the insular culture of the union, and specifically on the use of curtains on the job, she recalled that her "Daddy and Uncle Harold learned that way. They [were taken] behind the curtain while the others they'd send off to fetch supplies or get lunch. You had to be connected to see what went on behind that curtain." These practices contributed to the development of a brand identity, of sorts.[42] That brand—New Orleans Creole ornamental plasterwork—promised meticulous skill, cultivated from birth in its practitioners, who were, according to Mora Beauchamp-Byrd and John Michael Vlach, "raised to the trade" in families that became synonymous with New Orleans building arts.[43]

In the absence of any formal apprenticeships program, being raised to the trade within a network of artisanal families was the only way to achieve the absolute mastery of the plastering craft necessary to produce the sort of intricate ornamental designs associated with New Orleans plasterwork. Earl A. Barthé recalled in a 2005 interview that his "father was a plasterer, his father was a plasterer, his uncles and everybody else were plasterers. . . . The Barthé children knew they had to be plasterers. Daddy didn't want me to be a doctor, a lawyer or an Indian chief."[44] Barthé never wanted to be anything other than a plasterer: he was raised to be one. When describing the way his father administered training to him and his brother as children, Barthé recalled that

Daddy would come in after working on a Saturday tell my brother and I to clean the tools. He would leave pennies and nickels in his toolbox and say, "Whatever you all find, that's for you." So we'd dig in that bag, cleaning the tools and looking for them pennies and nickels. We realized later that he was training us. He would say, "Earl, give me that pointing trowel." And I'd say, "Pointing trowel?" He would pick it up and say, "You see this little tool. This is a pointing trowel. When I ask you for that that's what I want you to give me." . . . That was his way of educating us.[45]

Training a craftsman from childhood was a practice that accomplished two vital economic functions in the Creole community. The first function was the bequeathing of legacies from fathers to sons among people who, often, had more intellectual property to pass on than real property. The other, more practical and immediate, function was that it provided the Creole craftsman a pool of readily available free labor. A. P. Tureaud recalled that he was occasionally called upon by his father to work without pay on the "occasions when he went way in the hole in estimating" the costs of a project.[46] That remembrance informs the interpretation of Earl A. Barthé's account of the "deep sense of community and deep, deep, traditional moral family values" of the Creole community of his youth in New Orleans, where seemingly everyone had big families and where "sons were important to keep on the family trade and to keep the family name."[47] Taken with all sentimentality excised, sons (even partially trained sons) were important to the family business as sources of free labor. Similarly, "keeping the family name" seems much less a rustically nostalgic sensibility when one considers that family names often served the same function as trademarks.[48] Indeed, the advertising tag line of Earl A. Barthé's plastering company, Earl A. Barthé and Associates, directly illustrates this point: "Barthé: a name in plastering since 1850."[49]

Whether an accurate reflection of competence or not, the perception of one's competence as a craftsman was directly related to the reputation associated with the family names of those from whom an apprentice received instruction. Creole plasterer Allen Sumas explained in a 2003 interview the practical manifestation, on the job, of this sort of brand identity associated with family names. Sumas recalled that, if "you were a good plasterer, everyone wanted to know who was your teacher and what jobs you do" and if "you couldn't tell me you was taught by one of these great teachers, then you didn't learn from the best, so you are lacking in something."[50]

Pierre and Leon Barthé could not have learned their craft from their father, Antoine Barthé, who was a cooper by trade. Nor would the brothers have learned the plastering craft from their paternal grandfather, Jean Barthé, a Creole who served in Fortier's Native Militia at the Battle of New Orleans and who was in business with John Lafitte, trading slaves and other "scarce and valuable goods" between New Orleans and Baltimore. Although impossible to confirm, it seems most likely that Antoine Barthé, who was a member of Masonic Lodge Fraternité No. 20 in 1869 and l'Amite No. 27, secured an apprenticeship for his sons through his lodge fellowship. Alexander, Aubert, Dupart, Dupre, Gardette, Martinez, Meunier (Monier), Remy (Remey), and St. Cyr: these are all Creole families represented in one or both masonic lodges as well as New Orleans's Plasterers' Local 93. Arranging apprenticeships with skilled craftsmen for one's children through a lodge brother is exactly the sort of opportunity afforded through membership in such an organization.[51]

Membership patterns of Plasterers' Union Local 93 bore more than a superficial resemblance to the old Creole Masonic lodges, Fraternité No. 20 and l'Amite No. 27, though there were some crucial differences. All of those organizations were interracial sodalities composed of Whites and Creoles, for example. Unlike Fraternité No. 20 and l'Amite No. 27, however, Local 93 included Anglophone Irish American Whites (as opposed to white Creoles or Frenchmen) and, from the beginning, the official language of Local 93 was English. Conducting all official business of the union in English was almost certainly a necessary concession, not only to the white Anglophone members of Local 93, but also to the larger American economy that had finally begun to fully penetrate the borders of downtown New Orleans. English—'Mericain—was the language of commerce, and commerce demanded engagement on its own terms. These pressures informed the sensibilities of Creoles with aspirations of upward mobility and explain, in part, why they were less resistant to "English only" education. These realities did not dissuade Creoles from speaking their own language to one another within the union and on the job site, however, and it seems that Creoles intentionally used language as a mechanism of exclusion in Local 93.[52]

Creole master craftsmen used their language to delineate a separate Creole space in Local 93. Therein, they were able to safeguard their own privilege and intellectual capital from the encroachment of their white, Anglophone, union "brothers." Even as late as the 1950s, many of the old master craftsmen still spoke "gumbo-Creole French" among themselves without regard to the monolingual Anglophones around them.[53] Earl A. Barthé did not speak French or Louisiana Creole, yet he recalled that the generation before his own did. According to Barthé, his father could and did speak French with his mother and among his friends and coworkers when "they didn't want you to know what they were saying." After all, as Barthé went on to explain, "you didn't want everybody in your business"— only those people who spoke French and/or Creole, apparently.[54]

There were no African American members of the New Orleans Plasterers' Union for almost a half-century after its founding due to categorical exclusion. This is a circumstance that begs explanation, especially given the "one union or none" language that Earl A. Barthé employed when discussing the origins of the union. "One union or none" seems to imply an ideology of solidarity that would preclude the employ of Jim Crow–style practices of exclusion. In fact, although African Americans were definitely subjected to exclusion, it is not clear that the nature of that exclusion was rooted in racism or colorism.

Positing Creole colorism as the root of African American exclusion from Local 93 was not (and is not) a controversial proposition. There were definitely African Americans who perceived the discrimination against them to be a product of white racism and/or Creole colorism.[55] The biggest problem with the former proposition is that Whites did not have a controlling interest in the union, making white racism an unlikely cause for African American exclusion. Still, Creole colorism cannot account for African American exclusion, either. For example, even though Local 93 founder Pierre Barthé was passé blanc, his sons were not, and both of them were in the union.

Wendy Gaudin describes Creole colorism in integrated sodalities like Local 93 as a product of separatist Creoles utilizing their cultural capital to draw themselves closer to Whites through their exclusion of Blacks.[56] However, it is unclear to what extent Creoles were trying to "draw closer" to the Whites in Local 93. Louis Armstrong, later in life, recalled advice given to him when he was young by a neighborhood wise guy from New Orleans called "Black Benny" on the utility of having white allies in a white-supremacist society. That advice was: "as long as you live, no matter where you may be—always have a *White Man* (who like you) and can + will put his Hand on your shoulder and say—'This is "My" Nigger' and Can't Nobody Harm Ya.'" Having a white "patron" allowed some people of color to vicariously benefit from the privilege afforded to their white associates, and it was not uncommon for people of color to employ this strategy when overcoming structural obstacles to mobility and material advancement during the Jim Crow era. Given this reality, Creole relations with their white union "brothers" appears less of a desire to "draw closer" to Whites (politically or socially) and much more like a practical consideration, undertaken for direct, material, gain. Allowing Whites into Local 93, because of the political realities of the time, was just an additional cost of doing business in the Jim Crow South. Since there was no equivalent material benefit to allowing African American membership in the union, African Americans were excluded.[57]

Creoles understood the benefits of exploiting whiteness for material gain. Sometimes, even having a person of color who *looked white* with his hand on one's shoulder was enough to reap benefits. Earl A. Barthé recalled that, when traveling through the South as a young man while looking for work,

> there were these little highway diners. But if you were black, you might be able to stop and get gas but you couldn't go in to eat. You couldn't use the rest room. Not unless you were white. So, me and Harold [Earl A. Barthé's brother], we were travelling with a dark-skinned fella, we would sit in the back seat of the car and pretend he was the driver when we pulled in. We would get out and say "boy, fill up the tank while we get some sandwiches," and we would walk right in and order the food "to go." . . . They thought we was white. They didn't know. . . . A white man might look at you twice but he wouldn't ask you if you was white if you carried yourself like you were white. . . . we could be Mexican or we could be Indians or Italians and they was all white. . . . we just wanted to get our food and get on to the next job, man! We were looking for work! We weren't on vacation![58]

Earl A. Barthé's description of situational passing demonstrates a clear understanding of the relative (subordinate) social "place" of Blacks under the terms of Jim Crow (for example, drivers and servants to Whites). It also demonstrates an intuitive understanding that an investment in whiteness was, in part, based on a willingness to denigrate and humiliate black people (for example, in calling their coworker, and presumably their union brother, "boy" in a way meant to denigrate in order to evoke a sense of solidarity with onlooking white racists). Creoles like Earl Antoine and his brother, Harold, understood the arbitrary nature of racial identity and exploited their racial in-betweenness for their own profit and that of their dark-skinned coworkers. If Creoles were this calculated in their exploitation of white racial expectations, then it requires no leap of faith to accept that Creoles would understand the benefit of an alliance with Whites who could represent their interests in venues and markets where, as people of color, they were structurally barred from participation. Nothing in Earl A. Barthé's account suggests that his and his brother's responses were motivated by colorist bigotry, even if it is clear that they were prepared to situationally accommodate racist white expectations in order to advance their own interests.

Between 1918 and 1935, union records show instance after instance of plasterers rejoining the union after allowing their membership to lapse. Over and over again, the reasons given are the same: the World War I and/ or the Great Depression.[59] These two events, the war and the economic devastation that followed in its aftermath eleven years later, both had significant impacts on New Orleans's Creole community.

US military installations in New Orleans brought the reality of war home to Creoles in their downtown enclaves. Some Creoles signed up to fight for the United States, just as their fathers and grandfathers and great-grandfathers before them had. Clement Barthé was twenty-four years old and described his profession as "plasterer" when he filled out his registration for the draft at the Sixth Precinct station in the Sixth Ward on June 5, 1917. It was the same for Henry Tio, age twenty-two, who registered for the draft the same day as his union brother, Clement, but at the Tenth Precinct station in the Ninth Ward. The war was almost over in September of 1918 when Louis Lawrence, age thirty-three at the time, registered for the draft at St. Aloysius College on the corner of Rampart and Esplanade. All of these men were married with children, and all of them lived in downtown New Orleans. They were all Creoles, but the variance with which their racial identities were described is interesting. Lawrence and Tio are both recorded as "negro," although Tio's application bears the marks of a correction where he was originally marked as "colored." Despite his métis roots, and his phenotypical appearance, Clement Barthé was described as "African" on his draft registration. World War I brought Creoles into the American cultural fold in more ways than one, including through the sort of patriotic indoctrination that US military personnel were subjected to as a matter of course in their training, as well as through the imposition of Anglo-American racial identities, like "negro," upon them.[60]

During the Great Depression, many Creoles left the South to look for work in other parts of the country. Sometimes they left to relocate, never to return. At other times they left to find work and returned home after having earned enough money to do so. For Creole craftsmen, artisanal skill facilitated their efforts to find work, as did proficiency in English.

While discussing his time in Chicago as a young man, A. P. Tureaud described the status he enjoyed as a result of work experience he received from his father. Throughout Tureaud's account, we are reminded of the distance that he perceived between himself and African American laborers that he shared the experience of migration to Chicago with, especially as he describes scenes of African Americans in rural Mississippi running behind moving trains, "begging to be permitted to get on in order to escape peonage and . . . slavery."[61] While Tureaud is clearly sympathetic to the suffering of these African American migrants, he also made it clear that he did not share their experience. He may have been migrating to Chicago with a trainload of African Americans, but he did not perceive himself as one of them:

> I wasn't familiar with things like peonage or with these conditions of hiring a man's time and making him work it out under a condition which was really slavery. I knew nothing about the low wages of the unskilled laborer. I wasn't very skilled myself in anything except the work that I did with my father. I did do an apprenticeship with him as a carpenter. . . . Then, too, I had gone to school and I knew how to read and write. It gave me a sort of status that I suppose you would call at my age a middle-class life, which was of course my family's background too.[62]

Tureaud did not articulate the difference between himself and his fellow migrants in terms of race, or culture. Rather, he understood that difference as manifest in differing class identities. The educated Creole is posited as a contrast to the illiterate African American escaping bondage in the South; the sophisticated, skilled, city dweller is measured against the poor, desperate, Mississippi sharecropper. The plight of African Americans in the 1910s and 1920s was desperate, but Tureaud is keen to point out that, when it came to Creole immigrants in Chicago, a "lot of them had education, training," that set them apart from African Americans and that these Creoles typically "grouped together" and "had dinners and gumbos" in an attempt to recreate a semblance of the community they enjoyed in New Orleans, where, for the most part, they had lived separately from African Americans.[63] In Chicago, many older Creoles tended to be just as family oriented and "clannish, as they were known to be in New Orleans, and kept to themselves," and yet they were surrounded by Americans and embedded in a thoroughly American economy.[64]

In Illinois, where many people simply "wouldn't know that much difference" between a Creole or a southern European, many Creoles renegotiated their racial identity. Some, who were "too dark to be white in New Orleans," quietly passed into white identities in Chicago, according to A. P. Tureaud. In exchange, those Creoles enjoyed comparatively abundant professional opportunities as they availed themselves of the American Dream in a way that no person of color could. Some Creoles could not pass for white, however, and still other Creoles, like A. P. Tureaud for example, could pass for white but chose not to. Those Creoles who did not pass looked for opportunities in the same place that their African American co-migrants did and, despite their tendency to clannishness, eventually assimilated into the larger African American community.[65]

After World War I, labor agents representing the Pullman Company in New Orleans recruited workers on South Rampart Street, above Canal Street. Working as a Pullman porter, or as a car cleaner, was a lucrative opportunity, especially if one was comfortable with oleaginous kowtowing. For those without the temperament for unceasing professional obsequiousness, however, an industrial laborer driving spikes for the railroad could make more money than a carpenter in New Orleans. It was this opportunity that brought A. P. Tureaud to Chicago.[66] Despite his recollection of the middle class status afforded him as a result of his carpenter's apprenticeship, Tureaud worked as a manual laborer when he first arrived in Chicago. The most he had ever earned as an apprentice carpenter in New Orleans was three dollars a week, but working in Chicago as a scab for the railroad, he earned one dollar an hour. With his housing provided by Pullman at no cost, scabbing was very lucrative for Tureaud, but he was not content to be on the "wrong side of a picket line," at least in part due to his own family's participation in trade unions in New Orleans. The extent to which his apprenticeship helped to define his class status is dubious but, middle class or not, Tureaud was not without resources and, to the extent that he was able to resist his circumstances, he did.[67]

Tureaud's solution to his employment dilemma is a useful case study in the ways that Creoles leveraged Gemeinschaft connections in order to ensure their financial security. The first thing that Tureaud did, after he decided that he did not want to work as a scab, was to inform his mother of his concerns. His mother contacted his godfather, James Slater, who lived in New York. Slater contacted his friend Oscar Delarosa, a New Orleans Creole who had relocated to Chicago to ply his trade as a cigar maker. Delarosa invited Tureaud to quit his job and move into his family's home on East Forty-Second Street in Chicago. From New Orleans to New York to Chicago, Creole Gemeinschaft connections provided Tureaud with everything he needed in order to quit the most lucrative job he had ever had and move out of his company-provided housing with no adverse consequences. Through his business connections in the city, Oscar Delarosa got A. P. Tureaud a job at Western Steel Foundry, where he worked side by side with unionized European immigrants, yet Tureaud didn't stay at Western Steel Foundry very long. Ironically, and despite his pro-union sentiments, Tureaud was excluded from union membership at Western Steel on account of his race, a situation that compelled him to quit his job there after only a few days. Eventually, of course, Tureaud would find his calling in Washington, DC, where he studied under William Henry Harrison Hart, who trained him for a proper middle-class career as a lawyer.[68]

There is a general agreement among scholars that the effects of Roosevelt's New Deal policies on people of color in the United States was mixed, especially in the South. Abdelkrim Dekhakhena observed, for example, that the Dixiecrats often acted as a "bulwark to the advancement of Black rights and to the efforts of liberal New Dealers to include Blacks in their reforms."[69] Stephan and Abigail Thernstrom likewise noted that Dixiecrat congressmen did everything in their power to exclude Blacks from the benefits of New Deal legislation and did their best to ensure that even legislation that would have protected Blacks, in theory, could not be exploited for their benefit, practically.[70] Yet, as a result of Roosevelt's New Deal policies such as the National Labor Relations Act of 1935 (the Wagner Act), organized labor in New Orleans experienced a surge in participation. This surge ushered in an era in which Local 93 reached the height of its power.

The Plasterers exercised their power through striking and labor boycotts, even of projects for Roosevelt's Public Works Administration (PWA). Through one organized boycott in 1935, for example, Local 93 successfully forced the PWA to abandon the practice of hiring nonunion labor for government projects in New Orleans.[71] In another instance, when the city attempted to use unpaid poll taxes to disqualify plasterers from working on jobs for the Parish School Board in Algiers, Local 93 pulled plasterers off of every job in New Orleans where this tactic was being used to deprive men of work until the city abandoned the practice.[72] Such direct action by Local 93 strengthened the position of all the building-trade unions in the city, contributing to more extensive cooperation with other unions through associations like the New Orleans Master Plasterers' Association (MPA).

On Tuesday, July 9, 1935, a meeting of the MPA was held at Economy Hall on Ursuline Street, near Villere, in the Tremé. The MPA was composed of representatives from three building-trade unions: the Plasterers' Union Local 93, the Lathers Union Local 62, and the Laborers' Union Local 153. Including Johnny Monahan, an Irish American plasterer and the acting chair of the association, there were nine representatives from Local 93 at that meeting of the MPA. With the exception of Monahan and his cousin M. J. O'Keefe, every other plasterer present was a Creole. The meeting included both independent contractors and representatives from two large (white-owned) contracting companies in addition to representative committees from each of the three union locals.[73] Despite the insularity of Local 93, and its exclusion of African Americans from membership, the plasterers utilized their position of power in the MPA to advance the cause of equal opportunity in the building trades in New Orleans.

Lathers' Local 62 was a biracial union (a Whites-only union with a subordinate colored subdivision with a separate charter) and had come to a work agreement with the contractors. However, the plasterers rejected any agreement with the contractors or the lathers that did not allow for them all to "work like the Plasterers . . . as one, regardless of color." In the end, Lathers' Local 62 representative L. J. Pulfork capitulated, declaring that, as far as Local 62 was concerned, "any colored lathers that wants to join, the doors are open." Pulfork even went so far as to invite the committee of plasterers to the lathers' meeting the following Saturday, presumably to verify the Lathers' commitment for themselves.[74]

On July 24, 1935, a special committee meeting of representatives from the Plasterers' Union Local 93, the Lathers' Union Local 62, and the Laborers' Union Local 153 met to discuss the terms of a "Triple Agreement" to bind all three unions of the MPA into a semblance of an industrial union. Central to the Creoles' terms was a demand of respect from Whites on the job: "Lathers, Plasterers, and Laborers must at all times whilst working on Buildings or jobs treat the other with due respect and courtesy as Brothers of Unionism. Any violations of said law, the Brother thus found guilty of same, after proper investigation . . . will be fined $2.50 for each offense after it has been proven by evidence."[75] Creoles were familiar with the sorts of microaggressions that often occurred in a multiracial environment and, in contexts where they had the power to demand an environment free of such microaggressions, they did.

On August 7, 1935, the Triple Agreement was struck between the Plasterers, the Lathers, and the Laborers. S. Rousséve of the Plasterers' Union nominated J. Hoffman of the Lathers' Union as chairman of the group. Hoffman, a lather from the all-white suburb of Metairie Terrace, became the public face of the group for the first year of its existence and served as the Triple Agreement's white patron, protecting the Creole members with his metaphorical hand on their shoulders. There is no doubt, however, that Creole plasterers were the true force behind the union: both the vice chair and the recording secretary of the organization were Creoles and, in the three years following the initial establishment of the Triple Agreement, the chairmanship was transferred first to Louis Villa of the Plasterers and then to Louis Lawrence, also of the Plasterers, both of whom were Creoles.[76]

Given the activism of Local 93, it is hard to imagine that the union would discriminate against African Americans due to racist or colorist bigotry. However, there is no doubt that many African Americans perceived their exclusion as a result of racist and colorist discrimination. Among the first non-Creole-identified Blacks to attain membership in Local 93 was the late Herbert "the Wizard" Gettridge. In a 2009 interview, Gettridge remarked that, in the decades prior to his own entry, union membership was closed to African Americans. As he explained it: "a dark fella like me . . . with hair like me, you wouldn't get in. Among the Creoles, there was discrimination. I can't say why. . . . That's just the way it was back then." According to Gettridge, his entry into the Plasterers' Union in 1947 made him "one of the lucky ones," yet when asked about the presence of dark-skinned Creoles in the union, Gettridge acknowledged that there were some, including Etienne Jeanjacques, one of the three members who supported his application for membership. Obviously, this situation necessitates some clarification.[77]

When asked for clarification of the terms of union membership, Gettridge explained that there were no formal apprenticeship programs in the 1930s and early 1940s and that, in order to be considered for membership, "you needed to have a father, grandfather or somebody related to you." Even after an apprenticeship program was put in place after World War II, according to Gettridge, "the apprenticeships were closed to [you] unless you were related."[78] With no apprenticeship program, the only way a person could learn plastering in New Orleans was to be raised to the trade, which also informs the phenomenon of Creole artisanal clans. Herbert Gettridge may have been one of the "lucky ones" to be admitted to the insular professional community of Local 93, yet it seems that that was not the only manifestation of his good luck: Herbert Gettridge also had the good fortune to be raised to the plastering trade.

As a young man, Gettridge lived in the Seventh Ward with his mother, a native Francophone and Creolophone whose father, according to Herbert Gettridge, was a Choctaw. Gettridge's father was an African American

who worked on the waterfront as a "mule skinner," a hard and dangerous job that required few skills except a willingness to spend most of the
workday wading through feces and urine and the raw physical toughness
necessary to give a full day's work even after being kicked in the head, or
trampled, by large animals. Indeed, Herbert Gettridge would have likely
followed in his father's footsteps if it were not for his neighbor, a Creole
named Louis Jeffrion. In 1934, when he was only ten or eleven years old,
Herbert Gettridge got the chance of a lifetime: Jeffrion introduced him to
the plastering trade as a mortar mixer. By the time Gettridge was thirteen
years old, he was "spreading plaster on walls," and it was at that point
that he applied for membership to Local 93 as a plasterer (as opposed to
a modeler, shop hand, cement finisher, or apprentice) at a cost of $100.
Eventually he became known as "the Wizard" in recognition of his talent.[79]
By his own admission, he never learned the most intricate techniques of
Creole ornamental plastering, yet he still considered himself fortunate.
As he explained:

> Being in the union meant you couldn't get misused any kind of way. . . .
> They couldn't force you to work on a Saturday or a Sunday without pay-
> ing you double time. They couldn't work you overtime without paying
> you for it. I had four boys that were plasterers; I brought them all in. . . .
> I paved the way for a lot of other youngsters my age. Guys working ice
> wagons: I put them in a mortar box and I taught them how to get out
> of the mortar box, too. . . . I went to Chicago. I was up there, making
> money and sending it back home. Whenever things got bad here . . .
> you could go anywhere and get work. I worked for Tom Callahan out of
> Local 5 in Chicago. When we got to Chicago, there was a man who said
> we had to take a test. But then Callahan says—these guys don't need no
> test. They're from New Orleans![80]

There was a power in being a union man. To not be "misused any kind
of way" is an occupational perk, the value of which cannot be overstated,
especially to a black man during Jim Crow. Securing his position in the
union also allowed Gettridge to provide occupational opportunities for
his children, and for his friends, outside of manning ice wagons or "mule

skinning" and "trucking cotton" on the river. Membership in New Orleans Local 93 also allowed Gettridge to benefit from the brand identity established by generations of Creole artisans that came before him, even when he was searching for work in faraway places like Chicago.

African American membership in Local 93, by the late 1940s, was the result of a trend that began more than a half-century earlier. Gettridge joined Local 93 in 1947, along with another African American named Leo Green who would, in fact, become the first African American president of Local 93 in the early 1980s.[81] This was made possible, in part, due to a greater attention paid to the national struggle for civil rights and the role that organized labor played in that struggle. Still, the most important factor in contextualizing this liberalization of Creole attitudes, and corresponding diminishing of Creole clannishness, must be understood as the result of a process of Americanization that had been accelerated, in part, by thirty years of mandatory English-only education in Louisiana that had, by the late 1940s, produced at least two generations of Creoles who spoke "'Mericain" natively, and in some cases, exclusively. By 1947, Creoles in New Orleans did not perceive African Americans as foreigners or outsiders the way that their grandparents and great-grandparents had, in part, because by 1947, the Creole and African American communities in New Orleans were simply not as dissimilar culturally.

The power and prominence of the Plasterers' Union would gradually diminish over the course of the 1940s and 1950s due to the advent of drywall and the ubiquity of Sheetrock in new construction. As a result, Creoles from traditional artisanal clans began to take advantage of new educational opportunities previously unavailable to them. A.P. Tureaud recalled that, in the New Orleans of his youth, the "larger number of schoolteachers, were actually uptown American Negroes. The[y] had educational opportunities available to them in the uptown section through New Orleans University, the Methodist Church, and Straight College, which was an American Missionaries Association school. They also worked for a probably more aggressive set of people who were engaged in industry and acquired some of their habits of industry and thrift. The Creole Negro, on the other hand, was satisfied to live his own life in the community with his accustomed social attainments."[82]

Among those "accustomed social attainments" were, no doubt, institutions like the Plasterers' Union, which allowed Creoles to attain a "sort of middle-class status" for themselves. However, because of their proximity to African Americans who had deeply invested themselves in education, and whose community activism had included demands for educational resources ever since Emancipation, Creoles began to invest more resources in providing formal education for their children. By the late 1940s, more and more young Creoles were enrolling in college and universities, like Dillard and Xavier. There they received education and training, in English, that enabled them to transition into a modern, national economy, facilitating their assimilation into a modern, American, identity.[83]

5

LEARNING AMERICAN AT SCHOOL
(AND CHURCH)

Creoles were taught to be American in English-only, Jim Crow public schools that told them that they were Negroes and that they should be proud to be Negroes.[1] Regardless of the distinctions their parents may have made between themselves and African Americans, Creole children and African American children sat side by side in segregated classrooms, separate from Whites. Unlike the benevolent societies and labor organizations, Creoles had established no separate educational spaces for their children and so schools, both public and parochial, became the most significant loci for Creole assimilation into an American identity. During the fifty years or so between the *Plessy* verdict and World War II, segregated schools and churches, which did not distinguish between Creoles and African Americans, facilitated the transition from a Creole identity to an African American identity.

In part because African Americans in New Orleans were often barred from pursuing opportunities in skilled trades, many pursued formal education. A. P. Tureaud recalled to Joe Logsdon that during his youth, "the larger number of schoolteachers were actually uptown American Negroes" who had benefited from opportunities made available to them through New Orleans University, the Methodist Church, and Straight University. Tureaud characterized these "Uptown American Negroes" as industrious, thrifty, and aggressively business-minded, qualities that Creoles like Tureaud associated with Americans in general.[2] Indeed, the industrious pursuit of upward mobility was a part of the founding mythology of the country and, as African Americans finally gained recognition as citizens of the United States, many of them saw higher education as their key to that upward mobility. W. E. B. Du Bois observed that the "first great mass movement for public education at the expense of the state in the South, came from Negroes."[3] It should thus come as no surprise that many of the pioneers of public education for people of color in New Orleans were African Americans. Given the extent to which Creoles intentionally excluded African Americans from their social sodalities, and consciously distanced themselves from the "rough Negro element," it is clear that many Creoles were uneasy with the prospect of leaving their children to be educated by African American teachers.[4]

The relationship between the Creole community of New Orleans and the Catholic Church deteriorated after the Civil War. In 1888, however, Netherlander Francis Janssens was appointed archbishop of New Orleans and resolved to heal the rift and bring the city's Creole Catholics back into the fold. He was assisted in this effort by two missionary organizations: the Sisters of the Blessed Sacrament (SBS) and the Society of St. Joseph of the Sacred Heart (the Josephites, or SSJ). The church schools and parishes established through the efforts of these missionary orders, in conjunction with an archdiocese fully committed to racial segregation, would become integral to New Orleans's Creole identity but were not Creole institutions. On the contrary, they were thoroughly American institutions that, like public schools, functioned as vehicles of Americanization.

In 1890, Andrew Augustus Gunby of the Louisiana Bar Association observed that the "Southern States have continued to tax themselves for the support of negro schools but in many places the funds raised for this purpose have been indifferently and unfairly applied by incompetent or partisan school boards, and this evil is on the increase." Irrespective of the lip service paid to the importance of education, and the value of extending the benefits of education to all, there was still no true commitment to educating people of color. Indeed, the struggle for public education for people of color in New Orleans was long and arduous and produced only limited results. Gunby was an avowed segregationist who exhorted all "those who believe in and demand the highest and purest standard of Anglo-Saxon blood and manhood, [to] begin a crusade against the white men who would lower that standard by mixing their blood with that of an inferior race" which included not only "Negroes" but also "the Indian, the Chinaman and other inferior races." In this regard, Gunby's attitudes toward race and education were common among Whites, especially in the South. However, Gunby also held the exceptional belief that, through education and intellectual uplift, all people, regardless of race, were empowered to achieve their full potential. He was a white supremacist, yet he believed "the white man's burden [was] not to exterminate, but to uplift," and that "Anglo-Saxon supremacy itself is founded, not on might and blood, but on mental and moral enlightenment." In Gunby's view, to deny anyone fair access to education was to engage in acts of "inhumanity" and "oppression."[5]

In a 1904 article, "Along the Color Line," Lucy Semmes Orrick of Canton, Mississippi, offered another paternalistic view on providing educational opportunities for people of color. Orrick observed that "the expenditure of the South for the education of the Negro for the years 1900–1901 was $6,000,000 out of a total of $35,405,561." For Orrick, this financial expenditure stood as "a testimonial to the generous spirit of the Southern people who charge nothing up against the thousands of blacks still so dependent on them—for it must be remembered that the weight of the tax-paying falls almost entirely upon the white people." The fact that the greatest portion of that southern wealth was created by appropriated black labor, extracted through violence and slavery, for which no reparations were ever made, did not seem to register with Orrick, who gushed that "forty years are not long enough to root out of the heart of the white man that generations-grown idea and conviction that the negro . . . needs him and will need for a long time yet the kindly aid and affectionate interest of his one time master."[6] Unfortunately, the picture painted by Orrick of paternal southern kindness, affection, and generosity does not align well with other evidence from the period famously described as the "nadir of American race relations" by historian Rayford Logan.[7] Though it is fair to say that white southerners at the turn of the twentieth century may have been fairly united in their support of a white-supremacist sociopolitical order, within that ideological spectrum there was still room for disagreement on central questions of race and caste, like free, public, colored education.

Indeed, both Gunby's and Orrick's views seem rather at odds with the sentiments articulated by the governor of Orrick's home state of Mississippi as he communicated them in the February 1904 issue of *Leslie's Weekly*. Governor James K. Vardaman, the "Great White Chief" whose political movement of "Rednecks" dominated Mississippi politics until the middle of the 1920s, did not support colored education. He did not view denying educational opportunities to people of color as "inhumanity" or as "oppression." Nor did he evidence much in the way of kindness or affection for black people.[8] In his own words:

> I am the nigger's best friend. But I am friendly to him as a nigger whom I expect to live, act, and die as a nigger. A great deal of money, more than $250,000,000, has been spent since the years 1861–65 by the white people of the North and the South in a foolish endeavor to make more of the nigger than God Almighty ever intended . . . [and that] has demonstrated the fallacy of the contention of the superficial student who sees in the school-house and booklearning the panacea for the ills which render the nigger unfit to perform any other function in the economy of the world than that of a servant or menial.[9]

Vardaman fired off a flurry of statistics to bolster his claim that Negro education (like Negro freedom itself) was unconducive to a rightly or-dered society. Citing a joint study produced by Cornell University and the North Carolina Agricultural College, Vardaman argued that the "negro is nearly three times as criminal in the Northeast, where he has not been a slave for a hundred years, and three and a half times as criminal in the Northwest, where he has never been a slave, as in the South, where he was a slave until 1865." For Vardaman, and those who shared his racist opinions, the emancipation of enslaved black people from the tyranny of masterism represented the disruption of a system of control that had held innate black criminality in check.[10] It is ironic that Vardaman would argue that Blacks had not progressed since 1865 when his own opinions so clearly evoke the sentiments of one 1866 Tensas Parish planter who, invok-ing Divine Order, declared that "God intended the niggers to be slaves."[11]

Southern Whites would continue to argue among themselves as to the effectiveness or desirability of educating people of color for decades after Gunby, Orrick, and Vardaman had offered their views. Meanwhile, people of color seeking self-betterment and upward mobility struggled to acquire the means to achieve social and economic stability through education and professional development. In his famous work *The Mis-Education of the Negro,* Carter G. Woodson exhorted Blacks to "undergo systematic training for those professions in which they have shown special aptitude," including the arts but also the sciences, including medicine and dentistry.[12] Woodson believed that the study of the law was of paramount importance to Blacks, who he suggested "must become like English gentlemen who study the law of the land, not because they intend to study the profession, but because every gentleman should know the law."[13] In New Orleans, many Creoles followed their fathers and grandfathers in learning a family trade, but at the turn of the twentieth century, a growing number of Creoles also chose to pursue formal education.

African Americans may have been unable to look past the curtains of closed Creole trade societies like the Plasterers, but by the 1930s, they had certainly made their mark on public education in New Orleans. In many ways (colored) public education became the first economic market in the city that African Americans were able to dominate in the early twentieth century. English language skills gave African Americans a competitive educational advantage over some Creoles in the late nineteenth century that was fortified after the State Board of Education mandated English-only education in Louisiana in 1916. In her memoir, Beverly Jacques Anderson recalled that as late as the 1950s many Creole students at Jones School still "resisted putting the proper endings on words, some tended to speak in idioms, some used 'broken French phrases,' and others spoke too fast to be understood." Such students, according to Anderson, required special attention and instruction in how to speak and write "the King's English."[14] This is why Valena C. Jones and Fannie C. Williams, two African American women from Mississippi, emerged as such central figures in promoting education in New Orleans for people of color.

Valena C. Jones was a native of Bay St. Louis, Mississippi, and a pioneer of public education in New Orleans. Her husband, Bishop Robert E. Jones, was the first black man elected as general superintendent of the Methodist Episcopal Church in New Orleans. Between 1892 and her death in 1917, Jones was instrumental in providing educational opportunities both for

Creoles and for African Americans.[15] In recognition of her contributions, the Miro School, one of the most important schools for colored children in the city, built in the heart of Creole New Orleans's Seventh Ward, was renamed for her after her death.[16]

It is unclear why, but Valena C. Jones School would be commonly known by many in New Orleans as the "Bucket of Blood School." The school itself was housed in a former tenement building that was painted a deep red color which may have accounted for this nickname. Adam Fairclough discusses Valena C. Jones briefly in his 2001 work, *Teaching Equality,* where he repeats the legendary etymology for the nickname that A. P. Tureaud recalled to Joe Logsdon, which was that the school was built in a particularly violent part of town. Unfortunately, Tureaud contradicts himself in his account, wherein he suggested that Jones School was located "in a neighborhood where there were probably more fights and social disorders in the community," yet in the very next breath, he said that the school was "in a section of the city that was not heavily populated" and that in order to get to it, one "had to go through a lot of cow pastures."[17] How a remote community beyond "a lot of cow pastures" might be considered uncommonly violence-ridden in a city that has always been marked by areas of murderous violence in its urban center is unclear. With that said, the negative reputation of Valena C. Jones School endured nonetheless, even though Jones School produced scores of graduates who went on to programs at Straight and other historically black colleges and universities (HBCUs).

Fannie C. Williams, a native of Biloxi, Mississippi, was appointed principal of Valena C. Jones School in 1921. Though perpetually vexed by substandard facilities and an underfunded program, Fannie C. Williams's accomplishments as an educator at Jones School were dramatic. In addition to serving as principal of Jones School, Williams taught courses on education and pedagogy at Tuskegee Institute, Southern University (Baton Rouge), Alabama State College, West Virginia Institute, and Alcorn A&M (Mississippi). Over the course of her long and illustrious career as an educator, Williams was invited to educational conferences at the White House by Presidents Herbert Hoover, Franklin Delano Roosevelt, and Harry Truman in recognition of her expertise.[18]

From 1921 until her retirement in 1954, Fannie C. Williams presided over a school described as "90 per cent Creole" where "the students range in color and type from blue-eyed blondes to those so dark that only their names betray their Creole heritage." She was interviewed in 1953 by *Jet* magazine, wherein she described the experience of teaching Creoles in New Orleans for more than thirty years. Specifically, she described the challenge of "re-educating" Creole mothers who, according to Williams, "had an inborn dislike of anything black." Williams explained that in her experience it was not uncommon for a Creole mother to come to school and "peek in the door, and complain because her youngster was sitting by 'that funny child.' That 'funny child' was always dark [skinned]." One can only imagine what it was like for an African American woman, like Williams, to work in such an environment, with parents so apprehensive about "funny dark skinned people." Yet, Williams was mistress of her domain, and because she was a master of her craft, something Seventh Ward Creoles could certainly relate to and understand, she commanded the respect of the community she served. Fannie C. Williams served as a mentor and role model for generations of Creole children in New Orleans.[19]

Fannie C. Williams's account to *Jet* magazine suggests that tensions between Creoles and African Americans in the larger society did not end at the schoolhouse door. Indeed, there is every reason to believe that the same insularity and clannishness that ruled organizations like the Jeunes Amis and the Juvenile Cooperators were articulated in the schools as well. One older Creole, a Roman Catholic deacon named John Williams, offered an account to Wendy Gaudin in 2002 that paints a picture of Creole cliquishness at work in the public school he attended in the 1930s. Williams recalled that, "at that time, kids were put in various classes based on who their families were. Your family had some professional experience, odds are that you were in class with folk with families with professional experience. Families labeled as laborers: you were probably classed with those that were laborers. In many cases, there were kids from the Seventh Ward . . . who were favored in the public schools. Because the valedictorians and salutatarians [sic] were usually Seventh Warders. And it was based on who your dad or your grandfather or grandmother was."[20]

Williams's testimony suggests that Creoles attempted to maintain the borders of their social circles in public schools, much as they did in their own private clubs: the children of laborers were classed with the children of laborers; the children of the "aristocrats of labor" were classed with other children from similar backgrounds. The biggest difference between private Creole organizations like the Jeunes Amis and public schools like Valena C. Jones, however, was that Creoles exercised no exclusive operational control over the public schools that served their community. By the 1930s, the faculty of Valena C. Jones School included almost as many Creoles as African Americans, but it was Fannie C. Williams, an African American woman from Mississippi, who was in charge and tasked with educating Creole students (and parents) in important subjects like English and "re-educating" them in even more important subjects like American racial propriety.[21]

Creole mothers may have been apprehensive about their youngsters sitting next to funny dark-skinned children, but that was the price of a public education (and the nature of racial "re-education") in Jim Crow New Orleans. No doubt, part of the purpose of providing public education was to train young men and women to be productive citizens capable of contributing to the economy and to society at large. However, there is also no doubt that part of the purpose of providing public education was to facilitate the process of Americanization. As Frank Cody, superintendent of the Detroit public school system and instructor of Americanization classes for immigrants so succinctly put it in 1918, one of the most important functions of public education was to "weld the many peoples of any community into one body politic and create throughout the nation the unity and power that comes from common ideals, a common language and a uniform interpretation of citizenship."[22]

In the case of public schools that served New Orleans's Creole community, part of that "common language" and "uniform interpretation of citizenship" was a thoroughly American language of race and caste. As Upton Sinclair observed in *The Goslings: A Study of the American Schools,* it "is the thesis of the businessmen who run our educational system that the schools are factories, and the children raw material, to be turned out thoroughly standardized, of the same size and shape, like biscuits or sausages."[23] In New Orleans's public schools, Creoles and African Americans sat side by side and learned what it meant to be American and, perhaps more importantly, what it meant to be a "Negro." Whatever cultural distinction that may have existed between Creoles and African Americans was subordinated to the purpose of forging one people, one race, out of these two ethnic groups. This was the nature of the assimilative process at work in the city's public schools, and those Creoles who attended Valena C. Jones in the 1920s and 1930s, who learned in school how to be "Negroes," would form the generation that would ultimately stand united with African Americans to successfully challenge legal segregation in Louisiana in the 1950s.

By the 1930s, more than twenty-one thousand colored students were served by twenty public schools in New Orleans.[24] Or perhaps it would be more accurate to say that these students were underserved by the city's system. Huey Long became governor in 1928 after campaigning to make "every man a king" and, as part of his political program, he changed the face of public education in Louisiana. Still, people of color only marginally benefited from Long's programs.

As governor, Huey Long succeeded in wrangling educational resources for working-class people, presenting himself as a champion of the "poor man." Long biographer and historian T. Harry Williams points out that, even though Huey Long never took seriously the notion of allowing Blacks to vote in Louisiana (he demurred, referring to Negro suffrage as a "state's rights" issue), he consistently fought for policies that often brought direct, material benefit to people of color in the state. Still, Long was adamant that he not be portrayed as "pro-Negro." In a 1935 interview with *Crisis* magazine, the organ of the NAACP, Huey was clear: "don't say I'm working for niggers. I'm not, I'm for the poor man."[25] To his credit, Long achieved much for the poor man in Louisiana, white and black (but mostly white), and it is unfortunate that much of his "share the wealth" radicalism, which promised so much structural transformation of Louisiana's political economy, died with him after he was gunned down by Carl Weiss in September of 1935.

By 1940, a half-century after A. A. Gunby's observations, public education for people of color in New Orleans was still chronically underfunded and deprived of resources: Whites had opted for, in Gunby's terms, inhumanity and oppression. Indeed, even the monies allotted for nonteaching personnel in schools for people of color (white teachers in public schools for colored children were phased out during the 1890s) were funneled to Whites, much to the chagrin of the officers of (colored) Teacher's Union Local 527, who petitioned to replace white janitors and bus drivers with colored workers, citing, among other reasons, "the wholesome effect on the children" to see people of color in such productive, contributive, everyday roles.[26] A 1946 letter from the "Colored Educational Alliance" to the Orleans Parish School Board, pleading for resources, paints a grim picture of the state of colored education in New Orleans: "Finally, we bring to your attention the fact that several of our Negro Public Schools labor under great difficulty because of inadequate space. The F. P. Ricard School is the worst in that respect. For the past six years many children are withdrawn to be sent to various schools in the community. Classes are being conducted in an unheated basement, and a school of its size should be provided with industrial rooms. We recommend a ten (10) room addition for this school."[27]

To be fair, or rather to be clear, as a general rule, public education was undervalued and underutilized in Louisiana during the early twentieth century. Schools for colored students were starved for funding and resources, in part because all schools were starved for funding and resources. During World War II, Louisiana's deficient educational system threatened national security insofar as Selective Service reported that "too large a number both colored and white Louisianians" were rejected for military service "because they lacked basic education."[28] Still, in a state with an overabundance of ignorant, uneducated, impoverished communities, as T. Harry Williams observed, "the Negroes were poor, poorer even than the poorest whites," and the dilapidated, distressed, nature of the school facilities assigned to colored students served to psychologically reinforce the sense of Negro inferiority.[29] It should be no surprise, given all of this, that Creoles in New Orleans never fully invested themselves in public education.

The relationship between the Roman Catholic Church and the Creole community deteriorated after the Civil War.[30] Many Creoles, like A. P. Tureaud's father, Louis Tureaud, had abandoned the church rather than suffer the indignities and humiliations of racial segregation and, as was the case with A. P. Tureaud, they often passed on their critical attitudes to their children. A. P. Tureaud explained the chilled relations between the Creole community and the Catholic Church to Joe Logsdon, and offered insight on to the rejection of the Jim Crow church by his father's generation, saying "There was nothing in the church that catered to the parishioners who were Negro. We were in the church but we weren't really a part of it. . . . The priests simply didn't take any interest in us." Even at St. Augustine Parish in the Tremé, a church that was built with more than $25,000 contributed by free Creoles of color, Creoles were still forced to endure racist subordination to white parishioners. Regardless of their interest or contributions, Creoles were not allowed to take part in any official church organizations and were relegated to segregated pews. As a result of this situation, many Creoles abandoned the church for other faith traditions, including Spiritualism and Freemasonry.[31]

Despite the evacuation of Creoles from the folds of the Church of Rome, however, there were two church-affiliated institutions in Creole New Orleans that endured, despite the bad feelings that existed after the Civil War. Those two institutions were the Couvent School and the order of the Sisters of the Holy Family. Coincidentally, but unsurprisingly, the primary importance of both of these institutions to the Creole community was to provide Creoles with educational opportunities.

Known variously in French as l'Institute Catholique and l'Ecole des Orphelins Indigents, the Couvent School was founded according to the will of the widow Couvent, Marie Justine Cirnaire, and represents a point of contrast to the public schools that Creoles attended in New Orleans. Cirnaire was an African woman who was enslaved in Saint Domingue before coming to New Orleans, where she acquired her freedom. As a result of her marriage to Bernard Couvent, a free Creole of color who was a carpenter by trade, Madame Couvent inherited a fair amount of material wealth (including slaves) upon the death of her husband. In her will, she bequeathed property specifically for the purpose of establishing a school for children of color in New Orleans, and the result was l'Institute Catholique. Creoles had little voice in the management of the public schools that served their community, but this was not the case when it came to parochial schools.

The Couvent School was affiliated with the Catholic Church, but its board of directors was composed of prominent Creoles in the community.[32]

The Couvent School was a notable exception to the rule of unavailability regarding educational opportunities for Creoles in New Orleans in the nineteenth century. Unlike New Orleans's public schools, the Couvent School was a thoroughly Creole institution from its inception in 1847 and, because it served students from "all sections of the city" (that is, Creoles and African Americans), the school offered instruction in both French and English until pressured to convert to an English-only curriculum following the 1916 law. It was destroyed by a terrible storm in 1915, but the Creole community could not abide the destruction of the Couvent School, and by 1917 the school was reopened as St. Louis School of Holy Redeemer Parish with assistance from the SBS and the Sisters of the Holy Ghost of San Antonio, Texas.[33]

Even more than the Couvent School, the order known as the Sisters of the Holy Family is perhaps the most important educational institution established by Creoles of color in New Orleans. Unarguably, it is the most enduring. Its founder, Blessed Mother Henriette Delille, was a Creole from New Orleans and is presently a candidate for Roman Catholic sainthood (hence the title "Blessed") and was described in 2010 by then-Pope Benedict XVI as a woman of "heroic virtues."[34] Delille's candidacy for sainthood is based on her efforts to care for the sick, the elderly, and the indigent as well as her determination to provide Catholic educational opportunities for children of color in New Orleans, even when such an enterprise was directly in contravention of the law. As historian James B. Bennett observed, "the Holy Family Sisters was crucial to Black Catholicism in New Orleans. . . . In the face of the widespread white neglect, the sisters were often the only ones who regularly tended to the needs of Catholics of color."[35] Many generations of Creoles and African Americans in New Orleans owe their education to the efforts of Blessed Mother Henriette Delille and the religious order she established.

In 1894, Holy Family Sister Mary Bernard Deggs wrote of the sixth mother superior of the order, Mother Mary Austin, "who was in the world known as Mary Ellen Jones," as the "only American superior who has ever governed our dear little community since its founding."[36] Deggs's journals would form the basis for *No Cross, No Crown: Black Nuns in Nineteenth-Century New Orleans,* edited by Virginia Meacham Gould and Charles E. Nolan. Gould and Nolan observed in their notations that Austin's identification as an "American" referred not only to her place of birth (she was originally from Maryland), but more specifically to the fact that English was her primary language. It was under Austin that the Sisters of the Holy Family would acquire property in Gentilly and New Orleans East, where they would build the Lafon Nursing Facility in 1973 (originally established in 1841) and St. Mary's Academy in 1965 (originally established in 1867). It was also under Austin, the American, that the Sisters of the Holy Family would become missionaries to Belize.[37]

According to Gould and Nolan, the Holy Family Sisters "recognized that their French Creole culture was becoming extinct," and as they took on more and more English-speaking students, the dominant culture of the order shifted.[38] Though founded by Creoles, the culture of the Holy Family Sisters was more Catholic than Creole, more concerned with religious ministry than cultural production. The Sisters of the Holy Family is the oldest and most enduring institution established by Creoles in the city, but in 1900, the task of enduring required the order to relinquish its Creole character. To accomplish its evangelical mission, it was forced to assimilate and acquiesce in the face of the juggernaut of Americanization. In a letter to her order, the SBS, founder St. Katharine Drexel described meeting the Sisters of the Holy Family while purchasing property in New Orleans. She indicates that, even as late as 1915, many of the nuns "broken English, French being their language," yet those women represented the fleeting past of the order, not its future, a point underscored in 1916 when English-only education became law in Louisiana.[39]

Mandatory English-only education had a profound effect on St. Mary's Academy. Between 1881 and 1900, the school had maintained an enrollment of approximately two hundred, including students from Nicaragua, British Honduras (Belize), Panama, and Spanish Honduras. However, those numbers steadily declined, especially after Katharine Drexel established Xavier University Preparatory School. By 1930, enrollment at St. Mary's had fallen to only sixty-eight students across all grades between first through eleventh, prompting the principal, Mother Elizabeth, to restructure the school, adopting the state of Louisiana's program of studies and requiring all faculty to become state certified. In 1932, St. Mary's Academy applied for state certification and, in 1933, the school was ranked first in the state as a result of its students' performance on Louisiana's graduation examinations. Enrollment steadily grew under Mother Elizabeth's leadership. Accepting English as the dominant language, and adopting the state-approved English-only curriculum, had guaranteed the school's success and brought it back from the brink of closure.[40]

It is hard to imagine that Francis Janssens's upbringing in Tilburg, Netherlands, his seminary training in Belgium, his experience as a rector in Richmond, Virginia, or even his time as bishop in Natchez, Mississippi, prepared him for the dysfunctional morass that awaited him in the Archdiocese of New Orleans. When Janssens arrived in New Orleans from Natchez to replace Francis Xavier Leray as archbishop of New Orleans in 1888, he found his new flock to be deeply troubled by racial antagonism. The Creole Catholic community's relationship with the church was strained and had been since the André Cailloux affair, and it was Janssens's task to heal the rifts, as much as they could be healed.

Even though the culture of Catholicism in the city was, and always had been, interracial, the Third Plenary Council in Baltimore had recommended separate, racially segregated parishes for New Orleans in 1884. The archdiocese had been slow to act, however. This inaction had persisted throughout Leray's tenure, in part because few seemed to want segregated parishes, even as Whites and people of color remained largely at odds with one another in their conceptions of racial propriety. Creole Catholics resented segregation and, at the turn of the twentieth century, rejected "colored only" Jim Crow parishes, preferring equality before the altar. Whites did not demand racially segregated parishes, yet they expected, and demanded, that people of color stand in the back of integrated churches like St. Augustine in the Tremé, where Catholics of color were categorically excluded from organized parish life, a point of bitter contention among Creoles.[41]

In one 1892 report, Janssens explained to the Commission for Catholic Missions among Colored People and Indians that "Creole Catholics as they are called, are in language, manners, and ways of thinking quite different from the colored people elsewhere." Particularly, these Creole Catholics were different in that, according to Janssens, they resented that Whites wished "to draw the line of white and colored upon them."[42] From his correspondence, it is clear that Janssens's initial encounters with New Orleans's Creole community were challenging, and there is little to suggest that, in his nine-year tenure as archbishop of New Orleans, that relationship ever became easier to manage.

Creole Catholics were ignored by their parish priests and, even though the Archdiocese of New Orleans had the single largest population of colored Catholics in the United States, archdiocesan efforts to engage colored Catholics, through social organizations and parish life, were largely nonexistent. Janssens made rectifying that official neglect one of his top priorities, a decision motivated by both a genuine concern for the spiritual well-being of his charges, as well as the need for the financial support of affluent Creoles of color in the city in digging the archdiocese out from beneath a mountain of debt that it had accrued in the wake of the Civil War, a debt of more than $600,000.[43] By the time Janssens arrived, that amount had been reduced by half but was still a major concern that the new archbishop was expected to address aggressively. Part of Janssens's response was outreach to Creole Catholics who, in some parishes, represented the congregation's primary financial support.[44]

Janssens's greatest ally in his mission to the colored Catholics of New Orleans was Philadelphia heiress Katharine Drexel. Canonized by the Roman Catholic Church in 2000, St. Katharine Drexel founded the Sisters of the Blessed Sacrament upon the advice of Pope Leo XIII in 1891 as a missionary order dedicated to serving people of color, specifically African Americans and Amerindians. Together, Janssens and Drexel would change the culture of Catholicism in New Orleans through passionate, zealous engagement.[45] For their efforts, they were met with resistance from all sides.

In January of 1892, in a letter to Drexel, Janssens lamented both the lack of involvement on the part of his colored parishioners and the racism of his white parishioners. "The colored people take little interest in their own color. . . . The white people will give 25 cents to a colored asylum whereas they will give $5 to a white asylum. . . . Prejudices are hard to be removed."[46] Drexel, who in a private audience with Pope Leo XIII in 1887 had been charged with establishing a religious order to serve Blacks and Amerindians, responded with generous patronage, contributing thousands of dollars to the Archdiocese of New Orleans.[47]

In one letter dated January 22, 1892, Janssens thanks Drexel for a gift of $2,000.[48] In a February 29 letter he thanks her for a check for $600, apparently an advance on a $5,000 payment for a rectory, for her pledge of $1,000 to the maintenance of four colored schools in St. James Parish and for an additional $700 she gifted for two colored schools in the city.[49] In an April 10 letter Janssens thanks Drexel for her $2,000 contribution toward the cost of an orphanage for colored children and for an additional $1,200 for a new colored school in Breaux Bridge, Louisiana. He goes on to ask Drexel for the prayers of her order in support of his search for qualified priests as well as for an additional $1,750 to help with the construction costs of a new colored school in Gretna, Louisiana.[50] Long before she died, Katharine Drexel had established herself as a patron saint of parochial education in the state.

For all of the diligence of Francis Janssens, and for all of Drexel's generosity, the basic grievance the Creole community had with the Catholic Church, that it had cosigned the marginalization they suffered under Jim Crow, went unanswered. Janssens responded by denouncing those Creoles who were "up in arms" against him over the proposed colored parishes and whose leaders were "bright [fair-skinned] mulattoes who never set foot in church, some of them Freemasons."[51] Of course, among that troublesome bunch of bright-mulatto Creole Freemasons were people like the Rey brothers and Homer Plessy, people who had only ever turned away from the church because the church had first turned its back on them after the Civil War, punishing them for their aspirations to social and political equality by refusing anti-Confederate Creoles access to the sacraments, including Christian burial.[52] Francis Janssens and Katharine Drexel had the best intentions, but they were not prepared for the historical sociopolitical complexities of this community they had dedicated themselves to. Yet, as it is in many things in the United States, with enough money and enough determination, many things that seem impossible are nevertheless made to be.

In addition to the efforts of Janssens, Drexel, and the SBS, along with Sister Mary Austin and the Sisters of the Holy Family, there is one final group crucial to any discussion of Creole Catholicism in New Orleans, the priests and brothers of the Society of St. Joseph of the Sacred Heart (SSJ), or as they are commonly known, the Josephites. The Josephites were the answer to the prayers of many involved in the spiritual life of Catholics of color in Louisiana in the early 1900s. Though the order's origins were in England, many of the Josephites who came to New Orleans in the early 1900s were Anglophone Irish, or Irish American from the Northeast and Eastern Seaboard. A missionary order pledged to serve people of color, the Josephites ministered to their colored parishes with more careful attention than those communities had ever experienced before. It was hard work ministering to Blacks in the Jim Crow South. It tested the faith of the Josephite priests, and not all of them emerged from their trials unscathed.

Father John Slattery, the first superior general of the Josephites in the United States, took up his missionary vocation in 1893. His experiences with white racism in the course of his mission shook his faith to the core and led him to denounce as "uncatholic" those within the church who abided and, worse, abetted the racism that afflicted the people of color that he had dedicated his life to. Slattery would eventually turn away from the priesthood, indeed from the church altogether, sickened as he was by the rank bigotry he experienced in the course of his tenure with the Josephites. Slattery was convinced that black congregations required black priests to lead them and decried what he perceived as opposition within the church to the ordination of black priests.[53] It was not an easy mission to take up the struggles of people of color in Jim Crow Louisiana.

A. P. Tureaud recalled the Josephite father who "came into the community who was quite a builder and he got a lot of the Catholics in the community who probably had fallen out of the church."[54] Although Tureaud does not mention the priest by name, it is likely that he was referring to Father Samuel J. Kelly, SSJ. Kelly was tasked with organizing a new parish to replace the colored parish of St. Katharine's, Janssens's and Drexel's first experiment with a segregated church in New Orleans. That replacement parish was centrally located in the Seventh Ward and would quickly become the largest, most affluent, most successful colored parish anywhere in the United States: Corpus Christi, the second parish administered by Josephites in New Orleans.

Prior to the establishment of Corpus Christi, the Josephites ministered to colored Catholics at St. Dominic's, which is today Blessed Sacrament–St. Joan of Arc, located uptown near Riverbend, where their tenure began in 1909. When Father Peter Lebeau, the elderly pastor of St. Dominic's, took ill, he was replaced by Father Kelly, who excelled in his new position. Even when the structure of the church itself was destroyed by a tropical storm in September of 1914, Father Kelly persevered and supervised the erection of a temporary church for St. Dominic Parish. Having proven his mettle under such extreme conditions, Kelly must have seemed like exactly the sort of person needed at a parish meant to serve the Seventh Ward Creole community, where resided the greatest concentration of those "bright mulattoes" who had resisted segregated parishes so fiercely.[55]

In April of 1916, Katharine Drexel purchased a large plot of land between North Johnson and North Galvez and between St. Bernard Avenue and Onzaga. Two small buildings on the plot were made to serve as a rectory and temporary chapel. Archbishop James Blenk issued a canonical decree establishing Corpus Christi Parish on September 24, 1916, with Father Samuel J. Kelly as pastor. Father Kelly secured funds for the construction of a school and church by soliciting contributions from northern philanthropists as well as from local businessmen as he set about the task of improving the parish facilities. Kelly was fortunate in that Corpus Christi was located in the Seventh Ward, a neighborhood with one of the highest concentrations of skilled artisans in the entire state of Louisiana, and since the Corpus Christi Church and School were to serve their community, many of those Seventh Ward master artisans donated their labor.[56]

Earl A. Barthé was baptized at Corpus Christi in 1919. When asked about any possible role that his father, a master plasterer, might have played in the construction of Corpus Christi, Barthé suggested that "it was the [whole] community that came together for that. It wasn't just one man. Everyone in the community put in time. Sometimes on the weekends . . . well, mostly on the weekends but, back then especially, people had a deep sense of community."[57] The man most often credited with leading the construction of Corpus Christi Church and School is, in fact, Louis Charbonnet, who was Clement Barthé's father-in-law.[58] Unfortunately, the school has been closed since 2005 as it suffered major damage as a result of the flooding that accompanied the levee failure following Katrina. Yet, after almost a century, Corpus Christi Church and School are still standing and structurally intact, having withstood the fury of Hurricanes Betsy (1965), Camille (1969), and Katrina (2005); it is a testament to New Orleans Creole craftsmanship.

To offer an organized fellowship for his parishioners, Father Kelly introduced the Knights of Peter Claver, a Catholic fraternal organization that he had cofounded in Mobile, Alabama, in 1909. In the same way that the Knights of Columbus served as a Vatican-approved alternative to Freemasonry, the Knights of Peter Claver served as a Jim Crow alternative to the Knights of Columbus. The organization proved so popular that, in 1922, a Ladies Auxiliary division was added in Opelousas, the success of which prompted the adoption of a national Ladies Division in 1926. Despite the enduring discontent that Creoles experienced, and distaste that they expressed for Jim Crow segregation and the church's complicity in it, by the 1930s, the roster of the New Orleans branch of the Knights of Peter Claver was comprised mostly of Creole names like Amedee and Desvignes and Duvigneaud, and LaBeau and LaCroix and Richard and Rousséve.[59]

Corpus Christi Church and School are among the twentieth-century institutions that Nikki Dugar identifies as "socializing agents" for New Orleans's Creole community. Bennett argues that parishes like Corpus Christi "preserved and even strengthened Creole distinctiveness (from African Americans), even though separate black churches emerged from a white rejection of such differences," and further that Corpus Christi "became synonymous with Creole identity." Fairclough observed that "as [Creoles] ceased to speak French and their social status declined, allegiance to the Catholic Church became an increasingly important part of Creole self-identity in New Orleans" and that segregated parishes like Corpus Christi "reinforced a tendency in the Creole community to look inward, regarding itself separate and distinct." Yet, there is one crucial feature of Corpus Christi Church and School that all of these historians overlook which betrays the narrative of Corpus Christi being a Creole institution of any kind, traditional or otherwise: Corpus Christi School was administered, for the most part, by Irish and Irish American priests who spoke only English even though, when Corpus Christi was founded, the Seventh Ward Creole community was still largely Francophone and Creolophone. Just as the New Orleans public schools serving the Creole community facilitated the process of Americanization, so did the parochial schools (and churches) serving the Creole community.[60]

The Anglophone Irish and Irish American Catholic priests who staffed Corpus Christi were from northern states. Its first pastor was Father Samuel J. Kelly, SSJ. He was replaced in 1926 by Father Michael J. O'Neil, SSJ. Father Harry F. Kane, SSJ, replaced Father O'Neil in 1931 and was replaced by Father Edward V. Casserly, SSJ, in 1937. These pastors were joined over the years by scores of assistants and substitutes with names like Donahue, Murphy, McConnell, McKee, Sullivan, O'Brian, and Hennessey.[61] It would seem odd to assign Anglophone Irish priests to a predominantly Francophone/Creolophone community, unless of course the intention was to turn that community into an Anglophone community, which is exactly what happened in Corpus Christi Parish.

Far from being a Creole institution—that is, controlled by Creoles and designed to serve the needs of Creole people on their own terms—Corpus Christi Church and School were (Anglo-)American institutions. With all the best intentions, the Josephites and the SBS, through Corpus Christi, replaced Creole cultural and linguistic heritage with a simulacrum of ethnicity, articulated as an "achieved status" predicated on membership in an association controlled, ultimately, by English-speaking white people. At the same time, these Josephite priests, and the SBS who served as principals and teachers at Corpus Christi School, made no distinctions between Creole students and African American students, but instead regarded them all as "Negroes" whom they had pledged themselves to serve.

Staffing Corpus Christi with white, Anglophone personnel was, at least in part, a choice. Furthermore, it is clear that this choice was motivated, in part, by racist notions of the unsuitability of priests of color. Father John Joseph Plantevigne was a Creole from Pointe Coupée, Louisiana, and a graduate of Straight who was ordained as a Josephite priest in Baltimore in 1907. He came to New Orleans in 1909, hoping to say mass at St. Dominic's, but the pastor, Father Peter Lebeau, objected to Plantevigne preaching to his congregation because Plantevigne was a black man. Plantevigne protested to Archbishop Blenk, who responded by prohibiting him from saying mass anywhere in New Orleans. His faith shaken, Plantevigne was assigned to Palmetto, Louisiana, but before he could take his position, the archbishop extended the prohibition on Plantevigne's ministry to Palmetto as well. Though it might seem that Father Plantevigne would have made a perfect fit for a large Creole parish like Corpus Christi, being Creole himself, it was not to be: he returned to Baltimore, embittered and disillusioned. Father John Joseph Plantevigne died at forty-two. Historian Norman R. Smith describes Plantevigne at the time of his death in 1913 as "a broken man with a broken heart."[62]

At the same time that Katharine Drexel was building schools that facilitated the Americanization of Creoles in Louisiana, she was also building schools to facilitate the Americanization of Amerindians in Indiana and the southwestern United States. Among these were Saint Michael's Indian School in Arizona, St. Boniface Indian School in California, St. Joseph Indian Normal School in Indiana, and St. Catherine's Industrial Indian School in New Mexico. Indeed, according to Trafzer, Keller, and Sisquoc, Drexel was more influential in providing education to Amerindian people "than any other Catholic in the nineteenth or twentieth centuries" during her lifetime, and even after, through her legacy, "she supported nearly sixty schools and missions for Native American and African American people."[63] Throughout the first half of the twentieth century, in each of these schools, there are similar assimilative strategies at play, with the only significant difference between the Creole schools and the Indian schools being that the Indian schools, as a general rule, had boarding facilities. In all cases, students were instructed in English with mandatory lessons in Catholic catechism taught by primarily, if not exclusively, white faculty, which is significant because, as historian Amelia V. Katanski noted, among the signifying achievements marking the attainment of civilization, according to the white Anglo elites of the time, were "Christianization and literacy in English." While Creoles in New Orleans had been Christianized since the early French colonial period, it was through the efforts of missionaries like Katharine Drexel and orders like the Holy Family Sisters and the Josephites that they became literate in English.[64]

The success of Corpus Christi Parish, and of Corpus Christi School in particular, created a demand for a parochial high school for people of color in New Orleans. Once again, Katharine Drexel produced her checkbook. In a 1915 letter, Drexel communicated the urgency of establishing a Catholic institution for higher education to the sisters of her order, explaining that she was "to visit the Baptist and Strait [sic] Institute and Public schools to see what we must compete with. It is necessary to offset the protestant schools to have higher education." The end result of Drexel's efforts was Xavier University Preparatory School.[65]

The grounds and buildings of Xavier Prep were located at 5100 Magazine Street in uptown New Orleans at the previous site of Southern University and just a few blocks away from New Orleans University, which was located on St. Charles Avenue near Jefferson Avenue. The site of Xavier Prep School was purchased for $18,000 with an additional $4,000 allocated for repairs and improvements to the facility. In 1925, Xavier University added a college of liberal arts, becoming, in the process, the only Roman Catholic HBCU in the United States. By 1927, it added a college of pharmacy.[66]

The high-quality parochial education offered at Drexel-financed schools like Corpus Christi and Xavier Prep enticed the Creole community back to the church after many years of frosty relations. The facilities and grounds of those schools were of much higher quality and craftsmanship than those of the colored public schools, and a predominantly white faculty (who were often perceived as more competent than colored faculty, whether that impression was true or not) also played to Creoles' elitism. The New Orleans public school system was problematic for a lot of reasons, yet the Catholic school system in New Orleans was vibrant and high-performing. By 1946, Protestant Louisianians, leery of papist insurgency and sleeper agents, decried the prestige associated with the Catholic schools in the city in an anonymous letter to the New Orleans Teachers' Federation.

> Principals, and Teachers are not loyal to the Public School system but to the Parochial Schools. The Church has used the same method that was used in Europe to weaken the small nations, disloyalty or sabotage within the ranks. Catholic Supervisors and Teachers openly make the statement that Parochial Schools are superior. With such disloyalty how can you expect anything but condemnation from the Public, regardless of how efficient our system might be. . . . After the point that is put

across that our schools are inefficient, the next step will be to take taxes
from our schools to support Parochial schools. The teachers will only
have the disloyal Catholic Teachers to blame.[67]

It is hard to imagine Creoles seriously considering the objections of
anti-Catholic Protestants in Louisiana when it came to Catholic education. After all, Creoles were willing to give up their language—that which
most distinguished them from the ocean of Americans that surrounded
them—in exchange for that education. Creoles had been regarded as untrustworthy, foreign, and disloyal by Anglo-Americans since Washington
Irving's tour of the prairies: anti-papist accusations hurled at them in 1946
could only be described as banal. At least with high-quality education,
they had the chance to expand their economic opportunities in a new,
modernized, national economy.

No single factor contributed more to the changed nature of the dialogue on créolité and on blackness in New Orleans than the expansion of
opportunities for education. In fact, educational opportunities afforded to
Creoles during the Jim Crow era played a crucial role in diminishing the
Creole identity in New Orleans. Through English-only schools, Creoles
lost their linguistic distinctiveness. Through Anglo-American instructors,
both African American and white, Creoles were indoctrinated in the language and customs of American racial propriety and caste so that, as the
decades passed, more and more Creoles saw themselves less as Creoles
and more as "Negroes."

Educational opportunities fortified Creoles in their aspirations of upward mobility, aspirations that outweighed the value they placed on their
linguistic heritage. Through institutions like Valena C. Jones, Straight
University, Southern University, Xavier University Preparatory School,
and later Xavier University in New Orleans, Creoles were trained for
skilled professions such as teaching and pharmacy. Perhaps even more
significantly, education fortified Creoles in their struggle against racial
prejudice. In a state where, during World War II, dangerously large swaths
of the population (across racial lines) were illiterate, the acquisition of an
eighth-grade diploma was often a mark of profound distinction, especially
for a person of color.

Receiving a high-quality education while they sat next to African American students who, as native Anglophones, had an advantage in an all-English teaching environment forced younger generations of Creoles to challenge the insularity and bigotry of the older generation and drew them closer, psychologically and emotionally, to African Americans. In public schools, accomplished African Americans like Valena C. Jones and Fannie C. Williams commanded the respect of everyone in their community, and served as role models. In parochial schools staffed by mostly Irish Catholic Josephite Fathers and white Blessed Sacrament Sisters from the American Northeast, Creoles and African Americans were afforded a respect that did not conform to the racist conventions of southern white supremacy. In this environment, Creoles began to "unlearn" the prejudices that many of them held against African Americans and began, in fact, to understand themselves more and more as African Americans.

CONCLUSION
Creole Americans

The late Gilbert E. Martin Sr. recalled being a "young Creole growing up during the Great Depression and the Jitterbug era," not knowing why his elders hated the Americans so much.[1] For Martin, the American community and the Creole community were self-evidently distinct from one another with a "natural" resentment for the former embraced by the latter. This resentment, at times, was racialized, but not always so: sometimes, the "Americans" were white, but sometimes they were not. For Martin, the beginning of the true abatement of Creoles' hostility for their American neighbors, and a sign of the waning of a self-conscious Creole identity separate from American identity, was World War II. Wartime propaganda made it impossible to equivocate: Creoles in New Orleans were, nominally, citizens of the state of Louisiana and thus of the United States of America, and the government of the United States needed every man it could muster in the fight against the Axis powers. Service in World War II cultivated a truly American sensibility among many Creoles that had never existed before.

My great-uncle Henry Oubre was a cook in the US Navy during World War II. Before his time in the service, he had never ventured far from Vacherie, Louisiana, except to go to New Orleans. In a July 2013 interview, Oubre recalled a sense of camaraderie with his American crewmates both on the ship and at port that had a powerful influence on him. His quarters were not segregated, for example, and every night he slept between two white crewmates. Together, he and his fellow sailors went out on the town in northern cities in places like New York and Massachusetts and Quebec.[2]

This is not to say, however, that his experience was free of the stain of ethno-racial marginalization. He recalled that the "white boys" on ship treated him differently from his African American crewmates, who hailed from Memphis, Tennessee, and Cambridge, Massachusetts. Though Oubre would go drinking with his white crewmates, his white crewmates did not associate with the African American sailors, in part because the African American sailors were more antagonistic toward them. According to Oubre, his African American crewmates also viewed him with a sense of otherness as his self-identification as a Louisiana Creole aroused their suspicions that he might practice voodoo. Still, none of these stories, anecdotal as they are, address the larger issues of racial discrimination that Oubre experienced serving in the US military as a black man.[3]

Oubre described his struggle during World War II as a conflict against "two enemies . . . because they had the Germans that was the enemy and they had [American] Whites that was the enemy, too . . . white supremacists." Oubre was a cook because black men in the Navy could only be cooks or stewards. Oubre's voice took on a mournful tone when he recounted seeing black men with "two years of college" serving white officers as valets aboard ship. He also recalled the humiliation of arriving at the train station in Atlanta en route home to Louisiana and, though dressed in full uniform, being refused service in a restaurant where he saw German POWs eating and enjoying themselves. Oubre had served under the American flag in the North Atlantic and the South Pacific, but Atlanta was a more welcoming place for Nazis than it was for a person of color like himself.[4]

Just as their ancestors had at the Battle of New Orleans during the War of 1812, Louisiana Creoles stood shoulder to shoulder with white Americans during World War II only to find themselves denigrated and relegated to second-class citizens after the fighting was over. Henry Oubre was a sailor in the US Navy who had proudly served his country, but back home in New Orleans, dressed in his Navy uniform, he pretended to be from India in order to avoid racist victimization by a white man who had not served in the military himself and who instead stayed home where he "made big money all during the war." Oubre recalled visiting his sister after coming home from the war and taking his nieces to a movie theater in Jim Crow New Orleans:

Let me tell you something about how stupid segregation is. . . . I stayed in the South Pacific, on my ship, for over a year, you know. . . . I came back home. . . . [My nieces and I] walked to that little theater and I failed to realize where I was. . . . They had a bar and restaurant across the street [from the theater]. We got our tickets to go in the theater but we had to wait a while. I was out of cigarettes so I fooled around and walked across the street and went in [the segregated bar and restaurant] on the white side and asked for change for a dollar because cigarettes were maybe something like 40 cents. . . . the door happened to open and I saw all these black people because the kitchen was between the two—the white side and the black side. Well, when they opened the door, I must have shown some kind of expression because this white boy came to me and asked me, "Are you a nigger? What are you?" I said, "No, I was born in India, and raised in New York." This damn fool bought me two double whiskeys. He kept apologizing to me. . . . Believe it or not, you know, I was a candidate for an ass-whipping even in my uniform.[5]

By the end of World War II, Creoles in New Orleans had been thoroughly Americanized. The transformation of ethnic identity from Creole to American that began in 1803 was accelerated in the twentieth century through the imposition of Jim Crow segregation and English-only schooling, but by no means was Americanization always accomplished through coercive influences. The migration of Creole identity in the twentieth century was also facilitated by Creole encounters with African Americans who taught them how to play jazz and, later, how to dance the jitterbug. Creoles' sense of "Americanness" was also fortified as a result of Creole involvement in the American labor movement. Creoles participated in the Great Migration and started new lives, like millions of other immigrants, in American cities like Chicago, New York, and Los Angeles, where they reinvented themselves as Americans, sometimes as Whites. Like George Herriman, some acknowledged their African heritage privately, but others, like author, critic, and *New York Times* editor Anatole Broyard, divorced themselves completely from their identity as people of color. For these Creoles, the Great Migration included a journey from the black caste to the white caste that often demanded a renunciation of family ties and Creole identity, just as it had for many white Creoles after the Civil War.[6]

In post–World War II New Orleans, many Creoles still maneuvered in-between racialized color lines, situationally, just like their frontier ancestors, those twilight people who hovered "about the confines of light and darkness," like bats.[7] Yet, racial lines in Louisiana had hardened considerably by the end of World War II. Creoles in postwar New Orleans were sometimes regarded as white, but more often they were not. The persistence of racist marginalization directed at the Creole community compelled Creoles to embrace the struggle for black civil rights and to stand with other people of color in the United States in a solidarity based on an explicitly American articulation of racial identity. The struggle of Creoles in New Orleans after World War II was voiced less in terms of *liberté, égalité, fraternité* than in the sort utilized by Ernest Cherrie when he proclaimed himself a "race man" in 1933.[8]

From the first moment I heard my great-uncle Earl A. Barthé describe Plasterers' Union Local 93 as a "racially integrated" union, I knew that he was allowing his audience's racial expectations to inform their sense of the history he was relating to them. Americans speak race in black and white, and Earl was speaking to his American audience in American, but the story of Local 93 can't be fully contextualized within the confines of the binary divisions of the racialized American caste system. If anyone else in that audience suspected, as I did, that the story of Local 93 was more complex than the version my uncle was relating, no one was impolite enough to raise the question. Later, when Earl confirmed the details of African American exclusion, I heard the first words of a narrative that I have tried to give a voice to in this work, my best attempt to offer subtitles for a historical silence on Creole identity in New Orleans in the twentieth century.

NOTES

INTRODUCTION

1. A note on terminology used in this book: Proper nouns denoting caste orders (Whites, Blacks, etc.) are capitalized in every instance that I use them in my writing; adjectives are not. When I use "colored," "Negro/negro," and "Creole/creole" in original citations, or when referencing quotes of those citations, I follow the original form of the word without respect to contemporary discourses on the politics of capitalization. Finally, "Colored/colored" as a racial caste descriptor was a specific, legal term that was used historically to separate people of mixed ancestry from Whites and Blacks in Louisiana; it is impossible to discuss Creole people in Louisiana without recognizing that distinction.

2. See Arnold R. Hirsch and Joseph Logsdon, eds., *Creole New Orleans: Race and Americanization* (Baton Rouge: Louisiana State University Press, 1992); Gwendolyn Midlo Hall, *Africans in Colonial Louisiana: The Development of Afro-Creole Culture in the Eighteenth Century* (Baton Rouge: Louisiana State University Press, 1992); Caryn Cossé Bell, *Revolution, Romanticism, and the Afro-Creole Protest Tradition in Louisiana, 1718–1868* (Baton Rouge: Louisiana State University Press, 1995).

3. Wendy Ann Gaudin, "Autocrats and All Saints: Migration, Memory, and Modern Creole Identities," PhD diss., New York University, 2005; Nikki Dugar, "I Am What I Say I Am: Racial and Cultural Identity among Creoles of Color in New Orleans," MA thesis, University of New Orleans, 2009.

1. IDENTIFYING A HISTORIC LOUISIANA CREOLE COMMUNITY

1. Washington Irving, *A Tour on the Prairies* (London: John Murray Albemarle Street, 1835), 6–7.

2. Irving, *A Tour on the Prairies*, 19–20.

3. Irving, *A Tour on the Prairies*, 20–21.

4. Eva Martha Eckkrammer, "On the Perception of 'Creole' Language and Identity in the Netherlands Antilles," in *A Pepper-Pot of Cultures: Aspects of Creolization in the Caribbean,* ed. Gordon Collier and Ulrich Fleischmann (Amsterdam: Editions Rodopi, 2003), 85–87.

5. See Ira Berlin, "From Creole to African: Atlantic Creoles and the Origins of African-American Society in Mainland North America," *William and Mary Quarterly,* 3rd ser., vol. 53, no. 2 (April 1996): 284.

6. Ulf Hannerz, *Cultural Complexity* (New York: Columbia University Press, 1992), 264–65.

7. See José Pedro Machado, *Grande Dicionário da Lingua Portuguesa,* vol. 1 (Lisbon: Alfa Publications, 1991).

8. Charles Stewart, "Creolization: History, Ethnography, Theory," in *Creolization: History, Ethnography, Theory,* ed. Charles Stewart (Walnut Creek, CA: Left Coast Press, 2007), 1–18; and Rob Kroes, "American Empire and Cultural Imperialism: A View From the Receiving End," conference paper at American Impact on Western Europe: Americanization and Westernization in Transatlantic Perspective, German Historical Institute, Washington, DC, March 25–27, 1999, transcript, *Conference Papers on the Web.*

9. William W. Hening, ed., *The Statutes at Large: Being a Collection of All the Laws of Virginia, from the First Session of the Legislature, in the Year 1619* . . . [1809–23], vol. 2: 170, accessed at the Library of Virginia; and Edmund S. Morgan, *American Slavery, American Freedom: The Ordeal of Colonial Virginia,* (New York: W. W. Norton & Co., 1975), 155–56.

10. See George M. Fredrickson, *White Supremacy: A Comparative Study in American and South African History* (New York: Oxford University Press, 1981). Quote from David Fowler, "Northern Attitudes Towards Interracial Marriage: A Study of Legislation and Public Opinion in the Middle Atlantic States and States of the Old Northwest," PhD diss., Yale University, 1963, 37–39, quoted in Fredrickson, *White Supremacy,* 101–2, 307.

11. Jennifer M. Spear, *Race, Sex, and Social Order in Early New Orleans* (Baltimore: Johns Hopkins University Press, 2008), 19.

12. Mark Eastman, *Church and State in Early Canada,* quoted in Jerah Johnson, "Colonial New Orleans: A Fragment of the Eighteenth-Century French Ethos," in *Creole New Orleans,* ed. Hirsch and Logsdon, 22–35; Spear, *Race, Sex, and Social Order,* 33–34.

13. See Carolyn E. Frick, *The Making of Haiti: The Saint Domingue Revolution from Below* (Knoxville: University of Tennessee Press, 1990), and Kris E. Lane, *Pillaging the Empire: Piracy in the Americas, 1500–1750* (Armonk, NY: M. E. Sharpe, 1998).

14. See Pierre Le Moyne Sieur d'Iberville, *Iberville's Gulf Journals* (Tuscaloosa: University of Alabama Press, 1991); Robert V. Wells, *Facing the "King of Terrors": Death and Society in an American Community, 1750–1990* (Cambridge, UK: Cambridge University Press, 2000), 28–29.

15. Charles R. Maduell Jr., *The Census Tables for the French Colony of Louisiana from 1699 to 1732* (Baltimore, 1972), 16–22, cited in Richard Campanella, *Bienville's Dilemma: A Historical Geography of New Orleans* (Lafayette: Center for Louisiana Studies at University of Louisiana at Lafayette, 2008), 111.

16. Thomas N. Ingersoll, *Mammon and Manon in Early New Orleans: The First Slave Society in the Deep South, 1718–1819* (Knoxville: University of Tennessee Press, 1999), 10–11.

17. Ingersoll, *Mammon and Manon in Early New Orleans*, 10–11.

18. Demographic analysis of colonial Louisiana taken from James Pritchard, "Population in French America, 1670–1730: The Demographic Context of Colonial Louisiana," table 9.1 in *French Colonial Louisiana and the Atlantic World*, ed. Bradley G. Bond (Baton Rouge: Louisiana State University Press, 2005), 177. The estimated acreage of Louisiana is based on the territory acquired by the United States in the Louisiana Purchase Treaty of 1803 and does not include areas eliminated by the treaty with Spain in 1819 and are sourced from the website of the US Department of the Interior, Office of the Secretary, Areas of Acquisition to the Territory of the United States (Washington, DC: US Government Printing Office, 1992). Acreages therein are based on findings adopted February 2, 1912, by the secretary of the interior, www.blm.gov/natacq/pls02/pls1-1_02.pdf. See also Spear, *Race, Sex, and Social Order*, 1–2, 17–51.

19. Spear, *Race, Sex, and Social Order*, 129.

20. Virginia Meacham Gould, "The Free Creoles of Color of the Antebellum Gulf Ports of Mobile and Pensacola: A Struggle for the Middle Ground," in *Creoles of Color of the Gulf South*, ed. James H. Dormon (Knoxville: University of Tennessee Press, 1996), 33.

21. See Jean-Baptiste Duclos to Antoine de Cadillac, governor of Detroit, December 25, 1715, Archives de colonies, Archives nationales de France, ser. C13a, 3: 819–24, for conflation of the terms "métis" and "mulâtre." Jennifer Spear speaks to this discrepancy in usage between the Spanish and the French in *Race, Sex, and Social Order*, 236. See also Andrew Jolivette, *Louisiana Creoles: Cultural Recovery and Mixed-Race Native American Identity* (New York: Lexington Books, 2007), 7.

22. Ferdinand Stone, "The Law with a Difference and How It Came About," *The Past as Prelude: New Orleans, 1718–1968*, ed. Hodding Carter (Gretna, LA: Pelican Publishing, 2008), 52.

23. Kimberly S. Hanger, *Bounded Lives, Bounded Places: Free Black Society in Colonial New Orleans, 1769–1803* (Durham, NC: Duke University Press, 1997), 109–29.

24. Gwendolyn Midlo Hall, "The Formation of Afro-Creole Culture," in *Creole New Orleans*, ed. Hirsch and Logsdon, 82–84.

25. Nathalie Dessens, *From Saint-Domingue to New Orleans: Migration and Influences* (Gainesville: University Press of Florida, 2007), 35–38.

26. Adam Rothman, *Slave Country: American Expansion and the Origins of the Deep South* (Cambridge, MA: Harvard University Press, 2007), 37–40.

27. Bell, *Revolution, Romanticism, and the Afro-Creole Protest Tradition*, 87; Judith Kelleher Schafer, *Becoming Free, Remaining Free: Manumission and Enslavement in New Orleans, 1846–1862* (Baton Rouge: Louisiana State University Press, 2003), 97, 100.

28. John W. Blassingame, *Black New Orleans, 1860–1880* (Chicago: University of Chicago Press, 1973), 21.

29. Joseph Cardinal Ratzinger, "Congregation for the Doctrine of the Faith Declaration 'Dominus Iesus' on the Unicity and Salvific Universality of Jesus Christ and the Church," *The Vatican,* online.

30. "Hayti and Immigration Thither," *New Orleans Daily Picayune,* July 16, 1859.

31. Tregle, "Creoles and Americans," in *Creole New Orleans,* ed. Hirsch and Logsdon, 165–68; Randall M. Miller, "Immigration Through the Port of New Orleans," in *Forgotten Doors: The Other Ports of Entry to the United States,* ed. M. Mark Stolarik (London: Associated University Presses, 1988), 128.

32. Rodolphe Lucien Desdunes, *Our People and Our History: Fifty Creole Portraits* (Baton Rouge: Louisiana State University Press, 1973), 120.

33. Desdunes, *Our People and Our History,* 118–20.

34. Stephen J. Ochs, *A Black Patriot and a White Priest: André Cailloux and Claude Paschal Maistre in Civil War New Orleans* (Baton Rouge: Louisiana State University Press, 2000), 71. Family names of free Creole militiamen/guardsmen culled from muster rolls for Native Guards, James G. Hollandsworth, *The Louisiana Native Guards: The Black Military Experience During the Civil War* (Baton Rouge: Louisiana State University Press, 1995), and Marion John Bennett Pierson, comp., *Louisiana Soldiers in the War of 1812* (Baton Rouge: Louisiana Genealogical and Historical Society, 1963).

35. "Who Are the Creoles?" Marcus Christian Collection, Earl K. Long Special Collections (hereafter MCC), ACC 11, Literary and Historical Manuscripts, box 12, Historical C–F. See also Desdunes's recollections of André Cailloux from *Our People and Our History,* 124–25. The definitive account of the Fifty-Fourth Regiment Massachusetts Volunteer Infantry, the subject of a popular 1989 Hollywood film, is the first-person account written by Captain Louis F. Emilio, *A Brave Black Regiment* (Cambridge, MA: Da Capo Press, 1995).

36. "History of St. Rose of Lima Church," *St. Rose de Lima Catholic Church, New Orleans,* online.

37. "History of St. Rose of Lima Church."

38. W. S. Alexander, "Straight University, New Orleans," *American Missionary,* August 1882, 234–35.

39. S. A. Hurlbut, "Report of the Board of Education for Freedmen, Department of the Gulf, for the Year 1864," 3, "African American Perspectives: Pamphlets from the Daniel A.P. Murray Collection, 1818–1907," *American Memory,* Library of Congress, memory.loc.gov /cgi-bin/query/r?ammem/murray:@field(DOCID+@lit(lcrbmrpt2315divo)).

40. MCC, ACC 11, Literary and Historical Manuscripts, box 12, Historical C–F, folder "proposed booklet," *Louisiana Negroes,* "Dreams of an African Ex-Slave," unpublished manuscript, 20. A. P. Tureaud comments on Thomy Lafon's dealings with "the pirate Lafitte" in "Xerographic copy of typescript of interview of A. P. Tureaud by Dr. Joseph Logsdon," (hereafter "Tureaud-Logsdon"), box 164-1, A. P. Tureaud Collection, Earl K. Long Special Collections, 55–56.

41. Roger A. Fischer, *The Segregation Struggle in Louisiana, 1862–1877* (Urbana: University of Illinois Press, 1974), 22–26.

42. *Debates in the Convention for the Revision and Amendment of the Constitution of the State of Louisiana* (New Orleans, 1864), 493–99, quoted in Fischer, *The Segregation Struggle in Louisiana*, 25–26; see also Douglas M. Hall, "Public Education in Louisiana during the War between the States with Special Reference to New Orleans," MA thesis, Louisiana State University, 1940, 67–68.

43. "Legislature of Louisiana," *New Orleans Times*, November 15, 1864.

44. "Mr. Smith's Bill," *New Orleans Tribune*, November 16, 1864, 2.

45. Whitelaw Reid, *After the War: A Southern Tour, May 1, 1865–May 1, 1866* (London: S. Low, Son and Marston, 1866), 244.

46. *L'Union*, October 18, 1862, quoted and translated in Joseph Logsdon and Caryn Cossé Bell, "The Americanization of Black New Orleans," in *Creole New Orleans*, ed. Hirsch and Logsdon, 222.

47. David C. Rankin, "The Origins of Black Leadership in New Orleans During Reconstruction," *Journal of Southern History* 40, no. 3 (August 1974): 417–40.

48. Jay Gitlin, *The Bourgeois Frontier: French Towns, French Traders, and American Expansion* (New Haven, CT: Yale University Press, 2010), 169. One is reminded of Québécoise poet Michèle Lalonde's poem "Speak White," which referenced the Anglophone Canadian practice of admonishing Francophone Canadians to speak English by demanding that they "speak white."

49. David R. Roediger, *Working Toward Whiteness: How America's Immigrants Became White: The Strange Journey from Ellis Island to the Suburbs* (New York: Basic Books, 2005), 123.

50. "Eulogy of the Creoles," *New York Times*, April 27, 1885.

51. Justin A. Nystrom, *New Orleans After the Civil War: Race, Politics, and a New Birth of Freedom* (Baltimore: Johns Hopkins University Press, 2010), 142–51.

52. Christopher Benfey, *Degas in New Orleans: Encounters in the Creole World of Kate Chopin and George Washington Cable* (Berkeley: University of California Press, 1999), 118–19.

53. MCC, ACC 11, Literary and Historical Manuscripts, box 12, Historical C–F, draft of essay, "New Orleans Gumbo."

54. Joy J. Jackson, *New Orleans in the Gilded Age: Politics and Urban Progress, 1880–1896* (Baton Rouge: Louisiana State University Press, 1969), 14–19; Tregle, "Creoles and Americans," 184. The conflation of New Orleans Creoles with African Americans makes some studies, like Eric Arnesen's on waterfront workers for example, particularly difficult as much of the nuanced nature of New Orleans's race relations, especially in organized labor, is lost in the hegemonic inclusion of Creoles and African Americans in one racial category. Other historians with a firmer grasp of the cultural complexities of the communities of New Orleans people of color, like Caryn Cossé Bell or Gwendolyn Midlo Hall for example, have attempted to negotiate this nuance with the racialized qualifier "Afro-Creole," but Creoles

in New Orleans never referred to themselves in this way, and the qualifier only serves to indicate the nonwhiteness of the people as the "Afro-Creole culture" identified by Bell and Hall is expressed in music and food and experienced through other cultural practices and shared across racial lines in Louisiana. In Louisiana, both Blacks and Whites regard gumbo, a soup or stew which derives its name from the Bantu word for "okra," as a signature artifact of "authentic Louisiana culture" and Cajuns, many of whom deny any nonwhite ancestry, do not regard the practice of preparing gumbo as an expression of "Afro-Acadian" or "Afro-Cajun" culture. I am aware that there are people who have been racially categorized as "white" in Louisiana who identify as Creoles, but their number is far too small to justify the continuing use of racial qualifiers to distinguish Creoles of color from a "white" Creole community that had, for the most part, ceased to exist by 1900 in New Orleans. Therefore, racial qualification will be reserved for "white Creoles."

55. Fischer, *The Segregation Struggle in Louisiana*, 57; James Keith Hogue, *Uncivil War: Five New Orleans Street Battles and the Rise and Fall of Radical Reconstruction* (Baton Rouge: Louisiana State University Press, 2006), 66.

56. See Douglas C. M. Slawson, "Segregated Catholicism: The Origins of Saint Katharine's Parish, New Orleans," *Vincentian Heritage Journal* 17, no. 3 (October 1996): 141–84, passages relevant to this citation at 147–49. "Masterism" quote from Richard Follett, "Legacies of Enslavement," in *Slavery's Ghost: The Problem of Freedom in the Age of Emancipation*, ed. Richard Follett, Eric Foner, and Walter Johnson (Baltimore: Johns Hopkins University Press, 2011), 59.

57. Joel Williamson, "The Separation of the Races," in *After Slavery: The Negro in South Carolina during Reconstruction, 1861–1877* (Chapel Hill: University of North Carolina Press, 1965), 274–99.

58. "Who Are the Creoles?" MCC; Rodolphe Lucien Desdunes, *A Few Words to Dr. Du Bois: "With Malice Toward None"* (New Orleans, 1907), 13, quoted in Logsdon and Bell, "The Americanization of Black New Orleans, 1850–1900," 203.

59. MCC, ACC 11, Literary and Historical Manuscripts, Genealogy box 14, folder "White men and Negro women," numbered p. 185. On the same page of this unpublished manuscript, Christian offers another modernized nursery rhyme, reflecting the paradoxical coexistence of solidarity and caste inequality: "Yallah gals ride in automobiles; high-browns ride the train, Poor black gals ride old grey mules; but they get there just the same."

60. See Rebecca J. Scott, "Public Rights and Private Commerce: A Nineteenth-Century Atlantic Creole Itinerary," *Current Anthropology* 48, no. 2 (April 2007).

61. "Who Are the Creoles?" MCC.

62. J. Brown, "Brown, J., Opinion of the Court, Supreme Court of the United States, 163 US 537, Plessy vs. Ferguson" (hereafter J. Brown SCOTUS), *Cornell University Law School,* online.

63. J. Brown SCOTUS.

64. J. Brown SCOTUS.

65. David Brown and Clive Webb, *Race in the American South: From Slavery to Civil Rights* (Edinburgh: Edinburgh University Press, 2007), 224.

2. STRANGERS IN THEIR OWN LAND

1. Chief Justice Roger B. Taney, "The *Dred Scott* Decision: Opinion of Chief Justice Taney with Introduction by Dr. J. H. Van Evrie," *American Memory: Slaves and the Courts, 1740–1860,* Library of Congress Online.

2. See Theodore Roosevelt, *The New Nationalism* (New York: Outlook Publishing, 1910); Robert Wiebe, *The Search for Order, 1877–1920* (New York: Farrar, Straus and Giroux, 1967), 189.

3. Theodore Roosevelt to Richard Hurd, January 3, 1919, Transcript Division, Library of Congress Online.

4. Roosevelt to Hurd, January 3, 1919.

5. Rocky L. Sexton, "Cajun French Language Maintenance and Shift: A Southwest Louisiana Case Study to 1970," *Journal of American Ethnic History* 19, no. 4 (2000): 24–48; Shane K. Bernard, *The Cajuns: Americanization of a People* (Jackson: University of Mississippi Press, 2003).

6. "Roosevelt Bars the Hyphenated," *New York Times,* October 13, 1915.

7. Wiebe, *The Search for Order,* 257–58.

8. L. M. Harris, "The Creoles of New Orleans," *Southern Collegian* 30 (January 1898): 210, quoted in Jackson, *New Orleans in the Gilded Age,* 14.

9. "Is It Obtuseness or Perversity?" *Indianapolis Freeman,* November 23, 1901.

10. George Fredrickson, *The Black Image in the White Mind: The Debate on Afro-American Character and Destiny, 1817–1914* (New York: Harper and Row, 1971), 276–80.

11. See D. W. Griffith, dir., *The Birth of a Nation* (1915), available on *YouTube.* See also Thomas Dixon, *The Clansman: An Historical Romance of the Ku Klux Klan* (New York: Grosset & Dunlap, 1905).

12. Joel Waldo Finler, *The Hollywood Story* (New York: Wallflower Press, 2003), 47–48. Walt Disney's *Snow White and the Seven Dwarfs,* released in 1937, was the first US motion picture to gross more than *The Birth of a Nation.*

13. MCC, ACC 11, "Diary, Business Cards, notes, n.d. ca. 1924–ca. 1970," folder 4, "Diary, Notes, Business Cards, n.d."

14. *Niles Weekly Register,* November 5, 1825, p. 160, quoted in Bell, *Revolution, Romanticism, and the Afro-Creole Protest Tradition,* 76–78.

15. William M. Lewis, "Pencilings," *Indianapolis Freeman,* July 12, 1902.

16. There is no shortage of literature on Marie Laveau. Much of it is contradictory and sensationalized. Among the most commonly cited is Herbert Asbury, *The French Quarter: An Informal History of the New Orleans Underworld* (1936; New York: Thunder's Mouth Press, 2003), 265–80. Zora Neale Hurston offers an extremely colorful folkloric account of Laveau becoming "a god," "confounding enemies," and "putting curses" on them in *Mules and Men* (1936; New York: HarperCollins, 2009), which was produced from field research she conducted in New Orleans between 1928 and 1930, decades after the death of Marie, the widow Glapion. The extent of Laveau's legend endures to the present, and a fictional Laveau that

draws on details of the historical person exists today as a recurring superpowered character in the Marvel Comics franchises *Doctor Strange* and *Blade*. More scholarly sources on Marie Laveau include Martha Ward, *Voodoo Queen: The Spirited Lives of Marie Laveau* (Jackson: University Press of Mississippi, 2004), and Louise McKinney, *New Orleans: A Cultural History* (New York: Oxford University Press, 2006), 90–92, as well as Ina Johanna Fandrich, *Marie Laveau: The Mysterious Voodoo Queen* (Lafayette: University of Louisiana at Lafayette, 2012).

17. N. Y. Ledger, "How He Liked It," *Detroit Plaindealer,* June 27, 1890.

18. See Mary Gehman, "Visible Means of Support: Businesses, Professions, and Trades of Free People of Color," in *Creole: The History and Legacy of Louisiana's Free People of Color,* ed. Sybil Kein (Baton Rouge: Louisiana State University Press, 2000) 208–22; Hanger, "Landlords, Shopkeepers, Farmers, and Slave Owners: Free Black Female Property-Holders in Colonial New Orleans," in *Beyond Bondage: Free Women of Color in the Americas,* ed. David Barry Gaspar and Darlene Clark Hine (Urbana: University of Illinois Press, 2004), 221; and Judith K. Schafer, "'Open and Notorious Concubinage': The Emancipation of Slave Mistresses by Will and the Supreme Court of Antebellum Louisiana," *Louisiana History* 28, no. 2 (Spring 1987): 165–82.

19. "Something New in Breach of Promise," *Brooklyn Daily Standard-Union,* front page, March 10, 1890; "Promised to Marry a Negro Woman," *Marion* (New York) *Enterprise,* front page, March 13, 1890; *St. Paul Appeal,* front page, March 22, 1890; "The Race's Doings," *Cleveland Gazette,* March 29, 1890.

20. "Something New in Breach of Promise," *Brooklyn Daily Standard-Union,* March 10, 1890.

21. Thomas Mayne Reid, *The Quadroon, or, A Lover's Adventure in Louisiana* (London: George W. Hyde, 1856).

22. See Dion Boucicault, "The Octoroon: A Play in Four Acts," in *Dick's London Acting Edition of Standard English Plays and Comic Dramas* (New York: DeWitt Publishing House, 1859), 1–18.

23. Thomas S. Hischak, *American Literature on Stage and Screen: 525 Works and Their Adaptations* (Jefferson, NC: McFarland and Co., 2012), 188. See also Eve Golden, *Golden Images: 41 Essays on Silent Film Stars* (Jefferson, NC: McFarland and Co., 2001). See also Greta de Groat, "America's First Lady of the Screen: The Life and Career of Clara Kimball Young," *Clara Kimball Young,* web.stanford.edu/~gdegroat/CKY/cky.

24. "A Southern Romance," *Cleveland Gazette,* May 24, 1890.

25. "Elopes With a Creole," *Cleveland Gazette,* June 21, 1890.

26. "Dr. J. E. Hunter; Lexington; Will Hoffman; Xenia; Henry Bolden; Rev. J. H. Payne," *Cleveland Gazette,* July 15, 1890.

27. Information from the description of the scope and contents of "The Notarial Acts of Louis André Martinet," Louis A. Martinet Records, *New Orleans Notarial Archives,* www.notarialarchives.org/martinet.htm.

28. Alan Lomax, *Mister Jelly Roll* (London: Pan Books, 1952), 13, 64.

29. See Sister Frances Jerome Woods, *Marginality and Identity: A Colored Creole Family Through Ten Generations* (Baton Rouge: Louisiana State University Press, 1972), esp. 17–58.

30. J. D. Howard, "Gay Paris of America: A Month's Stay of Our Representative in the Crescent City—Facts Gleaned of Its Mongrel Population, Habits and Ways," *Indianapolis Freeman,* March 29 and April 12, 1902.

31. Howard, "Gay Paris of America," March 29, 1902.

32. "Tureaud-Logsdon," 12–14.

33. Irving, *A Tour on the Prairies,* 19–20.

34. See Gilbert E. Martin Sr., *French Creoles: A Shattered Nation* (Montgomery, AL: E-Booktime, 2006), quote from Martin, "The Creoles Promised Treaty Rights," FrenchCreoles .com.

35. Charles E. O'Neill, S.J., Foreword to Desdunes, *Our People and Our History,* xvii–xviii.

36. See Booker T. Washington, *The Negro Problem* (Radford, VA: Wilder, 2008), 11–26, for Du Bois's "Talented Tenth" essay, first published in 1903, wherein Du Bois argues that the "Negro race . . . is going to be saved by its exceptional men."

37. "Who Are the Creoles?" MCC.

38. Editorial, *Harrisburg* (PA) *Evening News,* November 22, 1926.

39. Alice Moore Dunbar-Nelson, "People of Color in Louisiana," in *Creole,* ed. Kein, 3, originally published in *Journal of Negro History* 2 (1917).

40. *State v. Treadaway et al.,* 126 La. 300, 52 So. 500–512 (1910). See also Virginia R. Dominguez, *White by Definition: Social Classification in Creole Louisiana* (New Brunswick, NJ: Rutgers University Press, 1986), 28–32; and Chief Justice Olivier O. Provosty, "Negro Definition," *Duhaime Legal Dictionary,* online.

41. Lomax, *Mister Jelly Roll,* 84. See also Gaudin, "Autocrats and All Saints," for her discussion of elitism among Creoles, specifically in her chapter "Making Middleness."

42. See Kerry Ann Rockquemore and David Brunsma, *Beyond Black: Biracial Identity in America* (Lanham, MD: Rowman & Littlefield, 2008); see 75–102 for their description of these reported approaches to identity negotiation and the forces associated with each approach, including phenotype, and socioeconomic background and reciprocity (that is, identities are transactions, and identifying oneself is only half of the process, the other half being that others accept your identity as presented). See also R. Bentley Anderson, *Black, White, and Catholic* (Nashville, TN: Vanderbilt University Press, 2005), 4–7, for analysis of Creole racial self-identification, specifically in Archbishop Jansenns's 1898 report on colored and Indian missions wherein Jansenns claims that Creoles resented "that we (whites) wish to draw the line of white and colored upon them." See also Jolivette, *Louisiana Creoles.*

43. "Tureaud-Logsdon," 8–9.

44. J. Brown SCOTUS.

45. "Tureaud-Logsdon," 72–73.

46. "Tureaud-Logsdon," 72–73.

47. Biographical information on John Harriman derived from "Lhota Family Tree: John Harriman," with source citations, trees.ancestry.com/tree/26105659/person/2038058367.

48. US Federal Census 1850, New Orleans Municipality 3 Ward 1, New Orleans, Orleans, Louisiana, roll M432_238, page 46B, image 97.

49. Amistad Research Center, Tulane University, New Orleans, George Longe Collection (hereafter George Longe Papers); minutes books for meetings of Fraternité No. 20 show George Herriman and George Herriman Jr. See also Bell, *Revolution, Romanticism, and the Afro-Creole Protest Tradition*, 290.

50. US Federal Census 1880, New Orleans, Orleans, Louisiana, roll 462, Family History Library microfilm 1254462, page 596B, enumeration district 051, image 0174.

51. Patrick McDonnell, Karen O'Connell, and Georgia Riley de Havenon, *Krazy Kat: The Comic Art of George Herriman* (New York: Abrams, 1986), 30.

52. Jeet Heer, "Racism as a Stylistic Choice and Other Notes," *Comics Journal*, March 14, 2011.

53. US Federal Census 1900, Los Angeles Ward 6, Los Angeles, California, roll 90, page 14B, enumeration district 0052, Family History Library microfilm 1240090.

54. Mr. John Williams, interview by Wendy Ann Gaudin, March 13, 2002, New Orleans, quoted in "Autocrats and All Saints," 68.

55. Williams interview by Gaudin.

3. CLIQUISH, CLANNISH, ORGANIZATION MINDED

1. Alan Lomax and Jelly Roll Morton, Library of Congress Narrative, Archived Folk Song 1648A, "Monologue of New Orleans funeral customs and the beginnings of Jazz, New Orleans Funeral Part 2 ('Flee as a Bird to the Mountain')."

2. See Ferdinand Tönnies, *Community and Society (Gemeinschaft und Gesellschaft)* (New Brunswick, NJ: Transaction Publishers, 2004), for further explanation of the difference between premodern communities (based on extended families, shared moral sensibilities, intimate interpersonal experiences, and low social mobility) and modern societies (based on impersonal, individual, voluntary associations often connected to one's professional life with opportunity for high social mobility). For more on the notion of "achieved status" (obtained through action, particularly meritorious action) as opposed to "ascribed status" (acquired and passed on hereditarily), see anthropologist Ralph Linton, *The Study of Man* (New York: D. Appleton Century Co., 1936), esp. chap. 2 on race and chap. 8 on status and role.

3. "Who Are the Creoles?" MCC.

4. Adam Fairclough, *Race and Democracy: The Civil Rights Struggle in Louisiana, 1915–1972* (Athens: University of Georgia Press, 1995), 15.

5. William Ivy Hair, *Carnival of Fury: Robert Charles and the New Orleans Race Riot of 1900* (Baton Rouge: Louisiana State University Press, 2008), 2.

6. Hair, *Carnival of Fury*, 177–78.

7. Lomax, *Mister Jelly Roll*, 59.

8. Asbury, *The French Quarter*, 430–55.

9. Alecia P. Long, *The Great Southern Babylon: Sex, Race and Respectability in New Orleans 1865–1920* (Baton Rouge, Louisiana State University Press, 2004).

10. Lomax, *Mister Jelly Roll*, 33.

11. Al Rose, *Storyville, New Orleans: Being an Authentic, Illustrated Account of the Notorious Red-Light District* (Tuscaloosa: University of Alabama Press, 1979), 159–60.

12. Rose, *Storyville, New Orleans*, 159–60.

13. Lomax, *Mister Jelly Roll*, 103–5.

14. Lomax, *Mister Jelly Roll*, 99.

15. Lomax, *Mister Jelly Roll*, 101.

16. "Who Are the Creoles?" MCC.

17. John R. Kemp, ed. *Martin Behrman of New Orleans: Memoirs of a City Boss* (Baton Rouge: Louisiana State University Press, 1977), 51.

18. Martin Behrman Collection, Main Branch, New Orleans Public Library, City Archives (hereafter Behrman Collection), ser. 1, carton 1, box 3, folder "Mayor Martin Behrman Papers, 1904–1920 Speeches, to Ladies of the Confederate Southern Memorial Association."

19. Behrman Collection, ser. 1, carton 1, box 2, folder "Mayor Martin Behrman Papers, 1904–1920 Correspondence Mithouard, A. (President of the Municipal Council of Paris, France)," letter (in English).

20. Kemp, *Martin Behrman of New Orleans*, 51.

21. Kemp, *Martin Behrman of New Orleans*, 52.

22. Kemp, *Martin Behrman of New Orleans*, 53.

23. Eric Arnesen, *Waterfront Workers of New Orleans: Race, Class and Politics, 1863–1923* (Urbana: University of Illinois Press, 1991), 148; Taney, "The *Dred Scott* Decision."

24. *State v. Treadaway et al.*, 126 La. 300, 52 So. 500–512 (1910). See also Dominguez, *White by Definition*, 28–32; and Provosty, "Negro Definition." Limited patronage for "negroes who knew their place" was not an uncommon philosophy of Jim Crow in Louisiana and elsewhere and represented a relatively moderate position when compared to the sort of draconian oppression expressed in massacres like the Tulsa Race Riots of 1921, for example. For more on philosophies of segregation, see Jack F. Davis, *Race against Time: Culture and Separation in Natchez since 1940* (Baton Rouge: Louisiana State University Press, 2001); Fredrickson, *White Supremacy*; Grace Elizabeth Hale, *Making Whiteness: The Culture of Segregation in the South, 1890–1940* (New York: Pantheon Books, 1998).

25. Mr. Alexander P. Tureaud, interview by Wendy Ann Gaudin, May 13, 2002, New Orleans, quoted in "Autocrats and All Saints," 64, brackets in original.

26. Gaudin, "Autocrats and All Saints," 68.

27. "Tureaud-Logsdon," 21–23.

28. Gaudin, "Autocrats and All Saints," 67–69.

29. Fairclough, *Race and Democracy*, 10.

30. Behrman Collection, ser. 1, carton 1, box 3, folder "Mayor Martin Behrman Papers, 1904–1920 Correspondence, Citizens Volunteer Ward Organizations," letter from the Sev-

enth Ward Improvement Association, December 11, 1918; Albert E. Arnoult, US Federal Census 1910, New Orleans Ward 4, New Orleans, Orleans, Louisiana, roll T624_520, page 1B, enumeration district 0061, Family History Library microfilm 1374533.

31. Behrman Collection, ser. 1, carton 1, box 3, folder "Mayor Martin Behrman Papers, 1904–1920 Correspondence," letter from St. Bernard Avenue Improvement Association, September 30, 1911, membership listed in letter for nominees to board of commissioners cross-referenced with data derived from US Federal Census of 1910 for racial background of members of St. Bernard Avenue Improvement Association. St. Bernard Avenue is the central thoroughfare of the Seventh Ward, extending from Rampart Street in the south (riverside) to the lake in the north.

32. Kemp, *Martin Behrman of New Orleans,* 52; Vanessa Flores-Robert, "Black Policemen in Jim Crow New Orleans," MA thesis, University of New Orleans, 2011.

33. Howard N. Rabinowitz, "The Conflict between Blacks and the Police in the Urban South, 1865–1900," in *Race, Ethnicity, and Urbanization: Selected Essays* (Columbia: University of Missouri Press, 1994), 167–80; Flores-Robert, "Black Policemen in Jim Crow New Orleans."

34. "Not for Negro Police," *New Orleans Times-Picayune,* July 26, 1923.

35. "Bust of Behrman Presented," *New Orleans Times-Picayune,* February 10, 1929.

36. Kemp, *Martin Behrman of New Orleans,* 51.

37. Behrman himself alludes to the race riots in Chicago in 1919, but the African American communities of Elaine and Tulsa both experienced devastating episodes of militarized, white violence after World War I. Elaine was a part of a larger string of race riots that erupted in the "Red Summer" of 1919. The "Black Wall Street" of Tulsa was probably one of the wealthiest African American communities in the United States when it was attacked by white mobs assisted by Oklahoma National Guardsmen, who earned the dubious honor of being the first men in history to subject an American city to aerial bombardment.

38. Gaudin, "Autocrats and All Saints," 68.

39. Fairclough, *Race and Democracy,* 383.

40. Fairclough, *Race and Democracy,* 15. The Dejoie family, though of Creole heritage, spoke English, lived in uptown New Orleans, and was (and still is today) a Protestant family, not a Catholic one. Thus, in many ways, the Dejoies represent a prototype for the Creole–African American fusion identity that predominates contemporarily in New Orleans.

41. Fairclough, *Race and Democracy,* 14; Alexander P. Tureaud, interview by Wendy Ann Gaudin, May 13, 2002, New Orleans, quoted in "Autocrats and All Saints," 128.

42. "NAACP: 100 Years of History," NAACP.org.

43. "NAACP: 100 Years of History."

44. "About the NAACP New Orleans Branch," *NAACP New Orleans Branch,* online.

45. Lee Sartain, *Invisible Activists: Women of the Louisiana NAACP and the Struggle for Civil Rights* (Baton Rouge: Louisiana State University Press, 2007), 50–55.

46. Fairclough, *Race and Democracy,* 18–19; Sharlene Sinegal-DeCuir, "Attacking Jim Crow: Black Activism in New Orleans, 1925–1941," PhD diss., Louisiana State University,

2009, iv; Rachel L. Emanuel and Alexander P. Tureaud Jr., *A More Noble Cause: A. P. Tureaud and the Struggle for Civil Rights in Louisiana* (Baton Rouge: Louisiana State University Press, 2011), 54–64.

47. "White's Speech Stirs Strife Between Creoles-Negroes," *Sepia Socialite* (New Orleans), May 28, 1938, 1–12.

48. "White's Speech Stirs Strife," 1–12.

49. "White's Speech Stirs Strife," 1–12.

50. From New Orleans Black Benevolent Associations Collection, Xavier University Archives and Special Collections (hereafter "XUNOBBA"), box "1872–1940 and n.d.," letter from Joseph Hirsch of the Federal Security Agency United States Public Health Service, April 10, 1940, to Professor of History D. J. Jackson at Xavier University; also Harry Joseph Walker, "Negro Benevolent Societies in New Orleans: A Study of Their Structure, Function, and Membership," MA thesis, Fisk University, 1937, 25–28.

51. XUNOBBA, box "1872–1940 and n.d.," scope notes arranged by Lester Sullivan; original booklet, "Constitution, By-Laws, and Rules of Order of The Zion Benevolent Sons and Daughters of Camparapet Incorporated June 8, 1872."

52. XUNOBBA, "Juvenile Cooperators Fraternals Mutual Aid Association Records Box 1" (hereafter Juvenile Cooperators), historical notes and bound vol., "Record."

53. Juvenile Cooperators, bound vol., "Record," 1.

54. Jeunes Amis 1887 membership list, Société des Jeunes Amis Collection, Earl K. Long Library Special Collections, University of New Orleans; MCC, Literary and Historical Manuscripts, Historical, folder "George Doyle," numbered pages 7–14; Certificate of Marriage, Henry Doyle to Eulalie Ducas, April 29, 1857, Louisiana Marriages, 1718–1925 database online, Provo, UT: Ancestry.com Operations, 2004; Certificate of Death, Henry Doyle, October 3, 1889, Orleans Death Indices 1877–1895, vol. 95: 1081, Ancestry.com. New Orleans Death Records Index, 1804–1949, database online, Provo, UT: Ancestry.com Operations, 2002. Original data: State of Louisiana, Secretary of State, Division of Archives, Records Management, and History, Vital Records Indices, Baton Rouge; Henry Doyle, US Federal Census 1880, New Orleans, Orleans, Louisiana, roll 461, Family History Library microfilm 1254461, page 326C, enumeration district 040, image 0456. Photo of George Doyle from family photo, Ancestry.com, trees.ancestry.com/tree/4276325/person/-14653695/mediax /b049bc3c-08b1-4b45-b6b0-d55abcd9e153?pg=32768&pgpl=pid.

55. St. Louis (Couvent) School Collection, box "CIOA [Couvent] / St. Louis School: Meeting Minutes for Board of Directors 1921–1942 v. 88," Archives of the Archdiocese of New Orleans, bound vol., *History of the Catholic Indigent Orphan Institute Dauphine and Touro Streets, Destroyed by the Hurricane September 1915 rebuilt in 1916,* published by the board of directors; "Tribute to be Paid to Negro Volunteers of 1815," *New Orleans Times-Picayune,* December 30, 1923; "Negro Military Body Plans Event, Patriotic League to Hold Celebration of Battle's Anniversary; "George Doyle," New Orleans, Orleans Parish Death Indices 1937–1948; vol. 210; page 1456; see also Flores-Robert, "Black Policemen in Jim Crow New Orleans."

56. "A Southern Romance," *Cleveland Gazette,* May 24, 1890.

57. MCC, ACC 11, Literary and Historical Manuscripts, Historical, folder "George Doyle," numbered pages 7–14; George Doyle, US Federal Census 1880, New Orleans, Orleans, Louisiana, roll 461, Family History Library microfilm 1254461, page 326C, enumeration district 040, image 0456; George Doyle, COLAS/COLIS Family Tree, Ancestry.com, trees. ancestry.com/tree/4276325/family?cfpid=-14653120; Mary Williams Coste, New Orleans, Louisiana Birth Records Index, 1790–1899, vol. 60: 459; National Park Service of the US Department of the Interior, "Troop Roster Tennessee Volunteers & Militia, Kentucky Volunteers & Militia, Battalion of Free Men of Color, Louisiana Volunteers and Militia," (hereafter "NPS Militia 1812"), www.nps.gov/jela/historyculture/upload/CHALTroopRoster.pdf.

58. Juvenile Cooperators, bound vol., "Record," 1–13.

59. Fairclough, *Race and Democracy,* 18.

60. Juvenile Cooperators, box 1, folder "correspondence 1915, 1918–1921, 1930–1935 and n.d.," letter from Ernest Cherrie, MD, September 6, 1933. It is fair to conclude that his utilization of capital letters for emphasis could be considered "shouting."

61. Dr. Ernest Cherrie to William L. Andrews, July 6, 1931, part 1, ser. G, container 82, Branch Files, NAACP Papers, Manuscripts Division, Library of Congress, quoted in Fairclough, *Race and Democracy,* 18.

62. "Who Are the Creoles?" MCC.

63. George Longe Papers, 1768–1971, and n.d., box 41, oversize, from Finding Aid and Scope Notes.

64. Bell, *Revolution, Romanticism, and the Afro-Creole Protest Tradition,* 283–94.

65. NPS Militia 1812.

66. George Longe Papers, minutes books for meetings of Fraternité No. 20 and its successor lodge, l'Amite No. 27, are all in French.

67. Walker, "Negro Benevolent Societies in New Orleans," 39–40; Société des Jeunes Amis Collection, Earl K. Long Library Special Collections, University of New Orleans (hereafter Jeunes Amis Collection), MS 25–2, envelope *Société des Jeunes Amis. Comité d'Elections* Reports, Jan.–Mar., Jun.–Jul., Sept.–Dec. 1887," membership list (hereafter "Jeunes Amis 1887 membership list"); Louis Andre Martinet Notarial Archives, Notarial Archives of the City of New Orleans, Martinet, Louis A. (hereafter Martinet Archives), vol. 2, act 37, November 23, 1899, Jeunes Amis amended charter.

68. "Jeunes Amis 1887 membership list"; Martinet Archives, vol. 2, act 37, November 23, 1899, Jeunes Amis amended charter, list of signatories. Names cross-referenced with Comité des Citoyens roster from Desdunes, *Our People and Our History,* 141.

69. Martinet Archives, vol. 2, act 37, November 23, 1899, Jeunes Amis amended charter. The building no longer exists today. Dumaine Street between North Villere Street and Marais Street, today, is contained within Armstrong Park.

70. *Woods Directory: A Classified Colored Business, Professional, and Trade Directory of New Orleans, Louisiana,* 2nd ed. (New Orleans: Alan T. Woods, 1912), 7–13.

71. *Woods Directory,* 7–13.

72. St. Martinville Parish Courthouse, conveyance #9716, "La Société des Francs Amis," August 6, 1876.

73. Names cross-referenced from Société des Francs Amis Collection, Earl K. Long Library, University of New Orleans, Special Collections (hereafter Francs Amis), MS 31–1, cashbook, dues and assessments; "Jeunes Amis 1887 membership list"; and Martinet Archives, vol. 2, act 37, November 23, 1899, Jeunes Amis amended charter, list of signatories.

74. Francs Amis, MS 31–1, cashbook, 14–24.

75. Francs Amis, MS 31–1, cashbook, dues and assessments.

76. Robert Sahr, "Inflation Conversion Factors for Years 1774 TO Estimated 2023, in Dollars of Recent Years," Oregon State University Department of Political Science website.

77. Francs Amis, MS 31–1, cashbook, dues and assessments, the transformation from French to "Franglish" to English happens between pages 134 and 214.

78. Gaudin, "Autocrats and All Saints," 29–30.

79. US Federal Census 1910, New Orleans Ward 5, Orleans, Louisiana, roll T624_521, page 7B, enumeration district 0082, Family History Library microfilm 1374534; US Federal Census 1920, New Orleans Ward 7, Orleans, Louisiana, roll T625_621, page 26B, enumeration district 123, image 546; US Federal Census 1930, New Orleans, Orleans, Louisiana, roll 804, page 35B, enumeration district 104, image 896.0, Family History Library microfilm 2340539.

80. Thomas Brothers, *Louis Armstrong's New Orleans* (New York: W. W. Norton, 2006), 178; Baby Dodds's story is also featured in Michael Eugene Crutcher, *Tremé: Race and Place in a New Orleans Neighborhood* (Athens: University of Georgia Press, 2010), 35.

81. Brothers, *Louis Armstrong's New Orleans,* 178.

82. Dominguez, *White by Definition,* 163; brackets and emphasis in original.

83. Desdunes, *Our People and Our History,* 85–86.

84. A "brown bag club" refers to a club which practiced the legendary "brown bag test" wherein if an individual's skin was darker than a brown paper bag, he or she would not be permitted entry. After poring over countless documents related to Creole organizations and sodalities, and after speaking with scores of Creole people born between 1920 and 1960, I have found no evidence at all for such a test. Wendy Gaudin concurs, dismissing the brown bag test as a "myth" in "Autocrats and All Saints" (95). Virginia Dominguez reports being "unable to find a single informant" to verify such a practice in *White by Definition,* 164. Fairclough maintains that stories of the "brown bag test . . . had no basis in fact" in *Race and Democracy,* 15. While it is possible that such a thing existed in places outside of the city, even in other communities in Louisiana perhaps, stories of "brown bag clubs" in New Orleans are not based in fact.

85. Desdunes, *Our People and Our History,* 85–86. See Jeunes Amis Collection, Earl Long MS 25–2, "Rapport du Premier Commissaire pour la Seance du 13 Juin 1887," and letter from Edmund Dédé to A. M. L. Perrault, in French: "J'ai reçu communication de la mission dont vous étiez chargé et les termes élogieux avec lesquels vous me l'avez fait savoir m'ont

sensiblement ému," and "oui, j'accepte d'être votre collègue. Recevez, Monsieur, pour vous, et tout les 'Jeunes Amis,' mes civilités empressées."

86. Francois Dédé , US Federal Census 1870, New Orleans Ward 6, Orleans, Louisiana, roll M593_522, page 239A, image 25, Family History Library microfilm 552021; and "Basile Dédé," US Federal Census 1870, New Orleans Ward 8, Orleans, Louisiana, roll M593_523, page: 725A, image 214; Family History Library microfilm 552022; Native Guard roster from Hollandsworth, *The Louisiana Native Guards,* "Appendix: Black Officers of the Native Guards." See also National Park Service of the US Department of the Interior, "Civil War Soldiers and Sailors System," searchable database (hereafter "NPS-CIVIL"), www.itd.nps.gov /cwss; Brothers, *Louis Armstrong's New Orleans,* 178.

87. Dugar, "I Am What I Say I Am," 15.

88. Gaudin, "Autocrats and All Saints," 29–30.

89. Mr. Alexander P. Tureaud, interview by Wendy Ann Gaudin, May 13, 2002, New Orleans, quoted in Gaudin, "Autocrats and All Saints," 66.

90. "Tureaud-Logsdon," 21–23.

91. "Our 12,000 Killings in 1926," *Literary Digest,* New York, July 2, 1927, 12–13. In 1926, the US cities with the highest murder rates per 100,000 people were all in the South, including Jacksonville, Florida (number one with a murder rate of 75.9); Tampa, Florida (number two with a murder rate of 67.6); Birmingham, Alabama (number three with a murder rate of 58.6); and Memphis, Tennessee (number four with a murder rate of 42.4).

92. Mary G. Rolinson, *Grassroots Garveyism: The Universal Negro Improvement Association in the Rural South, 1920–1927* (Chapel Hill: University of North Carolina Press, 2007), 198.

93. Rolinson, *Grassroots Garveyism,* 140–43.

94. See Marcus Garvey, "The Internal Prejudices of Negroes: Those Who Want to Be White and Those Who Want to Remain Black," *The Philosophy and Opinions of Marcus Garvey, Or, Africa for the Africans,* vol. 1 (Dover, MA: Majority Press, 1923), 84–87. See also Tony Martin, *Race First: The Ideological and Organizational Struggles of Marcus Garvey and the Universal Negro Improvement Association* (Dover, MA: Majority Press, 1976), specifically chapter 12, "The Ku Klux Klan, White Supremacy, and Garvey—A Symbiotic Relationship," 344–55. At the time of this writing, Marcus Garvey still appears on the website of the Knights Party, USA (Ku Klux Klan) as "A Black Moses" and "A Black Hero" whose memory deserves, in the words of the Klan's web editor, "respect by [sic] his fellow black brothers and sisters for whom he fought so hard." See: "Marcus Garvey: A Black Moses," Official Website of the Knight's Party, USA: Bringing a Message of Hope and Deliverance to White Christian America.

95. Rene Grandjean, Rene Grandjean Collection, Earl K. Long Special Collections, MSS 85–82, second bound vol. (black diary), letter to "Mr. B." The emphasized words appeared in the original letter. For more on the relationship on Henry Rey and Rene Grandjean, see Melissa Daggett, "Henry Louis Rey, Spiritualism, and Creoles of Color in Nineteenth-Century New Orleans," MA thesis, University of New Orleans, 2009.

96. Marcus Garvey, "W. E. Burghardt Du Bois as a Hater of Dark People," *The Philosophy and Opinions of Marcus Garvey*, 310–11.

97. Steven Hahn, "Marcus Garvey, the UNIA, and the Hidden Political History of African Americans," conference paper, Subaltern Citizens Conference, Emory University, October 2006; for the distribution of UNIA divisions, see Records of the Central Division, MS 20, boxes 22a–c, Schomburg Center for Research in Black Culture, New York.

4. THE AMERICAN LABOR MOVEMENT IN CREOLE NEW ORLEANS

1. Earl A. Barthé, "Interview 5.30.07," *Rebuilding New Orleans One Voice at a Time: Earl A. Barthé*, podcast (New Orleans: New Orleans PodCasting, 2007).

2. Covington Hall, *Labor Struggles in the Deep South & Other Writings* (Chicago: Charles H. Kerr Publishing Co., 1999), 27.

3. Blassingame, *Black New Orleans*, 2. The patterns observed by Blassingame and the circumstances of colored labor in New Orleans were not unique. Rather, these patterns remained consistent throughout the South, as is evident in Charles H. Wesley's *Negro Labor in the United States, 1850–1925* (New York: Vanguard Press, 1927). See also Paul Norgren and Gladys Louise Palmer, "Negro Labor and Its Problems: A Research Memorandum, Issues 1–3," Carnegie-Myrdal Papers, Schomburg Center, New York, microfilm collection for quantitative analysis that formed one pillar of Gunnar Myrdal's study on black labor in the United States in the early twentieth century, *An American Dilemma*, vol. 2: *The Negro Problem and Modern Democracy* (New York: Harper and Brothers, 1944). For more on skilled artisans among enslaved people in Louisiana, see Marcus Christian, *Negro Ironworkers in Louisiana: 1718–1900* (Gretna, LA: Pelican Publishing, 1972); see also Hall, *Africans in Colonial Louisiana*.

4. Lorenzo J. Green and Carter G. Woodson, *The Negro Wage Earner* (Chicago: Association for the Study of Negro Life and History, 1930), 3–5.

5. Robin Kelley, *Race Rebels: Culture, Politics, and the Black Working Class* (New York: Simon and Schuster, 1996), 32. For more on "nigger work" as racialized/caste-specific labor, see David G. Embrick and Kasey Henricks, "Intersections in Everyday Conversations: Racetalk, Classtalk, and Gendertalk in the Workplace," in *Routledge International Handbook of Race, Class, and Gender*, ed. Shirley A. Jackson (London: Routledge, 2014), 56–57.

6. Allyson Hobbs, *A Chosen Exile: A History of Racial Passing in American Life* (Cambridge, MA: Harvard University Press, 2014), 34.

7. Roediger, *Working Toward Whiteness*, 12–13.

8. "Hayti and Immigration Thither," *New Orleans Daily Picayune*, July 16, 1859.

9. Lomax, *Mister Jelly Roll*, 69–71.

10. Bruce Laurie, *Artisans into Workers: Labor in Nineteenth-Century America* (New York: Noonday Press, 1989), 215–16. Regarding the nature of the preindustrial economy of the southern United States, scholars like Adam Rothman (*Slave Country*), or William Dusinberre

in his study of rice on the East Coast, *Them Dark Days: Slavery in the American Rice Swamps* (Athens: University of Georgia Press, 2000), have argued that the American slave system was embedded in a much larger capitalist economy that dictated the nature of production on plantations just as much as it dictated the nature of production in factories. For other views, see Richard Follett, who, in *The Sugar Masters* (Baton Rouge: Louisiana State University Press, 2005), suggests that the American plantation system, while ruthlessly capitalistic, still employed preindustrial strategies of paternalistic control and exploitation of labor against enslaved workforces in Louisiana's sugar fields.

11. Laurie, *Artisans into Workers*, 215–16.

12. Laurie, *Artisans into Workers*, 215–16; and Myrdal, *The Negro Problem and Modern Democracy*, 1102–3.

13. Hall, *Labor Struggles in the Deep South*, 219. For extensive commentary from Roediger on the limitations of Hall's radical egalitarianism, see his foreword to Hall's book, 17–22.

14. Hall, *Labor Struggles in the Deep South*, 219.

15. Arnesen, *Waterfront Workers of New Orleans*, 32–33.

16. Roger W. Shugg, "The General Strike of 1892," *Louisiana Historical Quarterly* 21 (April 1938): 545–60, quote from page 547.

17. See Jackson, *New Orleans in the Gilded Age*, 226–30.

18. For primary accounts of the New Orleans General Strike of 1892, see "Labor Trouble in New Orleans," *New York Times*, November 5, 1892; "New Orleans' Big Strike," *Washington Post*, November 8, 1892; "The New Orleans Strike," *New York Times*, November 9, 1892; and "Labor's Defeat in New Orleans," *New York Times*, December 12, 1892. For the most comprehensive historiographical treatments of biracial unionism in New Orleans and other port cities, see Eric Arnesen, "Race and Labour in a Southern US Port: New Orleans, 1860–1930," in *Dock Workers: International Explorations in Comparative Labour History, 1790–1970*, vol. 1, ed. Sam Davies et al. (Aldershot, UK: Ashgate Publishing, 2000), 38–56; and Arnesen's "Biracial Waterfront Unionism in the Age of Segregation," in *Waterfront Workers: New Perspectives on Race and Class*, ed. Calvin Winslow (Urbana: University of Illinois Press, 1998), 19–61.

19. Arnesen's work on the New Orleans waterfront is definitive. For an alternate view, however, see Daniel Rosenberg, *New Orleans Dockworkers: Race, Labor, and Unionism 1892–1923* (Albany: State University of New York Press, 1988).

20. Arnesen, *Waterfront Workers of New Orleans*, 14–16.

21. Martinet Archives, vol. 1, act 27, December 9, 1891, Screwmen's Benevolent Association of Louisiana Act of Incorporation, 140; XUNOBBA, box "1872–1940 and n.d.," three booklets containing the names of officers of the Screwmen's Benevolent Association No. 1, including "Contract and Rules of Screwmen's Benevolent Association and Screwmen's Benevolent Association No. 1 (Colored)," and "Memorandum of Agreement Between Screwmen's Benev't Association and Screwmen's B. Ass'n No. 1 (Colored)" and "Constitution, Bylaws and Rules of Order of Screwmen's Benevolent Association No. 1 of Louisiana."

22. Lomax, *Mister Jelly Roll*, 84.

23. "Tureaud-Logsdon," 1–3.

24. "Tureaud-Logsdon," 1–3. Tureaud recalls his father "on more than one occasion" underestimating the costs of both materials and man-hours and being forced to draft his sons as free labor to deliver on projects that he had either underbid or mismanaged.

25. David Roediger, *The Wages of Whiteness: Race and the Making of the American Working Class* (New York: Verso, 1999), 142–46, esp. 145, where Roediger investigates the Irish immigrant laborer as the "white nigger." See also Laurie, *Artisans into Workers*, 26–27.

26. New Orleans Typographical Union No. 17 Collection, Earl K. Long Library, University of New Orleans; Calvin Moret, interview by author, October 20, 2010, notes in possession of author. Covington Hall also discusses New Orleans's Typographical Union in *Labor Struggles in the Deep South*, 27–29. Hall identifies Typographical Union No. 17 as a later iteration of an older syndicate called the New Orleans Typographical Society, which was in operation as early as 1811. See also Laurie, *Artisans into Workers*, 102.

27. Moret interview by author, and Christopher Porche West Papers, Amistad Research Center, box 2, folder 12, *Moret Mirror* (June 1960), "25 Years of Reliable Printing Service— January 1, 1932–1957: The Moret Press," 1, 4.

28. Kemp, *Martin Behrman of New Orleans*, 52.

29. Earl R. Barthé interview by author, July 20, 2013, notes in possession of author.

30. Kemp, *Martin Behrman of New Orleans*, 52.

31. William H. Davis Collection, Earl K. Long Library, University of New Orleans, ACC 74–1, Bricklayers, Masons, and Marble Masons' International Union No. 1 of Louisiana, Cash Ledger, July 16, 1908–November 2, 1911; ACC 74–3, Cash Ledger, July 1, 1920–June 19, 1930; ACC 74–6, Cash Ledger, January 6, 1949–June 19, 1958.

32. William H. Davis Collection, Earl K. Long Library, University of New Orleans, ACC 74–1, Bricklayers, Masons, and Marble Masons' International Union No. 1 of Louisiana, Cash Ledger, July 16, 1908–November 2, 1911.

33. William H. Davis Collection, Earl K. Long Library, University of New Orleans, ACC 74–1, Bricklayers, Masons, and Marble Masons' International Union No. 1 of Louisiana, Cash Ledger, July 16, 1908–November 2, 1911; ACC 74–3, Cash Ledger, July 1, 1920–June 19, 1930; ACC 74–6, Cash Ledger, January 6, 1949–June 19, 1958.

34. "Total for Year Reaches Nearly $30,000,000; Big Public Work," *New Orleans Times-Picayune*, May 20, 1923; front-page stories, *Times-Picayune*, May 20, 1923; "Co-operative Elects Cousins," *Times-Picayune*, May 20, 1923; "Five Apply at Italian," *Times-Picayune*, May 20, 1923; "Mutuals Closes Three," *Times-Picayune*, May 20, 1923; "Security Busy," *Times-Picayune*, May 20, 1923"; Eureka Approves Twenty-One," *Times-Picayune*, May 20, 1923; "Many Retailers Are Without Profit, Ad Men Are Told," *Times-Picayune*, June 7, 1923. See also Roger W. Babson, *Actions and Reactions: An Autobiography of Roger W. Babson* (New York: Harper and Brothers, 1935).

35. "Costs Have Doubled," *New Orleans Times-Picayune*, April 18, 1924; Hall, *Labor Struggles in the Deep South*, 219.

36. Barthé, *Rebuilding New Orleans.* Before he died, I asked Earl A. Barthé whether there were any records of the union dated prior to those available through the collection that he donated to the Earl K. Long Special Collections. He told me that there were some, along with other more personal artifacts, including photographs, but that these records were unsorted and in a box at his office on St. Bernard Avenue which was destroyed by the flood surge of Hurricane Katrina in 2005.

37. US Federal Census, Ancestry.com, 1860 Federal Census including Simon Ball accessed February 1, 2009. There is no census entry for either Simon or Jane Ball in the 1850 Census report for New Orleans. Aside from the Treadway case, which articulated the legal distinction between mixed-race people and "negros," Pierre Barthé appears listed as "mulatto" in every federal census between 1870 and 1920. Much of the inspiration for my research is rooted in a need to clarify that distinction between "negros/Blacks" and Creoles in Earl A. Barthé's narrative since he, himself, understood there to be a difference but was content to allow people to frame his narrative within the parameters of the dominant racial paradigm (that is, black/white) rather than engage what he knew to be a contentious debate over the "blackness" of Louisiana Creole people. Earl A. Barthé's obituary in the February 2, 2010, *New York Times* repeats a claim that he often made in interviews that he "integrated" the Plasterers' Union, but that claim begs the question: if the union included Creoles and whites (Irish) from the beginning, then who was there left to integrate if Creoles were "black"?

38. US Federal Census 1870, New Orleans Ward 5, Orleans, Louisiana, roll M593_521, page 73B, image 496, Family History Library film 552020. Earl A. Barthé incorrectly identifies Leon Barthé as his great-grandfather in a number of interviews, including the one published as a part of the Louisiana Folklife "Master Craftsmen of the Building Arts" series, available online. This erroneous version of his family history, including the story of the Barthé family roots in Haiti and Nice in the nineteenth century, also appears in Earl A. Barthé's entry page for National Heritage Fellows at the National Endowment for the Arts website, the NEA's "Master of Traditional Arts Education Guide," and at his entry page on KnowLa, the online encyclopedia of Louisiana culture and history. This is also the version of his family history publicized in his obituary in the February 2, 2010, *New York Times.* Leon Barthé is quoted in "The Labor Leagues. The Plasterers Hold A Special Meeting To Receive Their Bosses," *New Orleans Daily Picayune,* August 14, 1882. There are no existing records for this earlier Plasterers' Union.

39. Arthé Agnes Anthony, "The Negro Creole Community in New Orleans, 1880–1920: An Oral History," PhD diss., University of California, Irvine, 1978, 81–84.

40. Operative Plasterers' International Union of the US and Canada (hereafter OPIU) Local 93 Collection, Earl K. Long Library, University of New Orleans (hereafter "L93"), MSS 29–130, meeting minutes, bound vol., "November 1942–January 1945."

41. Cross-referencing rosters of Local 93 (from L93 correspondence), the meeting roll from minutes books of Fraternité No. 20 and l'Amite No. 27 (from the George Longe Papers), and NPS Militia 1812, www.nps.gov/jela/historyculture/upload/CHALTroopRoster.

pdf; Native Guard roster from Hollandsworth, *The Louisiana Native Guards,* "Appendix: Black Officers of the Native Guards." See also NPS-CIVIL, www.itd.nps.gov/cwss.

42. Terry Barthé, interview by author, June 7, 2009, notes in possession of author. I posed the clarifying question on the use of the curtain in response to an informal conversation I had with one of Herbert Gettridge's sons who mentioned that Creole "old timers" utilized the screen to protect their "secrets." I use a marketing term, "brand identity," to refer to that "unique set of brand associations that the brand strategist aspires to create or maintain" for purposes of promoting that brand on the open market.

43. "Raised to the Trade" was the common thematic motif of a collection of essays published by Beauchamp-Byrd and Vlach in a Louisiana Endowment for the Humanities publication, *Louisiana Cultural Vistas.* The article was a promotion for an eponymous exhibit at the Isaac Delgado Memorial Museum of Art in New Orleans, commemorated with a book by John Ethan Hankins and Steven Maklansky, *Raised to the Trade: Creole Building Arts of New Orleans* (Gretna, LA: Pelican Publishing Co., 2003). See also "Raised to the Trade: Creole Building Arts in New Orleans," *Louisiana Cultural Vistas,* Fall 2002, 26–39.

44. Earl A. Barthé, "2005 NEA National Heritage Fellowships: Creole Building Artisan Interview with Mary Eckstein," *National Endowment for the Arts,* July 2005, online (hereafter Barthé, Eckstein interview).

45. Barthé, Eckstein interview.

46. "Tureaud-Logsdon," 3.

47. Earl A. Barthé, interview by author, October 14, 2007, notes in possession of author (hereafter Earl A. Barthé interview 2007).

48. Barthé, Eckstein interview.

49. Advertisement, *Preservation in Print,* December 2007, 41.

50. Allen Sumas quoted in "Raised to the Trade: The Craftsmen," *Louisiana Cultural Vistas,* Fall 2002, 31.

51. US Federal Census 1870, New Orleans Ward 5, Orleans, Louisiana, roll M593_521, page 73B, image 496, Family History Library microfilm 552020; NPS Militia 1812, www.nps.gov/jela/historyculture/upload/CHALTroopRoster.pdf; Native Guard roster from Hollandsworth, *The Louisiana Native Guards,* "Appendix: Black Officers of the Native Guards." See also NPS-CIVIL, www.itd.nps.gov/cwss; advertisement for cotton blankets "suitable for New Orleans, Spanish Islands and West India Markets" by "Lafitte, Barthe and Co.," in *American & Commercial Daily Advertiser* (Baltimore), January 31, 1814; advertisement for fabrics in *Baltimore Patriot & Evening Advertiser,* December 14, 1814; Lafitte, Barthe & Co., Inward Slave Manifests for the Port of New Orleans, entry #10, record group 36, microfilm roll 1 of 25 (1818–20), National Archives. George Longe Papers, minutes books for meetings of Fraternité No. 20 and l'Amite No. 27 show Antoine Barthé joining the lodge with a man identified as F. Carriere. By 1880, Antoine Barthé is conducting meetings and directing orders of business. According to Earl Barthé, his family origins are in Nice, France, and Haiti, and it does seem that Antoine's wife, Louise Duval, had maternal roots in Haiti.

52. See L93; there are no documents or correspondence in the entire collection that are not in English. The OPIU, the parent union of Local 93, became affiliated with the AFL in 1908 as a part of the Building Trades Department and was a thoroughly Anglophone organization.

53. Herbert Gettridge, interview by author, February 21, 2009, notes in possession of author (hereafter Gettridge interview 2009).

54. Earl A. Barthé interview 2007.

55. Gettridge interview 2009.

56. Gaudin, "Autocrats and All Saints," 29–30.

57. Louis Armstrong, *Louis Armstrong: In His Own Words*, ed. Thomas Brothers, (New York: Oxford University Press, 1999), 160.

58. Earl A. Barthé interview 2007.

59. L93, 29–50, cashbook, bound vol., July 1925–March 1932 and May 1934–September 1935, showing dues paid with explanations of lapsed membership where applicable.

60. Draft-registration cards for Clement Barthé, Henry Joseph Tio, and Louis Adolphe Lawrence, Ancestry.com. US World War I Draft Registration Cards, 1917–18 database, Provo, UT, Ancestry.com Operations Inc., 2005, original data from US Selective Service System, World War I Selective Service System Draft Registration Cards, 1917–18, Washington, DC: National Archives and Records Administration, microfilm 1509, 4,582 rolls.

61. "Tureaud-Logsdon," 66–67.

62. "Tureaud-Logsdon," 67–68.

63. "Tureaud-Logsdon," 67–73.

64. Emanuel and Tureaud, *A More Noble Cause*, 26.

65. "Tureaud-Logsdon," 73.

66. Emanuel and Tureaud, *A More Noble Cause*, 24–25; Beth Thompkins Bates, *Pullman Porters and the Rise of Protest Politics in Black America, 1925–1945* (Chapel Hill: University of North Carolina Press, 2001), 18–20.

67. Emanuel and Tureaud, *A More Noble Cause*, 25.

68. Emanuel and Tureaud, *A More Noble Cause*, 25–33.

69. Abdelkrim Dekhakhena, *Blacks in the New Deal: The Shift from an Electoral Tradition and its Legacy* (Hamburg, Germany: Anchor Academic Publishing, 2014), 7.

70. See Stephan Thernstrom and Abigail Thernstrom, *America in Black and White: One Nation, Indivisible* (New York: Simon and Schuster, 1997), for a comprehensive treatment on the effect of New Deal legislation on Blacks in the United States and the role that institutionalized racism played in limiting Black access to New Deal benefits.

71. L93, MSS 29–126, meeting minutes, bound vol., August 1935–Sept. 1937, 76–80.

72. L93, MSS 29–127, 29–137, meeting minutes, bound vol., September 1937 and April 1963, 93–96.

73. L93, MSS 29–126, meeting minutes, bound vol., August 1935–September 1937, 59. Biographical information on John J. Monahan from New Orleans, Louisiana Birth Records

Index, 1790–1899, vol. 102: 1153; and John J. Monahan, US Federal Census 1930, New Orleans, Louisiana, roll 810, page 40A, enumeration district 0214, image 552.0, Family History Library microfilm 2340545.

74. L93, MSS 29–126, meeting minutes, bound vol., August 1935–September 1937, 59–63.

75. L93, MSS 29–126, meeting minutes, bound vol., August 1935–September 1937, 74–76.

76. L93, MSS 29–126, meeting minutes, bound vol., August 1935–September 1937, 94–96.

77. Gettridge interview 2009; Local 93 membership application, "Herbert Gettridge, 1947," L93, MSS 29–113, folder "membership applications." I describe Gettridge as "non-Creole identified" because, although he did not identify himself as Creole, his family still had historical social connections to the New Orleans Creole community. Given his mother's Creole roots, Gettridge himself certainly had a claim to a Creole identity. Yet, when I asked him why he did not consider himself Creole, his reply was that "no one ever asked me."

78. Gettridge interview 2009.

79. Gettridge interview 2009; Local 93 membership application, "Herbert Gettridge, 1947," L93, MSS 29–113, folder "membership applications." The job of a "mule skinner" consisted of entering the cargo hold of a ship, wrangling animals and unloading them from the vessel. Gettridge suggested that his father had suffered a number of concussions throughout his time working on the river in this capacity. Through my own experience working as a builder and painter in New Orleans, I encountered older craftsmen who all recognized the name "Gettridge" and who immediately associated that name with "the Wizard."

80. Gettridge interview 2009.

81. Gettridge interview 2009; Local 93 membership application, "Herbert Gettridge, 1947," L93, MSS 29–113, folder "membership applications"; Earl A. Barthé interview 2007.

82. "Tureaud-Logsdon," 21–23.

83. "Tureaud-Logsdon," 21–23.

5. LEARNING AMERICAN AT SCHOOL (AND CHURCH)

1. Adam Fairclough, *Teaching Equality: Black Schools in the Age of Jim Crow* (Athens: University of Georgia Press, 2001), 42–44; Kevin K. Gaines, "Racial Uplift Ideology in the Era of 'the Negro Problem,'" *Freedom's Story*, TeacherServe, National Humanities Center, online. Racial pride and uplift were crucial components of black education in New Orleans; see "A Tentative Approach to Negro History for Use in Grades 1–4 in New Orleans Colored Public Schools," George Longe Papers, box 2, folder 7; George Longe, "The Study of the Negro," *The Crisis*, October 1936, 304, 309.

2. "Tureaud-Logsdon," 21–23.

3. W. E. B. Du Bois, *Black Reconstruction in America: Toward a History of the Part That Black Folk Played in the Attempt to Reconstruct Democracy in America, 1860–1880* (New York: Simon and Schuster, 1935), 638.

4. Lomax, *Mister Jelly Roll*, 103–5.

5. A. A. Gunby, *Two Addresses on Negro Education in the South* (New Orleans: H.C. Thomason, 1890), 3–4.

6. Lucy Semmes Orrick, "Along the Color Line," *National Magazine*, November 1904, 172–75.

7. See Rayford Logan, *The Negro in American Life and Thought: The Nadir, 1877–1901* (New York: Dial Press, 1954).

8. See Albert D. Kirwan, *Revolt of the Rednecks: Mississippi Politics, 1876–1925* (Lexington: University Press of Kentucky, 2011).

9. James K. Vardaman, "A Governor Bitterly Opposes Negro Education," *Leslie's Monthly Magazine,* February 4, 1904.

10. Vardaman, "A Governor Bitterly Opposes Negro Education." The literature on black people's supposed biological predisposition to criminality is too extensive to list here, although Ernest Hooton's work stands out as the most significant of the early twentieth century, including *The American Criminal: An Anthropological Study,* vol. 1 (Cambridge, MA: Harvard University Press, 1939), and *Crime and the Man* (Cambridge, MA: Harvard University Press, 1939). One of the earliest works to assert essential criminality to people of African descent in the United States was Frederick Hoffman's *Race Traits and Tendencies of the American Negro* (New York: Macmillan Co., 1896). For critical treatments, see W. E. B. Du Bois, *The Philadelphia Negro* (1899; Philadelphia: University of Pennsylvania Press, 2007), and Khalil Gibran Muhammad, *The Condemnation of Blackness: Race, Crime, and the Making of Modern Urban America* (Cambridge, MA: Harvard University Press, 2010).

11. John T. Trowbridge, *A Picture of the Desolated States and the Work of Restoration, 1865–1868* (Hartford, CT, 1868), 392, quoted in Fischer, *The Segregation Struggle in Louisiana,* 23.

12. Carter G. Woodson, *The Mis-Education of the Negro* (New York: Start Publishing, 2013), 122–25.

13. Woodson, *The Mis-Education of the Negro,* 121.

14. Beverly Jacques Anderson, *Cherished Memories: Snapshots of Life and Lessons from a 1950s New Orleans Creole Village* (Bloomington, IN: iUniverse, 2011), 56–58.

15. "Valena C. Jones United Methodist Church," *Hancock County Historical Society,* online.

16. Fannie C. Williams Papers, 1882–1980, Amistad Research Center, Tulane University, New Orleans (hereafter Fannie C. Williams Papers), scope and biographical notes.

17. Fairclough, *Teaching Equality,* 43; "Tureaud-Logsdon," 52. It also bears saying that "bucket of blood" as an idiom or turn of phrase is not unique to Jones School or even the city itself and has been assigned to places known for violence in other locales as far removed from New Orleans as New York City (where it referred to a tenement house) and even Cornwall, UK, where a pub in Phillack, Hayle, bears the name. Even in contemporary times, the phrase "bucket of blood school" is used in New Orleans to denote schools with reputations for violence such as stabbings and shootings.

18. Fannie C. Williams Papers, scope and biographical notes. See also Fairclough, *Teaching Equality,* 43, and Emanuel and Tureaud, *A More Noble Cause,* 18–19.

19. A. S. "Doc" Young, "Are Creoles Negroes?" *Jet*, June 25, 1953, 12–15.

20. Mr. John Williams, interview by Wendy Ann Gaudin, March 13, 2002, New Orleans, quoted in Gaudin, "Autocrats and All Saints," 67.

21. Fannie C. Williams Papers, box 2, folder 10, "The Moving Finger," 1935–39, publication of the Senior Normal Class of Valena C. Jones Normal and Practice School of New Orleans.

22. See Frank Cody, "Americanization Courses in the Public Schools," *English Journal* 7, no. 10 (1918): 615–22.

23. Upton Sinclair, *The Goslings: A Study of the American Schools* (Pasadena, CA: Upton Sinclair, 1924), 26.

24. Sarah Towles Reed Collection, Earl K. Long Library, University of New Orleans (hereafter STR), box 121–27, bound pamphlet, "Statistical Report of the New Orleans Public Schools of the Parish of Orleans for the Session 1927–1928."

25. T. Harry Williams, *Huey Long* (New York: Alfred A. Knopf, 1969), 701–6.

26. STR, box 121–27, folder "File New Orleans Public Schools of New Orleans Oct 13, 1939," letter (unaddressed, unsigned) written on behalf of Negro workers and schools addressed to "Honorable members of Orleans Parish School Board." See also "Tureaud-Logsdon," 50–52, and Emanuel and Tureaud, *A More Nobel Cause,* 17–20.

27. STR, box 121–12, Union Correspondence 1946 and 1947, folder "N.O. Classroom Teachers Fed Correspondence," February 23–March 19, 1946, letter to Orleans Parish School Board from "The Colored Educational Alliance," March 6, 1946.

28. STR, box 121–11, Union Correspondence 1944 and 1945, folder July 14–16, 1945, letter from Classroom Teachers Association to Mrs. F. Gordon Eberle, President of New Orleans Federation of Clubs.

29. Williams, *Huey Long,* 702.

30. See also Ochs, *A Black Patriot and a White Priest,* and Bell, *Revolution, Romanticism, and the Afro-Creole Protest Tradition,* 242–46.

31. Emanuel and Tureaud, *A More Noble Cause,* 12–13; "Tureaud-Logsdon," 25–26.

32. Charles B. Rousséve Papers, Amistad Research Center, Tulane University, New Orleans, box 3, folder 11: "Collected Items Manuscript of history of St. Louis School [New Orleans] by Sister M. Georgiana Rockwell, 1987." See also Lucile L. Hutton Papers, 1850–1988, Amistad Research Center, Tulane University, New Orleans, ser. 9, box 17, folder 2: "Couvent Marie: Madame Veuve Bernard Couvent, address by Wilson Pecot; History and Origin of the Marie C. Couvent School at 2021 Pauger Street, by Lawrence A. Young, 1940, 1963." See also Desdunes, *Our People and Our History,* 101–5; and Elizabeth Clark Neidenbach, "Marie Couvent," In *KnowLa Encyclopedia of Louisiana,* ed. David Johnson, Louisiana Endowment for the Humanities, March 15, 2011, online.

33. St. Louis [Couvent] School Collection, box "CIOA [Couvent] / St. Louis School: Meeting Minutes for Board of Directors 1921–1942 v. 88," Archives of the Archdiocese of New Orleans, bound vol., "History of the Catholic Indigent Orphan Institute Dauphine and Touro Streets, Destroyed by the Hurricane September 1915 rebuilt in 1916," published by

the board of directors; Charles Rousséve Papers, "Collected Items Manuscript of History of St. Louis School [New Orleans] by Sister M. Georgiana Rockwell, 1987."

34. Carol Glatz, "Pope Brings African-American Foundress One Step Closer to Sainthood," *Catholic News Service,* March 29, 2010, online.

35. James B. Bennett, *Religion and the Rise of Jim Crow in New Orleans* (Princeton, NJ: Princeton University Press, 2005), 154–55.

36. Sister Mary Bernard Deggs, *No Cross, No Crown: Black Nuns in Nineteenth-Century New Orleans,* ed. Virginia Meacham Gould and Charles E. Nolan (Bloomington: Indiana University Press, 2001), 184–86.

37. See Edward T. Brett, *The New Orleans Sisters of the Holy Family: African American Missionaries to the Garifuna of Belize* (Notre Dame, IN: University of Notre Dame Press, 2012).

38. Brett, *The New Orleans Sisters of the Holy Family,* 217.

39. St. Katharine Drexel, Xavier University Archives Louisiana Corporation Minutes Books, folder 1, "Correspondence Archbishop Jansenns to Mother Katharine, Mother Katharine to the Sisters in New Orleans" (hereafter "Janssens-Drexel Correspondence"), letter from Katharine Drexel to Sisters, "1914 or 1915," numbered pages 681–84.

40. "History of St. Mary's Academy," *St. Mary's Academy,* online.

41. Bennett, *Religion and the Rise of Jim Crow,* 148–64.

42. Francis Janssens, 1892 report to the Commission for Catholic Missions among Colored People and Indians, quoted in John T. Gillard, *The Catholic Church and the American Negro* (Baltimore: Josephite Press, 1929), 122.

43. On archdiocesan debt after the Civil War, see Marie Louise Points, "New Orleans," *The Catholic Encyclopedia,* with original citations, vol. 11 (New York: Robert Appleton Co., 1911). Using data compiled by Sahr at University of Oregon, $600,000 in 1879 translates to $5,769,230.76 in 2014, which is certainly no small amount!

44. Bennett, *Religion and the Rise of Jim Crow,* 151.

45. Bennett, *Religion and the Rise of Jim Crow,* 174–200; John Allan Reyhner and Jeanne M. Oyawin Eder, *American Indian Education: A History* (Norman: University of Oklahoma Press, 2006), 85–86.

46. Janssens-Drexel Correspondence, letter to Katharine Drexel, January 14, 1892.

47. "Katharine Drexel (1858–1955)," *The Vatican,* www.vatican.va/news_services/liturgy /saints/ns_lit_doc_20001001_katharine-drexel_en.html.

48. Janssens-Drexel Correspondence, letter to Katharine Drexel, January 22, 1892.

49. Janssens-Drexel Correspondence, letter to Katharine Drexel, February 29, 1892.

50. Janssens-Drexel Correspondence, letter to Katharine Drexel, April 10, 1892.

51. Annemarie Kasteel, *Francis Janssens, 1843–1897: A Dutch American Prelate* (Lafayette: University of Southwestern Louisiana, 1992), 303; see also "Tureaud-Logsdon," 27–30.

52. See Ochs, *A Black Patriot and a White Priest,* 68–87, and Bell, *Revolution, Romanticism, and the Afro-Creole Protest Tradition,* 242–46.

53. John R. Slattery, "John Henry Dorsey, A Colored Man, Was Ordained a Priest by His Eminence Cardinal Gibbons," sermon, Josephite Fathers' Archives, John Dorsey File; Stephen J. Ochs, "The Ordeal of the Black Priest," *U.S. Catholic Historian* 5, no. 1 (1986): 45. For a more comprehensive treatment of the early years of the Josephite mission in New Orleans, see Stephen J. Ochs, *Desegregating the Altar: Josephites and the Struggle for Black Priests, 1871–1960* (Baton Rouge: Louisiana State University Press, 1990).

54. "Tureaud-Logsdon," 27.

55. Corpus Christi Parish, "Looking Back," September 16, 1941, historical pamphlet published in commemoration of the twenty-fifth anniversary of the founding of Corpus Christi Parish, copy in possession of author, 1–3; Bennett, *Religion and the Rise of Jim Crow*, 206–7.

56. Corpus Christi Parish, "Looking Back."

57. Earl A. Barthé interview 2007.

58. Ken Jenkins, Betty Charbonnet Reid Soskin, and Lisa Henderson, "Thirteen Generations of the Charbonnet Family Tree: Part Two, 1900–1960," *Safero: Collections of an African American Freedom Fighter, Journalist, Novelist and Teller of Stories,* online. See also Jari C. Honora, "1920 KPC Convention, Corpus Christi Parish, New Orleans," *Creolegen: Creole History and Genealogy,* online.

59. "Tureaud-Logsdon," 32; "Introduction," *The Claverite* 92 (Summer 2009): 2–3; roster from Knights of Peter Claver, Father John A. Clarke Council No. 29 Collection, Earl K. Long Library, University of New Orleans, bound journal, "Roll Call, Resolutions, Minutes, 1929–1938," 2–4. See also Bennett, *Religion and the Rise of Jim Crow*, 225–27.

60. Dugar, "I Am What I Say I Am," 17–19; Bennett, *Religion and the Rise of Jim Crow,* 227; Fairclough, *Race and Democracy,* 14.

61. Corpus Christi Parish, "Looking Back," 11.

62. Norman R. Smith, *Footprints of Black Louisiana* (Bloomington, IN: Xlibris, 2010), 12–13; see also Fairclough, *Race and Democracy,* 7.

63. Clifford E. Trafzer, Jean A. Keller, and Lorene Sisquoc, *Boarding School Blues: Revisiting American Indian Educational Experiences* (Lincoln: University of Nebraska Press, 2006), 155–57.

64. Mary J. Oates, *The Catholic Philanthropic Tradition in America* (Bloomington: Indiana University Press, 1995), 65–71; Amelia V. Katanski, *Learning to Write "Indian": The Boarding-School Experience and American Indian Literature* (Norman: University of Oklahoma Press, 2005), 32. See also "Saint Catherine Industrial Indian School," *New Mexico History.org,* online; and "St. Joseph Indian Normal School (also known as Drexel Hall) in Rensselaer, Indiana," *Faith Fabric Local History Books,* online; "The History of St. Michael Indian School," *St. Michael Indian School,* online.

65. Katharine Drexel, Janssens-Drexel Correspondence, letter from Katharine Drexel to Sisters, dated "1915," numbered pages 698–99.

66. Drexel to Sisters, dated "1915"; see also "The History of Xavier," *Xavier University of New Orleans,* online. A Louisiana historical marker on the building of De La Salle High

School at 5300 St. Charles Avenue identifies the location of New Orleans University, which would eventually merge with Straight College to form Dillard University.

67. STR, box 121–12, Union Correspondence 1946 and 1947, folder "N.O. Classroom Teachers Fed correspondence," June 30–August 30, 1946; anonymous anti-Catholic letter to New Orleans Teachers' Federation, August 5, 1946.

CONCLUSION: CREOLE AMERICANS

1. Martin, "The Creoles Promised Treaty Rights."

2. Henry Oubre, interview by author, July 28, 2013, recording in possession of author.

3. Oubre interview, July 28, 2013.

4. Oubre interview, July 28, 2013.

5. Oubre interview, July 28, 2013.

6. See Bliss Broyard, *One Drop: My Father's Hidden Life—A Story of Race and Family Secrets* (New York: Little, Brown and Co., 2014), and Joyce Johnson, "Passing Strange," *New York Times*, October 21, 2007.

7. Irving, *A Tour on the Prairies*, 19–20.

8. Juvenile Cooperators, box 1, folder "correspondence 1915, 1918–1921, 1930–1935 and n.d.," letter from Ernest Cherrie, MD, September 6, 1933.

BIBLIOGRAPHY

PRIMARY SOURCES

Archival Materials

Amistad Research Center, Tulane University, New Orleans.
    Hutton, Lucille L., Papers.
    Longe, George, Collection.
    Rousséve, Charles B., Papers.
    Tureaud, Alexander Pierre, Collection.
    West, Christopher Porche, Collection.
    Williams, Fannie C., Papers.
Archives Nationales de France.
    Archives de Colonies.
Archives of the Archdiocese of New Orleans.
    St. Louis School Collection (Couvent School).
Earl K. Long Library Special Collections, University of New Orleans.
    Boyer, A. P., Collection.
    Christian, Marcus B., Collection.
    Davis, William H., Collection.
    Grandjean, Rene, Collection.
    Knights of Peter Claver, Father John A. Clarke Council No. 29 Collection.
    National Association for the Advancement of Colored People (New Orleans Branch) Collection.
    New Orleans Typographical Union No. 17 Collection.
    Operative Plasterers and Cement Finishers International Union Local 93 Collection.

Reed, Sarah Towles, Collection.
Société des Francs Amis Collection.
Société des Jeunes Amis Collection.
Tureaud, A. P., Collection.
Howard-Tilton Library Louisiana Special Collections, Tulane University, New Orleans.
Augustin, Wogan, Labranche Family Papers.
King, Grace, Papers, 1906–1920.
The Negro South: Progress thru Understanding and Goodwill. New Orleans: Negro South, 1946.
Josephite Fathers' Archives, Josephite Headquarters, Baltimore.
Dorsey, John, File.
New Orleans City Archives, Main Branch New Orleans Public Library.
Behrman, Martin, Collection.
Schomburg Center for Research in Black Culture, New York.
Carnegie-Myrdal Papers.
United Negro Improvement Association, Records of the Central Division.
St. Martinville Parish Courthouse.
Conveyances.
Xavier University Archives and Special Collections, New Orleans.
New Orleans Black Benevolent Associations Collection.
Xavier University Louisiana Corporation Minutes Books.

Film

Griffith, D. W., dir. *The Birth of a Nation.* David W. Griffith Corp., 1915.

Historical Articles, Letters, Manuscripts, Memoirs, Pamphlets, and Plays

Alexander, W. S. "Straight University, New Orleans." *American Missionary,* August 1882.
Armstrong, Louis. *Louis Armstrong: In His Own Words,* ed. Thomas Brothers. New York: Oxford University Press, 1999.
Babson, Roger W. *Actions and Reactions: An Autobiography of Roger W. Babson.* New York: Harper and Brothers, 1935.
Boucicault, Dion. "The Octoroon: A Play in Four Acts." In *Dick's London Acting Edition of Standard English Plays and Comic Dramas.* New York: DeWitt Publishing House, 1859.

Christian Women's Exchange. *The Creole Cookery Book*. New Orleans: T. H. Thomason, 1885.

Cody, Frank. "Americanization Courses in the Public Schools," *English Journal* 7, no. 10 (1918): 615–22.

Corpus Christi Parish, New Orleans. "Looking Back." Historical pamphlet, September 16, 1941.

Deggs, Sister Mary Bernard. *No Cross, No Crown: Black Nuns in Nineteenth-Century New Orleans*, ed. Virginia Meacham Gould and Charles E. Nolan. Bloomington: Indiana University Press, 2001.

Desdunes, Rodolphe Lucien. *A Few Words to Dr. Du Bois: "With Malice Toward None."* New Orleans, 1907.

———. *Our People and Our History: Fifty Creole Portraits*. Baton Rouge: Louisiana State University Press, 1973.

Dixon, Thomas. *The Clansman: An Historical Romance of the Ku Klux Klan*. New York: Grosset & Dunlap, 1905.

Du Bois, W. E. B. *Black Reconstruction in America: Toward a History of the Part That Black Folk Played in the Attempt to Reconstruct Democracy in America, 1860–1880*. New York: Simon and Schuster, 1935.

———. *The Philadelphia Negro*. 1899. Philadelphia: University of Pennsylvania Press, 2007.

Dunbar-Nelson, Alice Moore. "People of Color in Louisiana." In *Creole*, ed. Kein.

Emilio, Louis F. *A Brave Black Regiment*. Cambridge, MA: Da Capo Press, 1995.

Garvey, Marcus. *The Philosophy and Opinions of Marcus Garvey, Or, Africa for the Africans*, vol. 1. Dover, MA: Majority Press, 1923.

Green, Lorenzo J., and Carter G. Woodson. *The Negro Wage Earner*. Chicago: Association for the Study of Negro Life and History, 1930.

Gunby, A. A. *Two Addresses on Negro Education in the South*. New Orleans: H. C. Thomason, 1890.

Hall, Covington. *Labor Struggles in the Deep South & Other Writings*, ed. David Roediger. Chicago: Charles H. Kerr Publishing Co., 1999.

Harris, L. M. "The Creoles of New Orleans." *Southern Collegian* 30 (January 1898).

Hearn, Lafcadio. *La Cuisine Creole*. Chicago: Hammond Press, 1885.

Hoffman, Frederick. *Race Traits and Tendencies of the American Negro*. New York: Macmillan Co., 1896.

Hooton, Ernest. *The American Criminal: An Anthropological Study*, vol. 1. Cambridge, MA: Harvard University Press, 1939.

———. *Crime and the Man*. Cambridge, MA: Harvard University Press, 1939.

Hurlbut, S. A. "Report of the Board of Education for Freedmen, Department of the Gulf, for the Year 1864." *American Memory: African American Perspectives,* pamphlets from the Daniel A. P. Murray Collection, 1818–1907, Library of Congress, memory.loc.gov/cgi-bin/query/r?ammem/murray:@field(DOCID+@lit(lcrbmrpt2315divo)).

Irving, Washington. *A Tour on the Prairies.* London: John Murray Albemarle Street, 1835.

Kemp, John R., ed. *Martin Behrman of New Orleans: Memoirs of a City Boss.* Baton Rouge: Louisiana State University Press, 1977.

Le Moyne, Pierre, Sieur d'Iberville. *Iberville's Gulf Journals,* trans. Richebourg McWilliams. Tuscaloosa: University of Alabama Press, 1991.

Lomax, Alan. *Mister Jelly Roll.* London: Pan Books, 1952.

Lomax, Alan, and Jelly Roll Morton. Library of Congress Narrative. Archived Folk Song 1648A, "Monologue of New Orleans funeral customs and the beginnings of Jazz, New Orleans Funeral Part 2 ('Flee as a Bird to the Mountain')."

Martin, Gilbert E., Sr. *French Creoles: A Shattered Nation.* Montgomery, AL: E-Booktime, 2006.

Olmsted, Frederick Law. *The Cotton Kingdom: A Traveller's Observations on Cotton and Slavery in the American Slave States, 1853–1861.* New York: Da Capo Press, 1996.

Orrick, Lucy Semmes. "Along the Color Line." *National Magazine,* November 1904, 172–75.

Points, Marie Louise. "New Orleans." *The Catholic Encyclopedia,* vol. 11. New York: Robert Appleton Co., 1911.

Reid, Thomas Mayne. *The Quadroon, or, A Lover's Adventure in Louisiana.* London: George W. Hyde, 1856.

Reid, Whitelaw. *After the War: A Southern Tour, May 1, 1865–May 1, 1866.* London: S. Low, Son and Marston, 1866.

Roosevelt, Theodore. *The New Nationalism.* New York: Outlook Publishing, 1910.

———. Letter to Richard Hurd, January 3, 1919. Transcript Division, Library of Congress Online. graphics2.snopes.com/politics/graphics/troosevelt.pdf.

Sinclair, Upton. *The Goslings: A Study of the American Schools.* Pasadena, CA: Upton Sinclair, 1924.

Trowbridge, John T. *A Picture of the Desolated States and the Work of Restoration, 1865–1868.* Hartford, CT, 1868.

Vardaman, James K. "A Governor Bitterly Opposes Negro Education." *Leslie's Monthly Magazine,* February 4, 1904.

Washington, Booker T. *The Negro Problem.* Radford, VA: Wilder, 2008.

Wilson, Harriet E. *Our Nig: or Sketches from the Life of a Free Black*. New York: Knopf, Doubleday Publishing Group, 2011.

Woods Directory: A Classified Colored Business, Professional, and Trade Directory of New Orleans, Louisiana. 2nd ed. New Orleans: Alan T. Woods, 1912.

Woodson, Carter G. *The Mis-Education of the Negro*. New York: Start Publishing, 2013.

Newspapers and Magazines

American & Commercial Daily Advertiser (Baltimore).

Baltimore Patriot & Evening Advertiser.

Brooklyn Daily Standard-Union.

Cleveland Gazette.

Detroit Plaindealer.

Harrisburg Evening News.

Indianapolis Freeman.

Jet.

New Orleans Bee.

New Orleans Daily Picayune.

New Orleans Times.

New Orleans Times-Picayune.

New Orleans Tribune.

New York Enterprise.

New York Times.

Niles Weekly Register.

Preservation in Print (New Orleans).

Sepia Socialite (New Orleans).

St. Paul Appeal. Washington Post.

Online Archival Collections

Ancestry.com.

"COLAS/COLIS Family Tree." trees.ancestry.com/tree/4276325/family?cfpid =-14653120.

"Lhota Family Tree." trees.ancestry.com/tree/26105659.

Louisiana Birth Records Index, 1790–1899.

Louisiana Marriages, 1718–1925.

New Orleans, Louisiana, Death Records Index, 1804–1949.

New Orleans, Louisiana, Death Records Index, 1877–1895.

Orleans Parish Death Indices, 1937–1948.

US Federal Census, 1850–1930.

Cornell University Law School.

"Brown, J., Opinion of the Court, Supreme Court of the United States, 163 US 537, Plessy vs. Ferguson." www.law.cornell.edu/supct/html/historics /USSC_CR_0163_0537_ZO.html.

Duhaime Legal Dictionary. www.duhaime.org.

Jim Crow Museum of Racist Memorabilia. www.ferris.edu/news/jimcrow/.

Library of Congress Online.

Taney, Chief Justice Roger B. "The *Dred Scott* Decision: Opinion of Chief Justice Taney with Introduction by Dr. J. H. Van Evrie." *American Memory: Slaves and the Courts, 1740–1860.* memory.loc.gov/cgibin/query/r? ammem/llst:@field%28DOCID+@lit%2811sto22d iv3%29 %29.

Library of Virginia.

Hening, William W., ed. *The Statutes at Large: Being a Collection of All the Laws of Virginia, from the First Session of the Legislature, in the Year 1619 ...* [1809–23]. www.lva.virginia.gov/public/guides/rn17_tithables.

National Archives and Records Administration, Washington DC.

Inward Slave Manifests for the Port of New Orleans, 1818–1820. www .afrigeneas.com/slavedata/Roll.1.1818-1820.html.

World War I Selective Service System Draft Registration Cards. www.archives .gov/research/military/ww1/draft-registration.

National Park Service of the US Department of the Interior.

"Civil War Soldiers and Sailors System." www.itd.nps.gov/cwss.

"Troop Roster Tennessee Volunteers & Militia, Kentucky Volunteers & Militia, Battalion of Free Men of Color, Louisiana Volunteers and Militia." 1812. www.nps.gov/jela/historyculture/upload/CHALTroopRoster.pdf.

Oral Histories and Interviews

Barthé, Earl A. "2005 NEA National Heritage Fellowships: Creole Building Artisan Interview with Mary Eckstein." *National Endowment for the Arts,* July 2005, arts. gov/honors/heritage/fellows/earl-barthé.

———. "Interview 5.30.07." *Rebuilding New Orleans One Voice at a Time: Earl A. Barthé.* New Orleans: New Orleans PodCasting, 2007. neworleanspodcasting .com/EarlBarthé.shtml/.

————. Interview by Darryl Barthé. New Orleans, October 14, 2007.

————. "More Than Just a Trade: Master Craftsmen of the Building Arts." *Folklife in Louisiana: Louisiana's Living Traditions,* ed. Laura Westbrook, 2004. www .louisianafolklife.org/Region5/noba/Ebarthe.html.

Barthé, Earl R. Interview by Darryl Barthé. Transcribed notes. New Orleans, July 20, 2013.

Barthé, Terry. Interview by Darryl Barthé. Transcribed notes. New Orleans, June 7, 2009.

Gettridge, Herbert. Interview by Darryl Barthé. Transcribed notes. New Orleans, February 21, 2009.

Oubre, Henry. Interview by Darryl Barthé. Recording. New Orleans, July 28, 2013.

Williams, Fannie C. Interview by A. S. "Doc" Young. In "Are Creoles Negroes?" *Jet,* June 25, 1953.

SECONDARY SOURCES
Chapters and Monographs

Aaker, David A. *Building Strong Brands.* New York: Simon and Schuster, 2009.

Adams, Christophe, Ian Peach, and Gregg Dahl, eds. *Metis in Canada: History, Identity, Law and Politics.* Edmonton: University of Alberta Press, 2013.

Andersen, Chris. *"Métis": Race, Recognition, and the Struggle for Indigenous Peoplehood.* Vancouver: University of British Columbia Press, 2014.

Anderson, Beverly Jacques. *Cherished Memories: Snapshots of Life and Lessons from a 1950s New Orleans Creole Village.* Bloomington, IN: iUniverse, 2011.

Anderson, R. Bentley. *Black, White, and Catholic.* Nashville: Vanderbilt University Press, 2005.

Arnesen, Eric. "Biracial Waterfront Unionism in the Age of Segregation." In *Waterfront Workers,* ed. Winslow, 19–61.

————. *Brotherhoods of Color: Black Railroad Workers and the Struggle for Equality.* Cambridge, MA: Harvard University Press, 2001.

————. "Race and Labour in a Southern US Port: New Orleans, 1860–1930." In *Dock Workers,* vol. 1, ed. Davies et al., 38–56.

————. *Waterfront Workers of New Orleans: Race, Class and Politics, 1863–1923.* Urbana: University of Illinois Press, 1991.

Asbury, Herbert. *The French Quarter: An Informal History of the New Orleans Underworld.* 1936. New York: Thunder's Mouth Press, 2003.

Bailey, Guy. "A Perspective on African American English." In *American Dialect Research: Celebrating the 100th anniversary of the American Dialect Society,*

1889–1989, ed. Dennis R. Preston. Philadelphia: John Benjamins Publishing Co., 1993.

Baron, Robert A., and Ana C. Cara, eds. *Creolization as Cultural Creativity.* Jackson: University Press of Mississippi, 2011.

Bastide, Roger. *The African Religions of Brazil: Toward a Sociology of the Interpenetration of Civilizations.* Baltimore: Johns Hopkins University Press, 1978.

Bates, Beth Thompkins. *Pullman Porters and the Rise of Protest Politics in Black America, 1925–1945.* Chapel Hill: University of North Carolina Press, 2001.

Beales, Carleton. *The Story of Huey P. Long.* Santa Barbara, CA: Greenwood Press, 1971.

Bell, Caryn Cossé. *Revolution, Romanticism, and the Afro-Creole Protest Tradition in Louisiana, 1718–1868.* Baton Rouge: Louisiana State University Press, 1995.

Bell, Caryn Cossé, and Joseph Logsdon. "The Americanization of Black New Orleans." In *Creole New Orleans,* ed. Hirsch and Logsdon.

Bellegarde-Smith, Patrick, ed. *Fragments of Bone: Neo-African Religions in a New World.* Urbana: University of Illinois Press. 2005.

Benfey, Christopher. *Degas in New Orleans: Encounters in the Creole World of Kate Chopin and George Washington Cable.* Berkeley: University of California Press, 1999.

Bennett, James B. *Religion and the Rise of Jim Crow in New Orleans.* Princeton, NJ: Princeton University Press, 2005.

Bernard, Shane K. *The Cajuns: Americanization of a People.* Jackson: University of Mississippi Press, 2003.

Berry, Jason . *The Spirit of Black Hawk: A Mystery of Africans and Indians.* Jackson: University Press of Mississippi, 1995.

Blanco, John D. *Frontier Constitutions: Christianity and Colonial Empire in the Nineteenth-Century Philippines.* Berkeley: University of California Press, 2009.

Blassingame, John W. *Black New Orleans, 1860–1880.* Chicago: University of Chicago Press, 1973.

Bond, Bradley G., ed. *French Colonial Louisiana and the Atlantic World.* Baton Rouge: Louisiana State University Press, 2005.

Boswell, Rosabelle. *Le Malaise Créole: Ethnic Identity in Mauritius.* New York: Berghahn Books, 2006.

Boyd, Michelle R. *Jim Crow Nostalgia: Reconstructing Race in Bronzeville.* Minneapolis: University of Minnesota Press, 2008.

Boulard, Gary. *Huey Long Invades New Orleans: The Siege of a City, 1934–1936.* Gretna, LA: Pelican Publishing, 1998.

Brandon, George. *Santeria from Africa to the New World: The Dead Sell Memories.* Bloomington: Indiana University Press, 1997.

Brasseaux, Carl A. *French, Cajun, Creole, Houma: A Primer on Francophone Louisiana.* Baton Rouge: Louisiana State University Press, 2005.

Brett, Edward T. *The New Orleans Sisters of the Holy Family: African American Missionaries to the Garifuna of Belize.* Notre Dame, IN: University of Notre Dame Press, 2012.

Brophy, Alfred L. *Reconstructing the Dreamland: The Tulsa Race Riot of 1921, Race Reparations, and Reconciliation.* New York: Oxford University Press, 2002.

Brothers, Thomas. *Louis Armstrong's New Orleans.* New York: W. W. Norton, 2006.

Brown, David, and Clive Webb. *Race in the American South: From Slavery to Civil Rights.* Edinburgh: Edinburgh University Press, 2007.

Brown, Leslie. *Upbuilding Black Durham: Gender, Class, and Black Community Development in the Jim Crow South.* Chapel Hill: University of North Carolina Press, 2008.

Brown, Ras Michael. *African-Atlantic Cultures and the South Carolina Lowcountry.* Cambridge, UK: Cambridge University Press, 2012.

Broyard, Bliss. *One Drop: My Father's Hidden Life—A Story of Race and Family Secrets.* New York: Little, Brown and Co., 2014.

Bumsted, J. M. *Dictionary of Manitoba Biography.* Winnipeg: University of Manitoba, 1999.

Burkholder, Zoë. *Color in the Classroom: How American Schools Taught Race, 1900–1954.* Oxford, UK: Oxford University Press, 2011.

Butel, Paul. *Histoire des Antilles Françaises: XVIIe–XXe siècle.* Paris: Perrin, 2007.

Bynum, Cornelius L. *A. Philip Randolph and the Struggle for Civil Rights.* Champaign: University of Illinois Press, 2010.

Campanella, Richard. *Bienville's Dilemma: A Historical Geography of New Orleans.* Lafayette, LA: Center for Louisiana Studies at University of Louisiana at Lafayette, 2008.

Canizares-Esguerra, Jorge, Matt D. Childs, and James Sidbury, eds. *The Black Urban Atlantic in the Age of the Slave Trade.* Philadelphia: University of Pennsylvania Press, 2013.

Cardoso, Hugo C., Alan N. Baxter, and Mário Pinharanda Nunes. *Ibero-Asian Creoles: Comparative Perspectives.* Amsterdam: John Benjamins Publishing, 2012.

Carter, Hodding, ed. *The Past as Prelude: New Orleans, 1718–1968.* Gretna, LA: Pelican Publishing, 2008.

Christian, Marcus. *Negro Ironworkers in Louisiana: 1718–1900.* Gretna, LA: Pelican Publishing, 1972.

Chute, Janet. "Ojibwa Leadership during the Fur Trade Era at Sault Ste. Marie." In *New Faces in the Fur Trade,* ed. Fiske, Sleeper-Smith, and Wicken.

———. *Shingwaukonse: A Century of Native Leadership.* Toronto: University of Toronto Press, 1998.

Clark, Emily. *The Strange History of the American Quadroon: Free Women of Color in the Revolutionary Atlantic World.* Chapel Hill: University of North Carolina Press, 2013.

Clemens, Elizabeth S., and Doug Guthrie. *Politics and Partnerships: The Role of Voluntary Associations in America's Political Past and Present.* Chicago: University of Chicago Press, 2010.

Clinton, Catherine, and Michael Gillespie, eds. *The Devils Lane: Sex and Race in the Early South.* New York: Oxford University Press, 1997.

Cohen, Robin, and Paola Toninato, eds. *The Creolization Reader: Studies in Mixed Identities and Cultures.* London: Routledge Press, 2009.

Collier, Gordon, and Ulrich Fleischmann, eds. *A Pepper-Pot of Cultures: Aspects of Creolization in the Caribbean.* Amsterdam: Editions Rodopi, 2003.

Collin, Rima and Richard H. *The New Orleans Cookbook.* New York: Knopf-Doubleday, 1987.

Conner, Randy P., and David Hatfield Sparks. *Queering Creole Spiritual Traditions: Lesbian, Gay, Bisexual, and Transgender Participation in African-Inspired Traditions in the Americas.* London: Routledge. 2004.

Cooper, William J., Jr., and Thomas E. Terrill. *The American South, a History.* Lanham, MD: Rowman and Littlefield, 2009.

Coppolaro, Lucia, and Francine McKenzie. *A Global History of Trade and Conflict Since 1500.* Basingstoke, UK: Palgrave-Macmillan, 2013.

Crichlow, Michaeline, and Patricia Northover. *Globalization and the Post-Creole Imagination: Notes on Fleeing the Plantation.* Durham, NC: Duke University Press, 2009.

Crouse, Nellis M. *Lemoyne D'Iberville: Soldier of New France.* Baton Rouge: Louisiana State University Press, 2001.

Crutcher, Michael Eugene. *Tremé: Race and Place in a New Orleans Neighborhood.* Athens: University of Georgia Press, 2010.

Curtin, Philip. *Africa Remembered: Narratives by West Africans in the Era of the Slave Trade.* Madison: University of Wisconsin Press, 1967.

Davies, Sam, et al., eds. *Dock Workers: International Explorations in Comparative Labour History, 1790–1970*, vol. 1. Aldershot, UK: Ashgate Publishing, 2000.

Davis, Jack F. *Race against Time: Culture and Separation in Natchez since 1940*. Baton Rouge: Louisiana State University Press, 2001.

Dekhakhena, Abdelkrim. *Blacks in the New Deal: The Shift from an Electoral Tradition and Its Legacy*. Hamburg, Germany: Anchor Academic Publishing, 2014.

Denton, Virginia Lantz. *Booker T. Washington and the Adult Education Movement*. Gainesville: University Press of Florida, 1993.

Dessens, Nathalie. *From Saint-Domingue to New Orleans: Migration and Influences*. Gainesville: University Press of Florida, 2007.

Dethloff, Henry C. *Huey P. Long: Southern Demagogue or American Democrat?* Lafayette: University of Southwestern Louisiana Press, 1976.

Dominguez, Virginia R. *White by Definition: Social Classification in Creole Louisiana*. New Brunswick, NJ: Rutgers University Press, 1986.

Dormon, James H., ed. *Creoles of Color of the Gulf South*. Knoxville: University of Tennessee Press, 1996.

Dray, Philip. *At the Hands of Persons Unknown: The Lynching of Black America*. New York: Random House, 2002.

Dusinberre, William. *Them Dark Days: Slavery in the American Rice Swamps*. Athens: University of Georgia Press, 2000.

Eckkrammer, Eva Martha. "On the Perception of 'Creole' Language and Identity in the Netherlands Antilles." In *A Pepper-Pot of Cultures*, ed. Collier and Fleischmann.

Edge, John T., Elizabeth S. D. Engelhardt, and Ted Ownby, eds. *The Larder: Food Studies Methods From the American South*. Athens: University of Georgia Press, 2013.

Emanuel, Rachel L., and Alexander P. Tureaud Jr. *A More Noble Cause: A. P. Tureaud and the Struggle for Civil Rights in Louisiana*. Baton Rouge: Louisiana State University Press, 2011.

Fabi, Maria Giulia. *Passing and the Rise of the African American Novel*. Champaign: University of Illinois Press, 2001.

Fairclough, Adam. *Race and Democracy: The Civil Rights Struggle in Louisiana, 1915–1972*. Athens: University of Georgia Press, 1995.

———. *Teaching Equality: Black Schools in the Age of Jim Crow*. Athens: University of Georgia Press, 2001.

Fandrich, Ina Johanna. *Marie Laveau: The Mysterious Voodoo Queen*. Lafayette: University of Louisiana at Lafayette, 2012.

Fichera, Sebastian. *Italy on the Pacific: San Francisco's Italian Americans.* Basingstoke, UK: Palgrave-MacMillan, 2011.

Finegan, Edward, Charles Albert Ferguson, Shirley Brice Heath, and John R. Rickford, eds. *Language in the USA: Themes for the Twenty-First Century.* Cambridge, UK: Cambridge University Press, 2004.

Finler, Joel Waldo. *The Hollywood Story.* New York: Wallflower Press, 2003.

Fischer, Roger A. *The Segregation Struggle in Louisiana, 1862–1877.* Urbana: University of Illinois Press, 1974.

Fiske, Jo-Anne, Susan Sleeper-Smith, and William Wicken. *New Faces in the Fur Trade: Selected Papers of the Seventh North American Fur Trade Conference, Halifax, Nova Scotia, 1995.* East Lansing: Michigan State University Press, 1998.

Follett, Richard. "Legacies of Enslavement." In *Slavery's Ghost,* ed. Follett, Foner, and Johnson.

———. *The Sugar Masters: Planters and Slaves in Louisiana's Cane World 1820–1860.* Baton Rouge: Louisiana State University Press, 2005.

Follett, Richard, Eric Foner, and Walter Johnson. *Slavery's Ghost: The Problem of Freedom in the Age of Emancipation.* Baltimore: Johns Hopkins University Press, 2011.

Folse, John. *The Encyclopedia of Cajun and Creole Cuisine.* Gonzales, LA: Chef John Folse & Co. Publishing, 2004.

Foster, Gaines M. *Ghosts of the Confederacy: Defeat, The Lost Cause, and the Emergence of The New South, 1865–1913.* Oxford, UK: Oxford University Press, 1987.

Franzen, Giep, and Sandra Moriarty. *The Science and Art of Branding.* Armonk, NY: M. E. Sharpe, 2008.

Fredrickson, George. *The Black Image in the White Mind: The Debate on Afro-American Character and Destiny, 1817–1914.* New York: Harper and Row, 1971.

———. *White Supremacy: A Comparative Study in American and South African History.* New York: Oxford University Press, 1981.

Frick, Carolyn E. *The Making of Haiti: The Saint Domingue Revolution from Below.* Knoxville: University of Tennessee Press, 1990.

Fugita, Stephen S., and David J. O'Brien. *Japanese American Ethnicity: The Persistence of Community.* Seattle: University of Washington Press, 1991.

Garrigus, John D. *Before Haiti: Race and Citizenship in French Saint-Domingue.* Basingstoke, UK: Palgrave-Macmillan, 2006.

Gaspar, David Barry, and Darlene Clark Hine, eds. *Beyond Bondage: Free Women of Color in the Americas.* Urbana: University of Illinois Press, 2004.

Gehman, Mary. "Visible Means of Support: Businesses, Professions, and Trades of Free People of Color." In *Creole,* ed. Kein.

Giggie, John M. *After Redemption: Jim Crow and the Transformation of African American Religion in the Delta, 1875–1915.* New York: Oxford University Press, 2007.

Gillard, John T. *The Catholic Church and the American Negro.* Baltimore: Josephite Press, 1929.

Gilroy, Paul. *The Black Atlantic: Modernity and Double Consciousness.* London: Verso Publishing, 1993.

Gitlin, Jay. *The Bourgeois Frontier: French Towns, French Traders, and American Expansion.* New Haven, CT: Yale University Press, 2010.

Gleeson, David T. *The Irish in the South, 1815–1877.* Chapel Hill: University of North Carolina Press, 2001.

Glissant, Éduard. *Poetics of Relation.* Ann Arbor: University of Michigan Press, 1997.

Gold, Martin B. *Forbidden Citizens: Chinese Exclusion and the U.S. Congress: A Legislative History.* Alexandria, VA: Capitol Net Inc., 2012.

Golden, Eve. *Golden Images: 41 Essays on Silent Film Stars.* Jefferson, NC: McFarland and Co., 2001.

Gomez, Michael Angelo. *Exchanging Our Country Marks: The Transformation of African Identities in the Colonial and Antebellum South.* Chapel Hill: University of North Carolina Press, 1998.

Gould, Virginia Meacham. "The Free Creoles of Color of the Antebellum Gulf Ports of Mobile and Pensacola: A Struggle for the Middle Ground." In *Creoles of Color of the Gulf South,* ed. Dormon.

Hair, William Ivy. *Carnival of Fury: Robert Charles and the New Orleans Race Riot of 1900.* Baton Rouge: Louisiana State University Press, 2008.

———. *The Kingfish and His Realm: The Life and Times of Huey P. Long.* Baton Rouge: Louisiana State University Press, 1991.

Hale, Grace Elizabeth. *Making Whiteness: The Culture of Segregation in the South, 1890–1940.* New York: Pantheon Books, 1998.

Hall, Gwendolyn Midlo. "African Women in French and Spanish Louisiana: Origins, Roles, Family, Work, Treatment," in *The Devil's Lane: Sex and Race in the Early South,* ed. Catherine Clinton and Michael Gillespie. New York: Oxford University Press, 1997.

———. *Africans in Colonial Louisiana: The Development of Afro-Creole Culture in the Eighteenth Century.* Baton Rouge: Louisiana State University Press, 1992.

———. "The Formation of Afro-Creole Culture." In *Creole New Orleans,* ed. Hirsch and Logsdon.

Hanger, Kimberly S. *Bounded Lives, Bounded Places: Free Black Society in Colonial New Orleans, 1769–1803.* Durham, NC: Duke University Press, 1997.

———. "Landlords, Shopkeepers, Farmers, and Slave Owners: Free Black Female Property-Holders in Colonial New Orleans." In *Beyond Bondage,* ed. Gaspar and Hine.

Hankins, John Ethan, and Steven Maklansky. *Raised to the Trade: Creole Building Arts of New Orleans.* Gretna, LA: Pelican Publishing Co., 2003.

Hannerz, Ulf. *Cultural Complexity.* New York: Columbia University Press, 1992.

Heinl, Robert Debs, and Nancy Gordon Heinl. *Written in Blood: The Story of the Haitian People, 1492–1995.* Lanham, MD: University Press of America, 2005.

Hele, Karl S. *Lines Drawn Upon the Water: First Nations and the Great Lakes Borders and Borderlands.* Waterloo, ON: Wilfrid Laurier University Press, 2008.

Hersch, Charles B. *Subversive Sounds: Race and the Birth of Jazz in New Orleans.* Chicago: University of Chicago Press, 2008.

Heywood, Linda M., ed. *Central Africans and Cultural Transformations in the American Diaspora.* Cambridge, UK: Cambridge University Press, 2002.

Hirsch, Arnold R., and Joseph Logsdon, eds. *Creole New Orleans: Race and Americanization.* Baton Rouge: Louisiana State University Press, 1992.

Hischak, Thomas S. *American Literature on Stage and Screen: 525 Works and Their Adaptations.* Jefferson, NC: McFarland and Co., 2012.

Hiyashi, Brian Masaru. *For the Sake of Our Japanese Brethren: Assimilation, Nationalism, and Protestantism Among the Japanese of Los Angeles, 1895–1942.* Palo Alto: Stanford University Press, 1995.

Hobbs, Allyson. *A Chosen Exile: A History of Racial Passing in American Life.* Cambridge, MA: Harvard University Press, 2014.

Hogue, James Keith. *Uncivil War: Five New Orleans Street Battles and the Rise and Fall of Radical Reconstruction.* Baton Rouge: Louisiana State University Press, 2006.

Hollandsworth, James G. *The Louisiana Native Guards: The Black Military Experience During the Civil War.* Baton Rouge: Louisiana State University Press, 1995.

Hughes, Cheryl C. D. *Mother Katharine Drexel: The Riches-To-Rags Life Story of an American Catholic Saint.* Grand Rapids, MI: Wm. B. Eerdmans, 2014.

Hurston, Zora Neale. *Mules and Men.* 1936. New York: HarperCollins, 2009.

Ingersoll, Thomas N. *Mammon and Manon in Early New Orleans: The First Slave Society in the Deep South, 1718–1819.* Knoxville: University of Tennessee Press, 1999.

Jackson, Joy J. *New Orleans in the Gilded Age: Politics and Urban Progress, 1880–1896.* Baton Rouge: Louisiana State University Press, 1969.

Jackson, Shirley A., ed. *Routledge International Handbook of Race, Class, and Gender.* London: Routledge, 2014.

Jacobson, Matthew Frye. *Whiteness of a Different Color: European Immigrants and the Alchemy of Race.* Cambridge, MA: Harvard University Press, 1999.

Jiobu, Robert M. *Ethnicity and Assimilation: Blacks, Chinese, Filipinos, Koreans, Japanese, Mexicans, Vietnamese, and Whites.* Albany: State University of New York Press, 1988.

Johnson, Jerah. "Colonial New Orleans: A Fragment of the Eighteenth-Century French Ethos." In *Creole New Orleans,* ed. Hirsch and Logsdon.

Johnson, Walter. *Soul By Soul: Life Inside the Antebellum Slave Market.* Cambridge, MA: Harvard University Press, 1999.

Jolivette, Andrew. *Louisiana Creoles: Cultural Recovery and Mixed-Race Native American Identity.* New York: Lexington Books, 2007.

Kane, Harnett Thomas. *Huey Long's Louisiana Hayride.* Gretna, LA: Pelican Publishing, 1971.

Kasteel, Annemarie. *Francis Janssens, 1843–1897: A Dutch American Prelate.* Lafayette: University of Southwestern Louisiana, 1992.

Katanski, Amelia V. *Learning to Write "Indian": The Boarding-School Experience and American Indian Literature.* Norman: University of Oklahoma Press, 2005.

Kein, Sybil, ed. *Creole: The History and Legacy of Louisiana's Free People of Color.* Baton Rouge: Louisiana State University Press, 2000.

Kelley, Robin. *Race Rebels: Culture, Politics, and the Black Working Class.* New York: Simon and Schuster, 1996.

Kellogg, Charles Flint. *NAACP: A History of the National Association for the Advancement of Colored People,* vol. 1. Baltimore: Johns Hopkins University Press, 1973.

Kelly, Brian. *Race, Class and Power in the Alabama Coalfields, 1908–1921.* Urbana: University of Illinois Press, 2001.

Kirwan, Albert D. *Revolt of the Rednecks: Mississippi Politics, 1876–1925.* Lexington: University Press of Kentucky, 2011.

Lachance, Paul F. "The Foreign French." In *Creole New Orleans,* ed. Hirsch and Logsdon.

LaFleur, John, Brian Costello, and Ina Fandrich. *Louisiana's French Creole Culinary & Linguistic Traditions: Facts vs. Fiction Before and Since Cajunization.* München, Germany: BookRix, 2013.

Lai, H. Mark. *Becoming Chinese American: A History of Communities and Institutions.* Walnut Creek, CA: AltaMira 2004.

Land, Mary. *Louisiana Cookery.* Jackson: University Press of Mississippi, 1954.

Lane, Kris E. *Pillaging the Empire: Piracy in the Americas, 1500–1750.* Armonk, NY: M. E. Sharpe, 1998.

Laurie, Bruce. *Artisans into Workers: Labor in Nineteenth-Century America.* New York: Noonday Press, 1989.

Law, Robin, and Paul E. Lovejoy. *The Biography of Mahommah Gardo Baquaqua: His Passage from Slavery to Freedom in Africa and America.* Princeton, NJ: Markus Wiener, 2007.

Letwin, Daniel. *The Challenge of Interracial Unionism: Alabama Coal Miners, 1878–1921.* Chapel Hill: University of North Carolina Press, 1998.

Linton, Ralph. *The Study of Man.* New York: D. Appleton Century Co., 1936.

Lofgren, Charles A. *The Plessy Case: A Legal-Historical Interpretation.* New York: Oxford University Press, 1987.

Logan, Rayford. *The Negro in American Life and Thought: The Nadir, 1877–1901.* New York: Dial Press, 1954.

Long, Alecia. *The Great Southern Babylon: Sex, Race and Respectability in New Orleans, 1865–1920.* Baton Rouge: Louisiana State University Press, 2004.

MacDougall, Brenda, Nichole St-Onge, and Carolyn Podruchny. *Contours of a People: Metis Family, Mobility, and History.* Norman: University of Oklahoma Press, 2012.

Machado, José Pedro. *Grande Dicionário da Lingua Portuguesa*, vol. 1. Lisbon: Alfa Publications, 1991.

Madigan, Tim. *The Burning: Massacre, Destruction, and the Tulsa Race Riot of 1921.* New York: Thomas Dunne Books, 2001.

Márquez, John D. *Black-Brown Solidarity: Racial Politics in the New Gulf South.* Austin: University of Texas Press, 2014.

Martin, Joan. "Plaçage and the Louisiana Gens De Couleur Libre: How Race and Sex Defined the Lifestyle of Free Women of Color." In *Creole*, ed. Kein.

Martin, Tony. *Race First: The Ideological and Organizational Struggles of Marcus Garvey and the Universal Negro Improvement Association.* Dover, MA: Majority Press, 1976.

Maselli, Joseph, and Dominic Candeloro. *Images of America: Italians in New Orleans.* Charleston, SC: Arcadia Publishing, 2004.

Matory, J. Lorand. *Black Atlantic Religion: Tradition, Transnationalism and Matriarchy in the Afro-Brazilian Condomblé.* Princeton, NJ: Princeton University Press, 2005.

McDonnell, Patrick, Karen O'Connell, and Georgia Riley de Havenon. *Krazy Kat: The Comic Art of George Herriman.* New York: Abrams, 1986.

McElvaine, Robert S. *Down and Out in the Great Depression: Letters from the Forgotten Man.* Chapel Hill: University of North Carolina Press, 2008.

McKinney, Louise. *New Orleans: A Cultural History.* New York: Oxford University Press, 2006.

Meeks, Eric V. *Border Citizens: The Making of Indians, Mexicans, and Anglos in Arizona.* Austin: University of Texas Press, 2007.

Merrill, Ellen C. *Germans of Louisiana.* Gretna, LA: Pelican Publishing, 2005.

Miller, Randall M. "The Enemy Within: Some Effects of Foreign Immigrants on Antebellum Southern Cities." In *The Making of Urban America*, ed. Mohl.

———. "'Immigration Through the Port of New Orleans': A Comment." In *Forgotten Doors: The Other Ports of Entry to the United States*, ed. M. Mark Stolarik. London: Associated University Presses, 1988.

Mirel, Jeffrey E. *Patriotic Pluralism: Americanization Education and European Immigrants*. Cambridge, MA: Harvard University Press, 2010.

Mitchell, Mary Niall. *Raising Freedom's Child: Black Children and Visions of the Future After Slavery*. New York: New York University Press, 2008.

Mohl, Raymond A., ed. *The Making of Urban America*. Oxford, UK: SR Books, 1997.

Morgan, Edmund S. *American Slavery, American Freedom: The Ordeal of Colonial Virginia*. New York: W. W. Norton & Co., 1975.

Muhammad, Khalil Gibran. *The Condemnation of Blackness: Race, Crime, and the Making of Modern Urban America*. Cambridge, MA: Harvard University Press, 2010.

Murphy, Joseph M. *Working the Spirit: Ceremonies of the African Diaspora*. Boston: Beacon Press, 1994.

Myrdal, Gunner. *An American Dilemma*, vol. 2: *The Negro Problem and Modern Democracy*. New York: Harper and Brothers, 1944.

Nau, John F. *The German People of New Orleans,1650–1900*. Leiden, Germany: Brill, 1958.

Nichols, Patricia. "Creole Languages: Forging New Identities." In *Language in the USA*, ed. Finegan et al.

Niehaus, Earl F. *The Irish in New Orleans, 1800–1860*. North Stratford, NH: Ayer, 1965.

Nystrom, Justin A. *New Orleans After the Civil War: Race. Politics, and a New Birth of Freedom*. Baltimore: Johns Hopkins University Press, 2010.

Oates, Mary J. *The Catholic Philanthropic Tradition in America*. Bloomington: Indiana University Press, 1995.

Ochs, Stephen J. *A Black Patriot and a White Priest: André Cailloux and Claude Paschal Maistre in Civil War New Orleans*. Baton Rouge: Louisiana State University Press, 2000.

———. *Desegregating the Altar: Josephites and the Struggle for Black Priests, 1871– 1960*. Baton Rouge: Louisiana State University Press, 1990.

Olmos, Margarite Fernández, and Lizabeth Paravisini-Gebert. *An Introduction from Voudou and Santeria to Obeah and Espiritismo*. New York: New York University Press, 2011.

O'Neill, Charles E., S.J. Foreword to Desdunes, *Our People and Our History*.

Pacyga, Dominic A. *Polish Immigrants and Industrial Chicago: Workers on the South Side, 1880–1922.* Chicago: University of Chicago Press, 1991.

Parks, Randy J. *The Two Princes of Calabar: An Eighteenth-Century Atlantic Odyssey.* Cambridge, MA: Harvard University Press, 2004.

Pierson, Marion John Bennett, comp. *Louisiana Soldiers in the War of 1812.* Baton Rouge: Louisiana Genealogical and Historical Society, 1963.

Pozetta, George E. *Americanization, Social Control, and Philanthropy.* London: Routledge, 1991.

Rabinowitz, Howard N. *Race, Ethnicity, and Urbanization: Selected Essays.* Columbia: University of Missouri Press, 1994.

Raimon, Eve Allegra. *The "Tragic Mulatta" Revisited: Race and Nationalism in Nineteenth-Century Anti-Slavery Fiction.* New Brunswick, NJ: Rutgers University Press, 2004.

Ray, Arthur J. *An Illustrated History of Canada's Native People: I Have Lived Here Since the World Began.* Montreal: McGill-Queen's Press, 2011.

Reyhner, John Allan, and Jeanne M. Oyawin Eder. *American Indian Education: A History.* Norman: University of Oklahoma Press, 2006.

Rockquemore, Kerry Ann, and David Brunsma. *Beyond Black: Biracial Identity in America.* Lanham, MD: Rowman & Littlefield, 2008.

Roediger, David R. *The Wages of Whiteness: Race and the Making of the American Working Class.* New York: Verso, 1999.

———. *Working Toward Whiteness: How America's Immigrants Became White: The Strange Journey from Ellis Island to the Suburbs.* New York: Basic Books, 2005.

Rolinson, Mary G. *Grassroots Garveyism: The Universal Negro Improvement Association in the Rural South, 1920–1927.* Chapel Hill: University of North Carolina Press, 2007.

Rose, Al. *Storyville, New Orleans: Being an Authentic, Illustrated Account of the Notorious Red-Light District.* Tuscaloosa: University of Alabama Press, 1979.

Rosenberg, Daniel. *New Orleans Dockworkers: Race, Labor, and Unionism 1892–1923.* Albany: State University of New York Press, 1988.

Ross, Marlon Bryan. *Manning the Race: Reforming Black Men in the Jim Crow Era.* New York: New York University Press, 2004.

Rothman, Adam. *Slave Country: American Expansion and the Origins of the Deep South.* Cambridge, MA: Harvard University Press, 2007.

Sanchez, George J. *Becoming Mexican American: Ethnicity, Culture, and Identity in Chicano Los Angeles, 1900–1945.* Oxford: Oxford University Press, 1993.

———. "Music and Mass Culture in Mexican-American Los Angeles." In *The Making of Urban America,* ed. Mohl.

Sansone, Livio, Boubacar Barry, and Elisée Soumonni, eds. *La construction trans-atlantique d'identités noires: Entre Afrique et Amériques.* Paris: Karthala Editions, 2010.

Sartain, Lee. *Invisible Activists: Women of the Louisiana NAACP and the Struggle for Civil Rights.* Baton Rouge: Louisiana State University Press, 2007.

Sawaya, Francesca. *The Difficult Art of Giving: Patronage, Philanthropy, and the American Literary Market.* Philadelphia: University of Pennsylvania Press, 2014.

Schafer, Judith Kelleher. *Becoming Free, Remaining Free: Manumission and Enslavement in New Orleans, 1846–1862.* Baton Rouge: Louisiana State University Press, 2003.

Schmid, Carol L. *The Politics of Language: Conflict, Identity, and Cultural Pluralism in Comparative Perspective.* Oxford, UK: Oxford University Press, 2001.

Schroeder, Jonathan, and Miriam Salzer Morling. *Brand Culture.* London: Routledge, 2006.

Schweninger, Loren. "Socioeconomic Dynamics among the Gulf Creole Populations: The Antebellum and Civil War Years." In *Creoles of Color of the Gulf South* ed. Dormon.

Sitkoff, Harvard. *A New Deal for Blacks: The Emergence of Civil Rights as a National Issue: The Depression Decade.* Oxford, UK: Oxford University Press, 1978.

Smith, Norman R. *Footprints of Black Louisiana.* Bloomington, IN: Xlibris, 2010.

Sollors, Werner, ed. *The Interesting Narrative of the Life of Olaudah Equiano, or Gustavus Vassa, the African, Written by Himself.* New York: Norton, 2001.

Spear, Jennifer M. *Race, Sex, and Social Order in Early New Orleans.* Baltimore: Johns Hopkins University Press, 2008.

Stewart, Charles. "Creolization: History, Ethnography, Theory." In *Creolization: History, Ethnography, Theory,* ed. Charles Stewart. Walnut Creek, CA: Left Coast Press, 2007.

St. James, Warren D. *The National Association for the Advancement of Colored People.* New York: Exposition Press, 1958.

Stockley, Grif, Jr. *Blood In Their Eyes: The Elaine Race Massacre of 1919.* Fayetteville: University of Arkansas Press, 2001.

Stolarick, M. Mark, ed. *Forgotten Doors: The Other Ports of Entry to the United States.* London: Associated University Presses, 1988.

Stone, Ferdinand. "The Law with a Difference and How It Came About." In *The Past as Prelude,* ed. Carter.

Stononis, Anthony J., ed. *Dixie Emporium: Tourism, Foodways, and Consumer Culture in the American South.* Athens: University of Georgia Press, 2008.

Sullivan, Patricia. *Lift Every Voice: The NAACP and the Making of the Civil Rights Movement*. New York: New Press, 2009.

Tallant, Robert. *Voodoo in New Orleans*. Gretna, LA: Pelican Publishing, 1946.

Tarry, Ellen. *Saint Katharine Drexel: Friend of the Oppressed*. San Francisco: Ignatius Press, 2002.

Taylor, Henry L., Jr., and Walter Hill. *Historical Roots of the Urban Crisis: Blacks in the Industrial City, 1900–1950*. London: Routledge, 2013.

Thernstrom, Stephen, and Abigail Thernstrom. *America in Black and White: One Nation, Indivisible*. New York: Simon and Schuster, 1997.

Thursby, Jacquelyn S. *Funeral Festivals in America: Rituals for the Living*. Lexington: University Press of Kentucky, 2006.

Tönnies, Ferdinand. *Community and Society (Gemeinschaft und Gesellschaft)*. New Brunswick, NJ: Transaction Publishers, 2004.

Trafzer, Clifford E., Jean A. Keller, and Lorene Sisquoc. *Boarding School Blues: Revisiting American Indian Educational Experiences*. Lincoln: University of Nebraska Press, 2006.

Tregle, Joseph G., Jr. "Creoles and Americans." In *Creole New Orleans*, ed. Hirsch and Logsdon.

———. *Louisiana in the Age of Jackson: A Clash of Cultures and Personalities*. Baton Rouge: Louisiana State University Press, 1999.

Tye, Larry. *Rising From the Rails*. New York: Henry Holt & Co., 2005.

Vaughan, Megan. *Creating the Creole Island: Slavery in Eighteenth-Century Mauritius*. Durham, NC: Duke University Press, 2005.

Ward, Martha. *Voodoo Queen: The Spirited Lives of Marie Laveau*. Jackson: University Press of Mississippi, 2004.

Wells, Robert V. *Facing the "King of Terrors": Death and Society in an American Community, 1750–1990*. Cambridge, UK: Cambridge University Press, 2000.

Wesley, Charles H. *Negro Labor in the United States, 1850–1925*. New York: Vanguard Press, 1927.

Wiebe, Robert. *The Search for Order, 1877–1920*. New York: Farrar, Straus and Giroux, 1967.

Williams, Lee E. *Anatomy of Four Race Riots: Racial Conflict in Knoxville, Elaine (Arkansas), Tulsa, and Chicago, 1919–1921*. Hattiesburg: University and College Press of Mississippi, 1972.

Williams, T. Harry. *Huey Long*. New York: Alfred A. Knopf, 1969.

Williamson, Joel. *After Slavery: The Negro in South Carolina during Reconstruction, 1861–1877*. Chapel Hill: University of North Carolina Press, 1965.

Wilson, Charles Reagan. *Baptized in Blood: The Religion of The Lost Cause, 1865–1920.* Athens: University of Georgia Press, 2011.

Winslow, Calvin, ed. *Waterfront Workers: New Perspectives on Race and Class.* Urbana: University of Illinois Press, 1998.

Woodrum, Eric Marc. *Japanese American Social Adaptation Over Three Generations.* Austin: University of Texas at Austin, 1978.

Woods, Sister Frances Jerome. *Marginality and Identity: A Colored Creole Family Through Ten Generations.* Baton Rouge: Louisiana State University Press, 1972.

Woodside, Arch G., Carol M. Megehee, and Alfred Ogle. *Perspectives on Cross-Cultural, Ethnographic, Brand Image, Storytelling, Unconscious Needs, and Hospitality Guest Research.* Bingley, UK: Emerald Group Publishing, 2009.

Wright, Richard D., Jr. *Kingfish: The Reign of Huey P. Long.* New York: Random House, 2006.

Yang, Fengang. *Chinese Christians in America: Conversion, Assimilation, and Adhesive Identities.* University Park: Pennsylvania State University Press, 2010.

Print Articles

Beale, Calvin L. "An Overview of the Phenomenon of Mixed Racial Isolates in the United States." *American Anthropologist* 74, no. 3 (1972): 704–10.

Beauchamp-Byrd, Mora, and John Michael Vlach. "Raised to the Trade: Creole Building Arts in New Orleans." *Louisiana Cultural Vistas,* Fall 2002, 26–39.

Bell, Caryn Cossé. "French Religious Culture in Afro-Creole New Orleans." *US Catholic Historian* 17, no. 2 (Spring 1999): 1–16.

Berlin, Ira. "From Creole to African: Atlantic Creoles and the Origins of African-American Society in Mainland North America." *William and Mary Quarterly,* 3rd ser., vol. 53, no. 2 (April 1996): 251–88.

Bonilla-Silva, Eduardo. "From Bi-racial to Tri-racial: Towards a New System of Racial Stratification in the USA." *Ethnic and Racial Studies* 27, no. 6 (2004): 931–50.

Bullock, Penelope. "The Mulatto in American Fiction." *Phylon* 6, no. 1 (1st qtr. 1945): 78–82.

Embrick, David G., and Kasey Henricks. "Intersections in Everyday Conversations: Racetalk, Classtalk, and Gendertalk in the Workplace." In *Routledge International Handbook of Race, Class and Gender,* ed. Jackson.

Freake, Rachelle, Guillaume Gentil, and Jaffer Sheyholislami. "A Bilingual Corpus-Assisted Discourse Study of the Construction of Nationhood and Belonging in Quebec." *Discourse and Society* 22 (2011): 21–47.

Ochs, Stephen J. "The Ordeal of the Black Priest," *U.S. Catholic Historian* 5, no. 1 (1986): 45–66.

Pollitzer, William S. "Analysis of a Tri-racial Isolate." *Human Biology* (1964): 362–73.

———. "The Physical Anthropology and Genetics of Marginal People of the South-eastern United States." *American Anthropologist* 74, no. 3 (1972): 719–34.

Rankin, David C. "The Origins of Black Leadership in New Orleans During Recon-struction." *Journal of Southern History* 40, no. 3 (August 1974): 417–40.

Richardson, Gary A. "Boucicault's 'The Octoroon' and American Law." *Theatre Journal* 34, no. 2 (May 1982): 155–64.

Schafer, Judith Kelleher. "'Open and Notorious Concubinage': The Emancipation of Slave Mistresses by Will and the Supreme Court of Antebellum Louisiana." *Louisiana History* 28, no. 2 (Spring 1987): 165–82.

Scott, Rebecca J. "Public Rights and Private Commerce: A Nineteenth-Century Atlantic Creole Itinerary." *Current Anthropology* 48, no. 2 (April 2007): 237–56.

Sexton, Rocky L. "Cajun French Language Maintenance and Shift: A Southwest Louisiana Case Study to 1970." *Journal of American Ethnic History* 19, no. 4 (2000): 24–48.

Shugg, Roger W. "The General Strike of 1892." *Louisiana Historical Quarterly* 21 (April 1938): 545–60.

Slawson, Douglas C. M. "Segregated Catholicism: The Origins of Saint Katharine's Parish, New Orleans." *Vincentian Heritage Journal* 17, no. 3 (October 1996): 141–84.

Spitzer, Nicholas R. "Monde Créole: The Cultural World of French Louisiana Creoles and the Creolization of World Cultures." *Journal of American Folklore* 116 (Winter 2003): 58–64.

Tregle, Joseph G., Jr. "Early New Orleans Society: A Reappraisal," *Journal of Southern History* 18, no. 1 (February 1952): 20–36.

Witkop, C. J. "A Study of Tri-racial Isolates in Eastern United States." *Human Heredity* 6, no. 3 (1956): 410–12.

Online Articles

"About the NAACP New Orleans Branch." *NAACP New Orleans Branch*, neworleansnaacp.org/about_us.

Albertson, Chris. "New Orleans '61 (The Journey Begins)." *Stomp Off,* stomp-off.blogspot.co.uk/2009/11/new-orleans-1961.html.

de Groat, Greta. "America's First Lady of the Screen: The Life and Career of Clara Kimball Young." *Clara Kimball Young,* web.stanford.edu/~gdegroat/CKY/cky.htm.

Gaines, Kevin K. "Racial Uplift Ideology in the Era of 'the Negro Problem.'" *Freedom's Story.* TeacherServe, National Humanities Center, nationalhumanitiescenter.org/tserve/freedom/1865–1917/essays/racialuplift.htm.

Glatz, Carol. "Pope Brings African-American Foundress One Step Closer to Sainthood." *Catholic News Service,* www.catholicnews.com/data/stories/cns/1001298.htm.

Heer, Jeet. "Racism as a Stylistic Choice and Other Notes." *Comics Journal,* March 14, 2011, www.tcj.com/racism-as-a-stylistic-choice-and-other-notes/.

"History of St. Mary's Academy." *St. Mary's Academy,* www.smaneworleans.com/site30.php.

"The History of St. Michael Indian School." *St. Michael Indian School,* stmichaelindianschool.org/about/history.

"History of St. Rose of Lima Church." *St. Rose de Lima Catholic Church, New Orleans.* www.neworleanschurches.com/StRose/history.htm.

"The History of Xavier." *Xavier University of New Orleans,* www.xula.edu/about-xavier/history.php.

Honora, Jari. "1920 KPC Convention, Corpus Christi Parish, New Orleans." *Creolegen: Creole History and Genealogy,* www.creolegen.org/2012/06/11/1920-kpc-convention-corpus-christi-parish-new-orleans/.

Jenkins, Ken, Betty Charbonnet Reid Soskin, and Lisa Henderson. "Thirteen Generations of the Charbonnet Family Tree: Part Two, 1900–1960." *Safero: Collections of an African American Freedom Fighter, Journalist, Novelist and Teller of Stories,* www.safero.org/family/charbonnethistory2.html.

Kroes, Rob. "American Empire and Cultural Imperialism: A View From the Receiving End." Transcript, *Conference Papers on the Web,* webdoc.sub.gwdg.de/ebook/p/2005/ghi_12/www.ghi-dc.org/conpotweb/westernpapers/kroes.pdf.

"Marcus Garvey: A Black Moses." Official Website of the Knight's Party, USA: Bringing a Message of Hope and Deliverance to White Christian America, www.kkk.bz/marcus_garvey.htm.

Martin, Gilbert E. "The Creoles Promised Treaty Rights." FrenchCreoles.com, www.frenchcreoles.com/Politics/Creole%20Treaty%20Rights/creole%20treaty%20rights.htm.

"NAACP: 100 Years of History." NAACP.org, www.naacp.org/pages/naacp-history.

Neidenbach, Elizabeth Clark. "Marie Couvent." *KnowLa Encyclopedia of Louisiana,* ed. David Johnson, www.knowla.org/entry/843/&view=summary.

"The Notarial Acts of Louis André Martinet." Louis A. Martinet Records. New Orleans Notarial Archives, www.notarialarchives.org/martinet.htm.

Ratzinger, Joseph Cardinal. "Congregation for the Doctrine of the Faith Declaration *'Dominus Iesus'* On the Unicity and Salvific Universality of Jesus Christ and the Church." *The Vatican,* www.vatican.va/roman_curia/congregations/cfaith /documents/rc_con_cfaith_doc_20000806_dominus-iesus_en.html.

Sahr, Robert. "Inflation Conversion Factors for Years 1774 TO Estimated 2023, in Dollars of Recent Years." Oregon State University Department of Political Science, oregonstate.edu/cla/polisci/sahr/sahr.

"Saint Catherine Industrial Indian School." *New Mexico History,* newmexicohistory .org/places/saint-catherines-industrial-indian-school.

"St. Joseph Indian Normal School (also known as Drexel Hall) in Rensselaer, Indiana." *Faith Fabric Local History Books,* www.faithfabric.com/tbh/history/st_joseph .htm (accessed September 7, 2014).

"Valena C. Jones United Methodist Church." *Hancock County Historical Society,* www.hancockcountyhistoricalsociety.com/vignettes/valena-c-jones-united -methodist-church/.

Theses and Dissertations

Anthony, Arthé Agnes. "The Negro Creole Community in New Orleans, 1880–1920: An Oral History." PhD diss., University of California, Irvine, 1978.

Daggett, Melissa. "Henry Louis Rey, Spiritualism, and Creoles of Color in Nineteenth-Century New Orleans." MA thesis, University of New Orleans, 2009. scholarworks.uno.edu/td/994.

Dugar, Nikki. "I Am What I Say I Am: Racial and Cultural Identity among Creoles of Color in New Orleans." MA thesis, University of New Orleans, 2009. scholar works.uno.edu/cgi/viewcontent.cgi?article=1926&context=td.

Flores-Robert, Vanessa. "Black Policemen in Jim Crow New Orleans." MA thesis, University of New Orleans, 2011. scholarworks.uno.edu/td/1392.

Fowler, David. "Northern Attitudes Towards Interracial Marriage: A Study of Legislation and Public Opinion in the Middle Atlantic States and States of the Old Northwest." PhD diss., Yale University, 1963.

Gaudin, Wendy Ann. "Autocrats and All Saints: Migration, Memory, and Modern Creole Identities." PhD diss., New York University, 2005.

Hall, Douglas M. "Public Education in Louisiana during the War between the States with Special Reference to New Orleans." MA thesis, Louisiana State University, 1940.

Sinegal-DeCuir, Sharlene. "Attacking Jim Crow: Black Activism in New Orleans, 1925–1941." PhD diss., Louisiana State University, 2009.

Walker, Harry Joseph. "Negro Benevolent Societies in New Orleans: A Study of Their Structure, Function, and Membership." MA thesis, Fisk University, 1937.

Worthy, Barbara A. "The Travail and Triumph of a Southern Black Civil Rights Lawyer: The Legal Career of Alexander Pierre Tureaud, 1899–1972." PhD diss., Tulane University, 1984.

Conference Paper

Hahn, Steven. "Marcus Garvey, the UNIA, and the Hidden Political History of African Americans." Subaltern Citizens Conference, Emory University, October 2006.

INDEX

Gemeinschaft social connections, 65, 93; leveraging of, 118
Germany, 65
Gesellschaft sodalities, 65
Gettridge, Herbert ("the Wizard"), 121–23, 173n42, 175n77, 175n79
Gitlin, Jay, 32
Goslings, The (Sinclair), 132
Gould, Virginia Meacham, 137
Grandjean, Rene, 90
Great Depression, 116
Great Migration, 59, 151–52
Great Southern Babylon, The (Long), 67
Green, Leo, 122
Greene, Lorenzo J., 96
Gregoir, Luchien, 79
Griffith, D. W., 44
Gulf Coast, 12
Gunby, Augustus, 126–27, 128, 133

Hahn, Steven, 91
Haitian Kréyol, 10
Haitian Revolution, 18, 54
Hall, Covington, 95, 100
Hall, Gwendolyn Midlo, 3, 17
Hanger, Kimberly, 22
Hannerz, Ulf, 11
Harrington, James, 79
Hart, William Henry Harrison, 118
Hearst, William Randolph, 60
hegemony, Anglo-American, 43
Harriman, George, Jr., 60, 61, 62, 151
Harriman, George, Sr., 60
Harriman, John, 60
Harriman, Stephen, 60
Hirsch, Arnold R., 3
historically black colleges and universities (HBCUs), 130, 146
Hobbs, Allyson, 97
Hoffman, J., 120

Holy Redeemer Catholic School, 80
Hoover, Herbert, 130
Houston, Alex, 79
Howard, J. D., 51–52
"How He Liked It" (Ledger), 46–47
Hurlbut, A. A., 27–28
Huron nation, 13
Hurricane Betsy, 143
Hurricane Camille, 143
Hurricane Katrina, 104, 143, 172n36

"I Am What I Say I Am" (Dugar), 3
identity negotiation, 161n42
Indianapolis Freeman, 51–52
industrialization, 94, 98–99
Industrial Workers of the World (IWW), 95
intellectual property/capital: multigenerational, 98; of New Orleans plastering craftsmanship, 109–10
International French Creole Cultural Society, 53
Irving, Washington, 6–8, 44, 51; characterization of the "French Creole" by, 7; on the image of the frontiersman, 7–8

Jackson, Alex, 79
Jackson, Andrew, 54
Jackson, James, 79
Jackson, Joy, 33–34
Jackson, Peter, 79
Janssens, Francis, 126, 138–39, 141
Jeanjacques, Etienne, 121
Jeffrion, Louis, 122
Jelly Roll Morton. *See* LaMothe, Ferdinand Joseph (Jelly Roll Morton)
Jim Crow era, 1, 38, 70, 88, 94, 104, 114; in New Orleans, 58, 59, 68, 73, 74, 75, 103, 132; social "place" of Blacks in, 114–15
Johnson, Jerah, 13
Jones, Robert E., 129